SONGS AND BALLADS
FROM NOVA SCOTIA

AT THE WHARVES, DEVIL'S ISLAND

SONGS AND BALLADS FROM NOVA SCOTIA

Collected by

HELEN CREIGHTON

Dover Publications, Inc., New York

Published in Canada by General Publishing Company, Ltd., 30
Lesmill Road, Don Mills, Toronto, Ontario.
Published in the United Kingdom by Constable and Company, Ltd.,
3 The Lanchesters, 162–164 Fulham Palace Road, London W6 9ER.

This Dover edition, first published in 1966 and reissued in 1992, is an
unabridged and corrected republication of the work first published by J.
M. Dent & Sons Limited, Toronto & Vancouver, in 1932. The "Post-
script, 1966" to the Introduction was written specially for this edition by
the author.

International Standard Book Number: 0-486-21703-5
Library of Congress Catalog Card Number: 66-26823

Manufactured in the United States of America
Dover Publications, Inc., 31 East 2nd Street, Mineola, N.Y. 11501

PREFACE

IN her Introduction, Miss Creighton tells the fascinating story of this fine collection of songs, gathered among the fisher-folk in the vicinity of Halifax, a story that confirms the testimony of Professor Mackenzie and others as to the folk-lore wealth of the Maritimes. Such collections as these from Nova Scotia will perhaps stimulate activity in other sections of English-speaking Canada on the part of those who may have been daunted hitherto by the unapproachable richness of our song heritage among French-speaking Canadians.

A word as to the grouping of the songs. Miss Creighton has wisely followed that most natural and useful of all folk-song collectors' conventions, the convention of arranging her groups with reference to Professor Child's great canon of balladry. Eleven of the Child ballads are to be found in this volume, including two of the precious Robin Hood pieces. I believe that *The Bold Pedlar and Robin Hood* has not appeared before among Robin Hood ballads found in North America. In her second group, of broadsides that reveal ultimate derivation from Child ballads, Miss Creighton has shown true Bluenose caution, for she has excluded several whose claim to admission among the lower nobility might have been allowed. This same severity has been followed in her selection of songs native to this continent.

In the inclusion of the tunes, seventeen of which have been specially designated by the English Folk-Song Society, Miss Creighton has recognized a fact that the majority of ballad collectors have strangely failed to take into account, the fact that a folk-song is not a poem. It is probable that some of the Border Ballads were originally recited, but in general a folk-song, whether it be ballad or broadside, should never be read or declaimed. No folk-song words are wedded in Heaven to one tune alone for ever, but a folk-song without any tune is a poor bereft half-thing, often pitifully ludicrous. Autolycus' ballad is a " passing merry one," and goes to the tune of *Two maids wooing a man :* rogue and all as he was, he was not rogue enough to try to palm off ballads without a tune.

There is an academic, clinical approach to folk-songs, and there is a sentimental approach, maudlin or mocking, as the case may be, but the ideal is a combination of the scientific and the sympathetic, and that is the one Miss Creighton has shown.

JOHN D. ROBINS.

Victoria College,
  Toronto,
    1932.

INTRODUCTION

THE compiling of this book has been as much a revelation to its author as she expects it to be to the reader who finds within its pages something of the wealth of Nova Scotia in traditional ballads and folk-songs of English and Scottish origin and songs native to this continent.

When it was suggested to me by Dr. Henry Munro, Superintendent of Education for the province, that I look for ballads in my search for literary material within this coast of adventure and romance, I thought the possibility of finding any such songs very remote indeed. For which my ignorance pleads humble forgiveness. Yet be it said in defence that until the early summer of 1929 I had never heard a ballad sung in this my native province.

It is interesting to watch the steps which lead to any undertaking, and who can gainsay the fact that a guiding hand points out the way when the eyes are open to observe the signposts? Else how explain the strange coincidence that followed Dr. Munro's suggestion? For I happened to be on a beach some few evenings later, and the evening being June, and the sky filled with the radiance of the setting sun, I walked on the sands with a companion, and communed upon Romance of the past. In such mood we returned to our bonfire to find a villager attending it, and here, where formalities are happily forgotten, we opened conversation by asking if treasure had ever been found upon this shore.

It was as we were going away that our informer mentioned songs. Our talk of pirates had made him think of them.

" The people down here will not only tell you stories," he said, " but they'll sing you songs as well."

" What kind of songs? " we asked indifferently.

" Pirate songs," he said. Could it be possible that I was to find them at my very door? So I took the names of those most likely to sing, asked him to prepare them for my coming, and went away wondering what I was to find.

Collecting can never be done in any hurry, as I discovered very soon. One or two visits were made in the day-time, when friendly contacts were established. But we soon saw that evening was the time for song. Evening, when the day's work is done and the hour of relaxation has come. Evening, when the workaday world is at rest and all people feel a kindly sense of companionship towards one another.

Let me describe the setting. Halifax Harbour is long and narrow, excellently protected from storm and little affected by tide. On the western side is the city of Halifax, its shore-line extending some fifteen miles to the sea. Directly opposite Halifax on the eastern side of the harbour is the town of Dartmouth, my home. From this point we set forth upon an evening early in July, following the shore for six miles to the district of Eastern Passage. Here there is a most picturesque fishing village with quaint little white cottages dotting low hills. Our objective was not to be found yet, however, so we followed this shore for another four miles past fishing shacks, past the long sand beach of South-East Passage, past a treacherous roadway where sand blows in great drifts, obstructing the way to such an extent that upon subsequent visits we were frequently obliged to push our car to firmer ground. Beyond all these we went to the very end of the land where the waters of the Atlantic Ocean meet those of Halifax Harbour and disport themselves gaily upon the shore. Here we turned to a private roadway which was rough and bumpy, and so came at last to the homes of the Hartlan family.

The Hartlan, or Hartley, estate is situated on a bluff below which the sea tosses upon a pebbled beach in all its many moods. To the east stands the favoured resort of bathers, the beloved sand beach of Cow Bay. Near by is a bluff where a lone tree guards reputed treasure. Far off are the red hills of Lawrencetown, and still farther, at the most distant visible point, the remains of a wreck cling to the rocky shore.

Back of the estate is a spruce grove, and beyond the shore at the very mouth of Halifax Harbour lies Devil's Island, whose kindly inhabitants have made this book a possibility, and of whom you will hear more very shortly. Far to the right lies the western shore of Halifax Harbour.

The houses of the Hartlans are grouped in a circle. In the centre stands the ghost house, ostracised for the unwelcome guest it harbours. Above the entrance may still be seen nails where the old grandfather used to place a board with nine letters taken from the German Bible to dispel witches who pursued them. Here you see a family of German descent whose forefathers came to Canada at the founding of Lunenburg in 1753, people who still possess that wealth of superstition which is found so often among German descendants in Nova Scotia. Yet strangely enough, it was among these people that some of my finest and oldest English songs were discovered.

We stopped at Mr. Enos Hartlan's door, where we were greeted most cordially. Here, by the warmth of his kitchen fire, we talked of songs, and strove to overcome the natural timidity which he felt in the presence of strangers, having none of his family at home at the time to support him. Personally I should be most embarrassed if a stranger came to my house and requested me to sing, so I readily sympathized with Mr. Hartlan. Furthermore, he was painfully conscious of the fact that age had robbed him of much of his vocal prowess, and he knew that the absence of teeth was a handicap not to be over-looked. However, Mr. Hartlan was a sportsman, and these things did not trouble him very long.

We had no trouble taking the words of Mr. Hartlan's song, for he gladly repeated and filled in the gaps our pencils had not been quick enough to catch at the first writing. We feared to weary him, for his memory was such that if he missed a word he had to go back to the beginning and sing his song through.

I soon learned in such cases to concentrate on the opening lines of each new verse, for when a man repeats very often he sometimes loses his thread, and a precious verse may be forgotten altogether. Most of my singers can recite their songs through from beginning to end without hesitation, but Mr. Hartlan is getting on in years, and to his great regret his memory is failing.

Indeed, the collecting of words is a comparatively simple matter. It was the recording of music that baffled me, and never did I realize my difficulty more than upon this first evening of collecting. Mr. Hartlan sang only one song, but so different was it from anything I had ever heard before that I knew it would be impossible to trust to memory to carry the tune away. My musical education had ceased with my schooling, and I had never attempted to take any music down by ear. There was no piano in his house, and I knew of no way to overcome the difficulty.

I often laugh now when I think of the suggestion made by one of our party, an eminent divine, who had in mind the organist of his cathedral. Viewing him in such predicament he thought of his most likely procedure, and suggested that we put dots on our paper to signify the rising and falling of the voice thus : .·˙·.·˙.. In theory this sounded excellent, but alas, when I tried it my untrained ear could not detect when the voice was going up and when down. Try it yourself at the next concert you attend, and when you get your dotted paper home, you will find it, no doubt, as meaningless as I did. That is unless you are a trained musician.

Thus the first evening passed with only one song secured, and that incomplete, for the music was still a problem. Many more prolific evenings followed, however, when the good Hartlans walked several miles to Mr. Thomas Osborne's house, where we frequently met. Here Mr. Enos Hartlan would bask as entertainer-in-chief, for when his voice grew too husky to sing he told many tales of ghosts, pirates, and witches as only he could relate them. My cordial thanks are due Mr. and Mrs. Osborne, whose house I have always felt free to use, and such is the hospitality of people in these parts that it mattered not how many I brought with me, all were welcome, and the house was mine for the time being.

Here, after much thought and questioning, I took a little melodeon, upon which, in the course of its short life, some one hundred tunes were finally worked out—a quaint little instrument measuring about three feet in length and one foot in width. It has a keyboard like an organ, but its great handicap is that the left hand must work a key up and down to pump air, while the right hand plays the notes. It has an interesting historic background, for it had been used by the Rev. Robert Murray among the Micmac Indians in Nova Scotia, and is the property of his son, Mr. R. H. Murray of Dartmouth. To Mr. and Mrs. Murray I am grateful indeed, for this treasure was given me to use as long as I found necessary. Many an evening it was tucked in its little wooden box and carried to the house wherein I was to collect.

At the end of its reign, however, I'm afraid it got rather puffed up with conceit, for wherever we went, people made a great fuss over it. It was not until later, when we had been on Devil's Island for some time, however, that it finally raised strenuous objection, when a blow was given to its pride. It had been necessary to push it over the bumps and rocks of the island, conveying it by the plebeian method of the wheelbarrow. There had been no objection when pirate songs had been played on its pious keys, but its heart was broken by the ignominy of this mode of transportation. Thus it gave a weary groan, a wheeze and a heavy sigh, but not until all had been accomplished that I required of it. For by this time a dictaphone had been tried and found infinitely more satisfactory. Without embarrassment the melody is sung into the mouthpiece, and the singer is always thrilled to know that the next moment will see the key pushed back, when he will hear his own voice returned to him. Repetition is disposed of altogether, and I was sure to have time and notes correct, with all the difficult work of transcribing done in the quiet atmosphere of my own home with nobody but myself to suffer if my brain were slow to function.

As a saving of precious time the dictaphone was invaluable, as was testified on the first evening of its use when I took it to Mr. Richard Hartlan's house. Here, with his two sons to assist him, I got twenty-six songs in one evening alone, when I might have had only six before. To the musician whose ear is trained so that he can write the notes on paper without need of musical instrument this must seem a very strange method of collecting, but untrained for this task as I was, I had to do the best I could.

For some weeks I culled songs from the mainland in the Eastern Passage district, finding my singers most cordial and hospitable, and always ready to oblige with a song. But wherever I went people said :

" Why don't you go out to Devil's Island and see Mr. Ben Henneberry ? They'll sing you lots of songs over there."

Devil's Island. There it lay at the very harbour's entrance, no tree upon its naked back to shelter it from storm or blusterous wind. Often from the Hartlans' place I looked over towards it. On clear days I could just see it from the ferry which plies between Halifax and Dartmouth. Its lights from the shore twinkled bravely at night, but it looked lonely in the extreme. Such a desolate island it seemed.

Yet I had now some thirty-five songs. It had been thrilling to get them, and knowing little of their worth myself, it had been still more thrilling to take them to Dr. Archibald McMechan of Dalhousie University, and to learn that they were good. So I realized Devil's Island must be visited.

Until that time I had met nobody who had ever been on the island. There is little to take one there, and its position is so remote that many are unaware of its existence. Following the Hartlans' advice I drove to the end of the land and left my car at Mr. Neiforth's place, which he said I might do, " as often as I liked and for as long as I liked." Here we waved to the island, and eventually a boat came across and two lads took us in.

My companion of the day, and also of many previous visits on the mainland, was Miss Helen O'Connor of Halifax. In those early days her assistance and that of her sister, Miss Juanita, meant more to me than I can ever express. Our feelings upon this occasion may be imagined as the friendly shore slipped away and we felt the splash of sea water beating beneath our boat. What would we find when we got there ? Yet we were destined to cross on stormier seas than this when fear was not without reason. This day, however, was calm and beautiful, and as we rowed into the little harbour formed by two government breakwaters, we saw a number of women seated upon a wharf. It seemed that their whole lives had been spent waiting for this moment to come, so cordial was their greeting. So we exchanged felicitations, and then told them that we wished to see Mr. Ben Henneberry, from whom we hoped to hear ballads. Immediately old " Aunt Jane," so called to designate her from all the other Henneberrys on the island, constituted herself escort-in-chief, but alas, the famous Ben of whom we had heard so much was not then to be found.

It happened, however, that the lightkeeper's wife had heard of our arrival, and by virtue of the fact that I had once told bedtime stories to her children over the local radio, she begged us to go to her house that she might return my hospitality. Consequently a pleasant contact was formed, and in their dwelling between the two lighthouses Mr. Faulkner sang for us, and Mr. Edmund Henneberry dropped in informally and gave us that delightful sea song, the *Mary L. MacKay.*

Afternoon passed and evening came, and still we were on the island. Such a funny little island we found it, with a total circumference of only one mile. There are seventeen houses, fourteen of which are occupied. The inhabitants are all fisher-folk, of English, Irish, and Welsh descent, the Henneberrys probably having come out with Alexander McNutt early in the nineteenth century, when he brought 300 Irish settlers over. They find their catch in the waters that lie near at hand. There is also a government lifeboat of which Mr. Ben Henneberry is coxswain.

We had lingered in this pleasant and altogether unique environment until the long shadows of the sun warned us that darkness was fast approaching. So with an escort which grew with every house we passed, we bade farewell to the Faulkners, intending to take our leave. As we reached the pier, however, we saw several men seated upon a log, and it occurred to me that one might be Mr. Henneberry. Consequently we asked, and the singer, whose memory was to astound me as the weeks went by, was introduced. Of course I asked him to sing, which he did very gladly, and here I heard folk singing as I have heard it neither before nor since.

Picture the little island at your back with its miniature hills and dales, its houses perched so insecurely that you feel a breath of wind might come at any moment and blow them all away. Facing the harbour is a row of fishing shacks in which the gear of the men is kept. In front of them is a path.

Behind the log on which the men are sitting the Devil's Island harbour lies, the fishing boats rocking cosily in the soft cradle of the sea. Far away are Lawlor's and McNab's Islands, heavily wooded in vivid contrast to this island upon which we stand. Far, far away is Citadel Hill at Halifax, very familiar, but now seeming as part of a different world, so unlike is the atmosphere here at the harbour's mouth. Behind Citadel Hill is the setting sun ; a glorious sun in the full pride of colourful beauty.

All is quiet among the islanders, save for the voice of Mr. Henneberry. His theme is the long, sad story of " Meagher's Children," the tale of two little tots lost in the woods near Dartmouth. The island listeners all know the song, and their sympathy is felt as the hardships of the children are related, and one feels that their hearts are throbbing for the little lasses who suffered so cruel a fate. One by one other islanders join the group, coming noiselessly between the fishing shacks in phantom silence, attracted by the beloved voice of Mr. Ben. Anon old Aunt Jane, perched upon a barrel, recalls a familiar phrase, and then her high falsetto joins the deep bass of Mr. Henneberry at the end of a well-known line. The air is tense and vibrant, for the ballad singer is an artist among his people, but upon this occasion the islanders are divided in thought between pleasure in hearing this dear old song again, and pride in the one who is singing it. Often have I wished I might repeat that precious moment.

There were many more visits to the island, but by the time October came I realized that I must go there to stay if I wished to accomplish anything worth while. I had thought a day or two might suffice, but there followed a week more strenuous than any I have ever put in. Every day began with a visit to the fishing shacks at about ten a.m., where the men sang as they mended their nets. (It was usually Mr. Ben who sang.) In the early afternoon the children came to the Faulkners' house, singing in their sweet voices about " Villikens and His Dinah," and how " he kissed her cold corpus a thousand times o'er." Later in the afternoon Mr. and Mrs. Henneberry could be found in their house, and here in a quiet atmosphere much could be accomplished.

At five-thirty I would rush home for food and rest, but at seven the unmistakable voice of Mr. Ben would be heard, when hospitality demanded that I arise and take down the songs he had so kindly come to sing for me. He usually remained until nine, and during the evening others would come in, and the singing would continue until three a.m. With nodding head I would work strange tunes out upon the little melodeon, for the magic dictaphone was yet unknown to me. Some of the songs were easy enough, but some of them, oh, so difficult. But how worth while it all was. At the end of the week nearly one hundred new songs were added to my collection, and many were treasures indeed.

Strange it seems that so minute an island should bear so rich a fruit. Yet perhaps it is not so strange. The people here have little contact with the outside world, for winter winds are cold and treacherous, and although the fisherman makes frequent trips to town he does not linger lest nightfall finds him upon the water in a storm. Here the ballad singer is a god among them; a being exalted by virtue of his superior gift of memory and voice. All is silent when he sings, and oftentimes his song recalls a wreck whose gruesome story is so well known that the islanders cling a little more closely to one another, hoping such fate may never come to them. No islander among them but turns with proud finger pointed towards Mr. Ben. Here is a prophet honoured most in his own country, and indeed he is worthy of his fame, as I realize the further I go in my collecting. Mr. Ben has sung no less than ninety songs to me, all of them interesting, most of them long and of infinite variety, and one, *The Courtship of Willie Riley*, possessing some seventy-eight verses in all.

Many, many are the thanks that are due these good people who gave me so unstintingly of their store, and to the Faulkners there is an especial thanks for the latch that was never down, enabling me to entertain all I would in the hospitality of their home.

Later, when the dictaphone came into use, Mr. Ben Henneberry, at great trouble to himself, came to my father's house and sang his melodies, working as long as four hours at a stretch without rest. Space does not permit me to tell of other kind friends who contributed, nor of the Will Edwards' at Eastern Passage where my dictaphone is always welcome upon their table.

All was not finished yet, however. The music had only been written as best I could do it, my idea being to put down the notes so that I should be able to read them myself, and then interpret them exactly as I heard them to a musician skilled in the knowledge of folk-music. Fortunately I found such a man in Dr. Healey Willan, Vice-Principal of the Toronto Conservatory of Music, who, with Mr. Campbell McInnes of Toronto, has spent many hours going over these songs that the music may be presented to you correctly. From the whole collection they chose a number which they considered most interesting from the musician's point of view, and these I sent at their instigation to the English Folk-Song Society, which reports the songs marked in the contents list (A) as " Good and worthy of publication." Those marked (B) they report as " Genuine, but better variants known elsewhere."

In passing let me add that the notation of the tune is that which will approximately fit the words of the first verse, but in singing these songs one must remember that while the metrical outline of the tune should be preserved, the exact values of the notes may be varied to suit the individual line or stanza ; the folk-singer has no set accompaniment to follow, and if four words must be sung to one note he has no difficulty in adapting them, so that for him the music continues to run smoothly.

How can I express my thanks to people so kind ? How can I ever tell them how their labour in the interest of folk-song has inspired me ? To Dr. Willan and Mr. McInnes I bow in deepest gratitude. To the members of the English Folk-Song Society who have given me such a faithful report I extend most gracious thanks.

Another phase of the collector's work must also be explained—that of classifying the songs, weeding out those which do not properly belong to such a collection, noting references elsewhere, and making the comparisons which accompany the songs in this volume. By a curious chain of circumstances I found that I must do all this work myself—a task I had never dreamed of doing during my period of collecting, but one which has taught me much. Fate led me to Toronto for this, where the library of the University of Toronto was placed at my disposal through the kindness of the librarian, Mr. Stewart Wallace. I have also used the public reference library freely, exhausting everything on ballads I could find in either of these sources, often longing for further volumes to consult, but thankful for the many valuable collections placed in my hands.

Here in Toronto I was most fortunate at the outset of my research in getting in touch with Professor John D. Robins of Victoria College in the University of Toronto, whose kindly guidance and advice have cheered me through the long hours of study and kept me from many pitfalls. Being himself possessed of an extensive library, he at once placed all his books at my disposal, and much that I have learned of ballad literature is due to the knowledge he imparted.

Professor Robins is a student of folk-songs, and at one time had a collection of his own which, alas, while still in manuscript, was destroyed by fire. It has been the greatest pleasure to take my ideas to him, and to have him check over my notes, and so tactful have been his criticisms that even while he pointed out mistakes I felt that I was being patted on the back. Is that not the essence of tact and diplomacy? It is with the greatest pleasure that I publish the preface he has been kind enough to write for this volume, in which the value of this collection is explained from the scholar's point of view. As for the classifying of the songs, you will find them arranged thus :—1–11, Variants of genuine English and Scottish Popular Ballads ; 12–14, closely related to Child Ballads ; 15–26, Songs of Love ; 27–30, Songs on the theme of the broken ring token ; 31–51, Songs of Love and the Sea ; 52–66, Songs of the Sea ; 67–72, Songs of Battle ; 73–88, Irish ; 89–93, Nursery Songs ; 94–97, Miscellaneous, having no claim to any especial grouping ; 98 ff., Songs native to the Province of Nova Scotia, or to this continent.

I must not close without conveying my gratitude to those who have helped make this book a possibility ; whose interest has always been a stimulus when the task seemed overwhelming. To Dr. Munro who started me on my way ; for his guidance throughout and ever-ready assistance. To Dr. McMechan aforementioned, who not only interpreted a number of sea terms for me, but also himself contributed a song. To Mr. and Mrs. R. H. Murray for the use of their melodeon. To the Soulis Typewriter Co. of Halifax, who allowed me to experiment with their dictaphone at a very negligible rate of payment. To Mr. Murray Gibbon, Chief Publicity Agent of the Canadian Pacific Railways, whose practical advice has been invaluable.

To Miss Maud Karpeles and Mrs. M. E. Hobbs of the English Folk-Song Society for interesting and helpful letters, including a number of references contributed by the latter. To the English Folk-Song Society for notes made upon the music. To Mr. Campbell McInnes of Toronto for his perusal of my songs in the early days when I knew little of their value, and for his kindly assistance in putting me in touch with him who has become musical editor of this volume, namely, Dr. Healey Willan. And last but far from least, to Professor Robins of Victoria College.

Thus this book is given you, and it may be that among its pages you will find old friends in song once loved but long forgotten. And while you read, the alert mind of the Nova Scotia fisher-folk will continue to create folk-songs in honour of its people. For although the old ballads of former days may be forgotten, there is no doubt that as long as fishing is carried on in the remote districts of this province, so will folk-songs be composed in remembrance of tragedy or mirth upon the coast of Nova Scotia.

HELEN CREIGHTON.

" Evergreen,"
   Dartmouth,
      Nova Scotia,
         1932.

POSTSCRIPT, 1966

LOOKING back it seems incredible that when *Songs and Ballads from Nova Scotia* was published in 1932 I thought my work as a collector was finished. I soon discovered this was only a beginning, and have been collecting ever since. In time my interest broadened to include the whole fascinating field of folklore. Much of the material lay within thirty miles of my home and although I have combed the province of Nova Scotia from Yarmouth to Cape North, Halifax County where I live has always proved the most lucrative for songs. A fisherman explained it this way: " Men in Halifax County fish in the summer and go into the lumber woods in winter. When fishermen have time to put in away from home they sing, and in the lumber woods they stay in camp for two or three months and this is how they entertain themselves. This means songs are always being exchanged, and that is what has kept them alive." To-day of course radio and television do most of the entertaining and the men are not away from home for such long periods, but this explanation seems a valid one. There is so much folk music and folklore in this area that I have never had to go further afield than the three Maritime Provinces, Nova Scotia, New Brunswick, and Prince Edward Island.

Collecting songs is much easier to-day when music need no longer be worked out in the singer's presence. It was a great joy in 1943 and again in 1948 when the Library of Congress asked me to record for them on one of their disc machines. From 1928 to 1947 collecting was a hobby financed by my far-seeing and generous parents and also by three fellowships from the Rockefeller Foundation. In 1947 I joined the staff of the National Museum of Canada and now one of their tape recorders accompanies every trip. Three Canada Council grants eventually made it possible to have all tapes and discs re-recorded so that I now have a complete set in Halifax; it also provided for having most of the tunes transcribed on paper. Original discs are at the Library of Congress in Washington, original tapes at the National Museum in Ottawa.

It was eight years before our songs appeared in print again, this time in a small volume, *Twelve Folk Songs from Nova Scotia* (collected by Creighton and Senior), Novello, London, 1940, with piano accompaniments by Doreen H. Senior. In 1950 my *Traditional Songs from Nova Scotia*, Ryerson Press, Toronto, appeared, with music noted by hand by Miss Senior. It contains

137 songs. This was followed in 1962 by *Maritime Folk Songs*, collected by me, Ryerson Press, Toronto, and Michigan State University Press, East Lansing, with 169 songs. This has a companion record with the same name published by Folkways, New York, who also published an earlier ethnic record called *Folk Music from Nova Scotia*. An opera, *The Broken Ring* (by Trevor Jones to a text by Donald Wetmore), and a ballet, *Sea Gallows* (by Eric Hyrst to music by Michel Perrault), have been based on music from my collection. My latest book, *Gaelic Songs in Nova Scotia*, National Museum of Canada, 1964, has for its Gaelic editor Major Calum MacLeod of St. Francis Xavier University, Antigonish, and contains 93 songs in Gaelic with English translations. All follow the general pattern of this first book.

In other folklore, 1950 saw the publication of my monograph, *The Folklore of Lunenburg County*, National Museum Bulletin 117, and in 1957 there appeared my *Bluenose Ghosts*, Ryerson Press, Toronto. (Bluenose, incidentally, is a nickname for a Nova Scotian.) For the last three years I have been working on a book to be called *Popular Beliefs and Superstitions in Nova Scotia*. The years have been full and have yielded over 4000 songs and thousands of items of folklore. In this rich field there are also other tongues, French, Gaelic as mentioned before, Micmac Indian, a few German, and a number of interesting Negro songs and stories. For singing Nova Scotians prefer the older imported songs; those they make up locally use familiar traditional melodies.

A word now about the music in the volume you are reading. By force of necessity (or was it a case of fools rushing in where angels fear to tread?) I wrote down all the music for this first book myself. I soon learned, however, that folk tunes are not simple and uncomplicated but need a competent musician to capture the time changes, embroideries, and strange intervals that provide so much of their charm. Fortunately, after the book was published I was able to record most of its music, and these tunes have been gone over by Mrs. Eunice Sircom and rewritten where advisable. Not all needed rewriting, but I feel much happier in this new edition knowing that such songs as " The Dark-Eyed Sailor," which completely defeated me so many years ago, are now given as the singers rendered them. Words needed occasional rearrangement, too, under the music notes and also in the text.

There have been many interesting field trips and warm friendships made with singers in the intervening years, but no memories are as dear to my heart as those of the early days described in the first part of this introduction.

H. C.

" Evergreen,"
  Dartmouth,
    Nova Scotia,
      1966.

ABBREVIATIONS

Barry . . . Barry, Eckstorm, Smyth, *British Ballads From Maine*, Yale University Press, 1929.

Baring-Gould . S. Baring-Gould, H. Fleetwood Sheppard, F. W. Bussell, *Songs Of The West*, Folk-Songs of Devon and Cornwall; Methuen & Co., London, 1922.

Bell . . . . Robert Bell, The Annotated Edition of *The English Poets*, John W. Parker & Son, London, 1875.

Child . . . Francis James Child, *The English and Scottish Popular Ballads*, Boston, 1882 ff. (Dover reprint).

Colcord . . . Joanna C. Colcord, *Roll and Go, Songs of American Sailormen*, Indianapolis, 1924.

Cox . . . . John Harrington Cox, *Folk-Songs of the South*, Cambridge, 1925.

Davis . . . Arthur Kyle Davis, Jr., *Traditional Ballads of Virginia*, Cambridge, 1929.

Dean . . . M. C. Dean, *The Flying Cloud, and* 100 *Other Old Time Songs and Ballads*, Virginia, Minnesota, 1922.

Dixon . . . J. H. Dixon, *Ancient Poems, Ballads and Songs*, vol. xvii, edited for the Percy Society, London, 1844.

Eckstorm . . Fanny Hardy Eckstorm and Mary Winslow Smyth, *Minstrelsy of Maine. Folk-Songs and Ballads of the Woods and the Coast*, Boston and New York, 1927.

EFSSA . . . Olive Dame Campbell and Cecil J. Sharp, *English Folk-Songs from the Southern Appalachians*, New York, 1914.

Fuller-Maitland J. A. Fuller-Maitland and L. E. Broadwood, *English Country Songs*, London, 1893.

Gray . . . Roland Palmer Gray, *Songs and Ballads of the Maine Lumberjacks with Other Songs from Maine*, Cambridge, 1924.

Harland . . . Harland and Wilkinson, *Ballads and Songs of Lancashire*, 1875.

J.A.F.L. . . *The Journal of American Folk-Lore*.

Journal . . . *Journal of the Folk-Song Society*, London.

Joyce . . . P. W. Joyce, *Old Irish Folk-Music and Songs*, Dublin, 1909.

Kidson, G. . . Frank Kidson, *A Garland of English Folk-Songs*, London.

Kidson, T. T. . Frank Kidson, *Traditional Tunes*, A Collection of Ballad Airs, Oxford, 1891.

Lomax . . . John A. Lomax, *Cowboy Songs and Other Frontier Ballads*, New York, 1922.

Mackenzie . . W. Roy Mackenzie, *Ballads and Sea Songs From Nova Scotia*, Cambridge, 1928.

Newell . . . William Wells Newell, *Games and Songs of American Children*, New York, 1883 (Dover reprint).

O'Conor . . Manus O'Conor, *Com-All-Ye's and Ballads of Ireland, A Repository of Ancient Irish Songs and Ballads*, New York, 1901.

Ord . . . . John Ord, *The Bothy Songs and Ballads of Aberdeen, Banff and Moray Angus and the Mearns*, Paisley, 1930.

Pound . . . Louise Pound, *American Ballads and Songs*, New York, 1922.

Rickaby . . . Frank Rickaby, *Ballads and Songs of the Shanty-Boy*, Cambridge, 1926.

Sandburg . . Carl Sandburg, *The American Songbag*, New York, 1927.

Sharp . . . Cecil J. Sharp, *One Hundred English Folk-Songs*, Oliver Ditson.

Stone . . . Christopher Stone, *Sea Songs and Ballads*, Oxford, 1906.

Yeats . . . E. C. Yeats, *A Collection of Broadsides*, published at the Cuala Press, Churchtown, Dumdrum, County Dublin.

CONTENTS

xxi

SONGS AND BALLADS
FROM NOVA SCOTIA

1.

False Knight Upon the Road

Very quickly in jig time.

"Oh what have you in your bag? Oh what have you in your pack?"

Cried the false knight to the child on the road. "I have a little

primer and a bit of bread for dinner," Cried the pretty little child only

seven years old. Hi diddle deedle dum, deedle diddle deedle dum

Deedle deedle deedle diddle deedle deedle dum. Diddle diddle diddle

dee deedle deedle deedle dum diddle diddle diddle deedle diddle

dee de dum

Sung in part by Mr. Faulkner, Devil's Island, and completed by Mr. Ben Henneberry. The singer dances to the chorus.

1. " Oh, what have you in your bag?   Oh, what have you in your pack ? "
    Cried the false knight to the child on the road.
    " I have a little primer and a bit of bread for dinner,"
    Cried the pretty little child only seven years old.

Chorus.

Hi diddle deedle dum, deedle diddle deedle dum,
Deedle deedle deedle diddle, deedle deedle dum,
Diddle diddle diddle dee, deedle deedle deedle dum,
Diddle diddle diddle deedle diddle dee de dum.

2. " What is rounder than a ring ?   What is higher than a king ? "
Cried the false knight to the child on the road.
" The sun is rounder than a ring.   God is higher than a king,"
Cried the pretty little child only seven years old.   Cho.

3. " What is whiter than the milk ?   What is softer than the silk ? "
Cried the false knight to the child on the road.
" Snow is whiter than the milk.   Down is softer than the silk,"
Cried the pretty little child only seven years old.   Cho.

4. " What is greener than the grass ?   What is worse than women coarse ? "
Cried the false knight to the child on the road.
" Poison is greener than the grass.   The devil's worse than women coarse,"
Cried the pretty little child only seven years old.   Cho.

5. " What is longer than the wave * ?   What is deeper than the sea ? "
Cried the false knight to the child on the road.
" Love is longer than the wave.   Hell is deeper than the sea,"
Cried the pretty little child only seven years old.   Cho.

6. " Oh, a curse upon your father and a curse upon your mother,"
Cried the false knight to the child on the road.
" Oh, a blessing on my father, and a blessing on my mother,"
Cried the pretty little child only seven years old.   Cho.

No. 1. *False Knight Upon the Road.*   Child 3.

The riddle ballad, of which this is an excellent example, goes back to remote times, and riddle tales still live as they did in the days of Samson, Œdipus and Apollonius of Tyre. Frequently a suitor wins a lady's hand by the clever solving of riddles she has propounded (see *Captain Wedderburn's Courtship* in this volume), and occasionally a lass wins a crown by solving difficult riddles of state for her king.

The Nova Scotia variant contains many of the questions found in " Riddles Wisely Expounded," Child 1, revealing a close relationship with the oldest and finest type of riddle ballads. Compare *Harpkin*, Chambers' *Popular Rhymes of Scotland*, p. 66 ; *Motherwell's Minstrelsy*, Appendix, p. xxiv ; Graves, *The English Ballad*, p. 43 ; etc.

For American texts see EFSSA, No. 1 ; Barry, pp. 11–14 ; Pound, No. 20 ; Davis, No. 2 ; J.A.F.L. 24, 344.

* Or, way.

2.

Cruel Mother

Allegro

There was a lady came from York All a-lone and a-loney She fell in love with her father's clerk Down by the greenwood siding.

Sung by Mr. Ben Henneberry, Devil's Island, who, when he sings this song, swings his right arm back and forth as the line repeats, " Down by the greenwood siding." The word " siding " is long drawn out.

1. THERE was a lady came from York,
    All alone and a-loney,
  She fell in love with her father's clerk
    Down by the greenwood siding.

2. She loved him well, she loved him long,
    All alone and a-loney,
  Till at length this young maid with child she did prove,
    Down by the greenwood siding.

3. She leaned her back against her yoke,
    All alone and a-loney,
  When first it bowed and then it broke,
    Down by the greenwood siding.

4. She leaned herself against a thorn
    All alone and a-loney,
  And there her two pretty babes were born
    Down by the greenwood siding.

5. She had nothing to wrap them in,
    All alone and a-loney,
  But her apron.   It was thin,
    Down by the greenwood siding.

3

6. She took the cap from off her head,
   All alone and a-loney,
   And tied those pretty babes' arms and legs,
   Down by the greenwood siding.

7. She took her penknife keen and sharp,
   All alone and a-loney,
   And she pierced it through their innocent hearts,
   Down by the greenwood siding.

8. She stuck her penknife in the green,
   All alone and a-loney,
   The more she rubbed the blood was seen
   Down by the greenwood siding.

9. Then she threw it far away,
   All alone and a-loney,
   The farther she threw it the nearer it came,
   Down by the greenwood siding.

10. As she entered her father's hall,
    All alone and a-loney,
    She saw those pretty babes playing ball,
    Down by the greenwood siding.

11. " Oh babes, oh babes, if you were mine,
    All alone and a-loney,
    I would dress you up in silks so fine,
    Down by the greenwood siding."

12. " Oh mother, oh mother, when we were thine,
    All alone and a-loney,
    You did not dress us up in silks so fine,
    Down by the greenwood siding.

13. " But you took your penknife, keen and sharp,
    All alone and a-loney,
    And you pierced it through our innocent hearts,
    Down by the greenwood siding."

14.   " Oh, pretty maidens, can you tell,
       All alone and a-loney,
   Whether I'll reign in heaven or hell?
     Down by the greenwood siding."

15.   " No, mother dear, we can't tell well,
       All alone and a-loney,
   But your body's here, but your soul's in hell,
     Down by the greenwood siding.

16.   " Seven years a beast in the woods,
       All alone and a-loney,
   And seven more a fish in the sea,
     Down by the greenwood siding.

17.   " And seven more did toll the bell,
       All alone and a-loney,
   Before you can be redeemed from hell,
     Down by the greenwood siding."

No. 2. *Cruel Mother.*   Child No. 20.

My variant of this early ballad, which is known as far afield at least as Denmark, is particularly interesting for the knife which would not be thrown away, and the blade of which it says,

" The more she rubbed the blood was seen."

The magic stain which cannot be washed away with any amount of scouring, and which Shakespeare used so effectively in the sleep-walking scene in *Macbeth*, Act V, Scene 1, is found in occasional variants of this song. Barry gives it from Maine, and Sharp has it from the Appalachians, but to find this superstition combined with that of the knife which,

" The farther she threw it the nearer it came,"

is to find treasure indeed.

The seven-year penances properly belong to the ballad of *The Maid and the Palmer*, Child 21, the story of Our Lord's meeting with the woman of Samaria. Numerous texts have been found in Great Britain and on this continent, but none is more interesting than this variant from Nova Scotia.

According to Wimberley, *Folklore in the English and Scottish Popular Ballads*, p. 33 ff., this and the ballad of *The Maid and the Palmer* are the only instances found in balladry of metempsychosis for retribution.

3.

Captain Wedderburn's Courtship

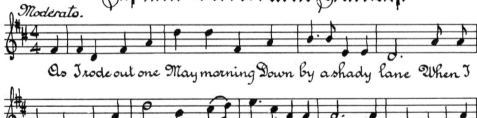

Sung by Mr. Richard Hartlan, South-East Passage.

1. As I rode out one May morning
   Down by a shady lane,
   When I met with Captain Woodstock,
   The keeper of the game,
   He said unto his servant,
   " If it was not for the law
   I would have that maid in bed with me
   As she lay next to the wall."

2. " Oh, before you lay one night with me
   You must answer my questions six.
   What is rounder than a ring,
   What's higher than a tree ?
   Oh, what is worse than woman's tongue,
   What deeper than the sea ?
   What tree buds first and what bird sings best ?
   Come answer my questions all
   Before you lay one night with me
   At either stock or wall."

6

3.   " Oh, the world is rounder than a ring,
      Heaven's higher than a tree,
      The devil is worse than a woman's tongue,
      Hell's deeper than the sea.
      The oak buds first and the thrush sings best,
      I've answered your questions all,
      So shake you up that old straw bed,
      You must lay next to the wall."

4.   " Oh, it's for my breakfast you must get
      Me chickens without bones,
      And for my dinner you must get
      Me cherries without stones,
      And for my supper you must get
      A bird without a gall
      Before I lay one night with you
      At either stock or wall."

5.   " Oh, when a chicken is in the egg
      I'm sure it has no bones,
      And when a cherry's in blossom
      I'm sure it has no stones.
      The dove she is a gentle bird,
      She flies without a gall,
      So shake me up that old straw bed,
      We must lay close to the wall."

6.   " Oh, bring to me a silken gown,
      A web that never went through,
      And you must get me a priest unborn
      To join us one and all,
      Before I lay one night with you
      At either stock or wall."

7.   " Oh, my mother's got a silken gown,
      A web that never went through ;
      Melchisedec is a priest unborn,
      He will join us one and all,
      So shake you up that old straw bed,
      You must lay next to the wall."

No. 3. *Captain Wedderburn's Courtship.* Child 46.

This riddle ballad, known by Mr. Hartlan as " Captain Woodstock," is, like *The False Knight Upon the Road*, of very early origin. The story of a suitor who wins the daughter of a king by answering riddles is found in the *Gesta Romanorum*, No. 70, while the custom of asking riddles when a prize is to be obtained goes back at least to the third century. It is interesting that this variant and that of Barry, pp. 93–94 (C), give Melchisedec as the priest, for he is spoken of by St. Paul, Hebrews vii. 3, as Priest without father or mother. This may be a later refinement of the Cæsarean birth of the Child variants.

See also Whitelaw, *Scottish Songs*, pp. 70–72 ; Sidgwick, *Popular Ballads of the Olden Time*, Second Series, pp. 162–169 ; Ord., pp. 416–420 ; etc.

For American texts see Mackenzie, No. 4 ; J.A.F.L. 24, 335–336 ; 29, 157–158 ; 30, 309.

4.

Lord Thomas and Fair Ellinor

Sung by Mrs. William McNab, Halifax.

1. LORD THOMAS he was a warrior bold
   And wore a broadsword by his side,
   Fair Ellinor she was a fair woman,
   He wanted her for his bride.

2. " Come riddle my riddle, dear mother," said he,
   " And riddle us both in one,
   Whether I shall marry with fair Ellinor
   Or bring the brown girl home."

8

3. " The brown girl she has housin and lands,
    Fair Ellinor she has none ; "
" Betide my life, and betide my living,
    I'll bring the brown girl home."

4. " Come riddle my riddle, dear mother," she said,
    " And riddle it all in one,
Whether I'll go to Lord Thomas' wedding,
    Or whether I'll stay at home."

5. " There's many that are our friends, daughter,
    And many that are our foes,
Therefore I charge thee on my blessing
    To Lord Thomas' wedding don't go."

6. " There's many that are our friends, mother,
    If a thousand were our foes,
Betide my life, betide my death,
    To Lord Thomas' wedding I'll go ! "

7. She dressed herself in rich array,
    Her merry men all in green,
And every bower that she rode by
    They took her to be a queen.

8. When she came to Lord Thomas' gate
    She knocked so bold at the ring,
And who was so ready as Lord Thomas himself
    To arise and let her in.

9. He took her by the lily-white hand
    And led her through the hall,
And he sat her on a golden chair
    Among the ladies all.

10. " Is this your bride ? " fair Ellinor said,
    " Methinks she looks wonderful brown,
She might have had as fair a colour
    As ever the sun shone on."

11. This brown girl had a knife in her hand
    Which was both keen and sharp,
    And 'twixt the long ribs and the short
    She pierced fair Ellinor's heart.

12. Lord Thomas he had a sword by his side
    Which was not sharp at all,
    He cut the brown girl's head right off
    And dashed it against the wall.

13. " O dig my grave," Lord Thomas he cried,
    " Dig it both wide and deep,
    And lay fair Ellinor by my side
    And the brown girl at my feet."

No. 4. *Lord Thomas and Fair Ellinor.* Child 73.

Child informs us that the English variant of this ballad is a broadside of Charles the Second's time, although this ballad would be, of course, much older. It is still widely current in England, Scotland and Ireland, and the story is found in similar detail in Norse and in other European ballads. Child considers Percy's Scottish variant, *Lord Thomas and Fair Annet,* one of the most beautiful of all ballads. References are too numerous to give in detail. It may be found in almost any English or Scottish collection such as Fuller-Maitland's *English County Songs.* It is also very widespread on this continent. Sharp found it in the Appalachians, EFSSA, No. 16, and Mackenzie has two variants from Nova Scotia. The text as sung by Mrs. McNab is similar to Child D, which, however, has 19 stanzas, making the details of the story a little more complete.

5.

Little Musgrave and Lady Barnard

Sung by Mrs. William McNab, Halifax.

LITTLE MATHA GROVE

1. HE took his lady by the hand
   And sat her on his knee,
   And said, " Come tell to me which you love best,
   Is it Little Matha Grove or me ? "

2. " It's well do I like his cheek," said she,
   " And it's well do I like his chin,
   And it's better do I like his little finger
   Than Lord Arnold and all his kin."

3. He took his lady by the hand
   And led her o'er the plain,
   And he never spoke another word
   Till he split her head in twain.

4. Lord Arnold has killed his wife to-day
   And he shall be hanged to-morrow.

No. 5. *Little Musgrave and Lady Barnard.*   Child 81.

Unfortunately Mrs. McNab could only recall a fragment of this well-known ballad.   Stanzas somewhat similar to my Nova Scotia text may be found in Child 81, G and I, while E agrees that " Lord Barnaby " shall be " hanged on the morrow."   The usual title is the above, but my singer knows it as *Little Matha Grove.*   Mackenzie, No. 8, has five variants from Pictou County, Nova Scotia.

6.

Bold Pedlar and Robin Hood

There chanced to be a pedlar bold A pedlar bold there chanced to be He
put his pack up-on his back And so merrily trudged o'er the lee

Sung by Mr. Ben Henneberry, Devil's Island.

PEDLAR BOLD. (Singer's title.)

1. THERE chanced to be a pedlar bold,
    A pedlar bold there chanced to be,
    He put his pack upon his back
    And so merrily trudged o'er the lee.
    By chance he met with two troublesome men,
    Two troublesome men they chanced to be,
    One of their names was bold Robin Hood
    And the other Little John so free.

2. " Pedlar, pedlar, what's in thy pack ?
    Come speedilie and tell to me."
    " I have several suits of the gay, green silk,
    And silken bow-strings one, two, and three."
    " If you have several suits of the gay, green silk,
    And silken bow-strings one, two and three,
    Then by my body," cried Little John,
    " Half your pack belongs to me."

3. The pedlar then took his pack
And placed little below his knee,
And demanded, " Moves me one perch from this
The pack and all shall gang to thee."
Little John he pulled forth the sword
And the pedlar by his pack did stand,
They swaggered swords till the sweat did flow
And he cried, " Pedlar, pray hold your hand."

4. Robin Hood, he being standing by,
He did laugh most heartilie,
" I could find a man of smaller scale
Could whip the pedlar and also thee."
" Go try, master," cried Little John,
" Go try, go try most speedilie,
There is not a man in fair Nottingham
Can beat the pedlar and also me."

5. Bold Robin Hood he drew forth his sword
And the pedlar by his pack did stand,
Where they swaggered swords till the blood did flow,
When he cried, " Pedlar, pray hold your hand.
Oh pedlar, pedlar, what is thy name ?
Come speedilie and tell to me."
" The devil a one of ye my name shall know
Before both your names ye have told to me."

6. One of our names is bold Robin Hood,
The other one Little John so free."
" Now," said the pedlar, " it's my good will
Whether my name I should tell to thee.
* I am Gamble Gold of the gay green woods,
I have travelled far and o'er the sea,
And for killing of a man in my father's court
From my country I was forced to flee."

* Mr. Faulkner of Devil's Island remembers this line as,

" Now my name it is young Gamwell."

13

7. " If you're Gamble Gold of the gay, green woods
   And have travelled far and o'er the sea,
   You are my mother's own sister's son,
   What nearer cousins then can we be ? "
   They sheathed the swords with friendly words,
   So merrilie they did agree,
   They went to a tavern and did they dine
   And cracked a bottle most merrilie.

8. Then these three they took hold of hand,
   Merrilie danced round the green tree.
   You drink water while your money lasts,
   There's a time you'll die, lads, as well as me.

No. 6. *The Bold Pedlar and Robin Hood.* Child 132.

As far as I can learn, this is the first time this ballad has been found upon this continent. Child says it seems to have been built up on a portion of the ruins of the fine old tale of Gamelyn. (See Skeat's *Chaucer*, 14, 645 ff.) Anthony à Wood and Pepys had it in their collections, and it was in the *Robin Hood Garland* of 1663 and 1670. It is a traditional variation of Child 128, *Robin Hood Newly Revived*, or *The Meeting and Fighting with his Cousin Scarlet*. It is significant that Mr. Faulkner remembers the name " Gamble Gold " as " Young Gamwell." The last stanza given by Mr. Henneberry, and which I have not found with any other variant of this ballad, is from *Little John A Begging*, Child 142, B, v. 21.

7.

Robin Hood's Progress to Nottingham

Robin Hood he bent his noble good bow And his broad arrow let

fly Till fourteen of those fifteen foresters Dead on the ground did

lie. Hi down Hi derry derry down.

1. ROBIN HOOD he bent his noble good bow
   And his broad arrow let fly,
   Till fourteen of those fifteen foresters
   Dead on the ground did lie.

   Chorus.

   Hi down, hi derry derry down.

2. Ten men they came from brave Nottinggame
   To take up Robin Hood,
   Some lost arms and some lost legs
   And more they lost their blood.   Cho.

3. Ten men they came from brave Nottingham
   To take up Robin Hood,
   But he picked up his noble good bow
   And he's off to the merry greenwood.   Cho.

All that Mr. Ben Henneberry could remember of this old song of *Robin Hood*.

This is all Mr. Henneberry could recall of a ballad which was widely current in England in the mid-seventeenth century.   The story according to Child is that when Robin Hood was about fifteen years of age he fell in with fifteen foresters who were drinking together at Nottingham. He made a wager that he would kill a hart at a hundred rod, but when it was done the foresters refused to pay.   Robin therefore killed them all, as well as others who had come from Nottingham to take him.   See *Roxburghe Ballads*, 111, 270, 845.   The story is told in the life of Robin Hood in Sloane MS. 715, 7, fol. 157, written towards the end of the sixteenth century.   Compare this fragment with Child 139, stanzas 12, 16, and 17.

8.

Sung by Mrs. William McNab, Halifax.

1. IT rains, it rains in merry Scotland,
    It rains in bower and ha',
    And all the boys in merry Scotland
    Are playing of the ba'.

2. They tossed it high, so very high,
    They tossed it high and low,
    They tossed it into a Jew's garden
    Where many a flower did grow.

3. Then out came one of the Jew's daughters,
    She was all dressed in green,
    " Come in, come in, my little boy,
    And get your ball again."

4. " I won't come in ; I daren't come in ;
I won't come in at all.
I can't come in ; I won't come in
Without my schoolfellows all."

5. She gave him an apple green as the grass,
She gave him a gay, gold ring,
She gave him a cherry as red as the blood
Until she enticed him in.

6. She sat him on a golden chair
And gave him sugar sweet,
She laid him on a dresser board
And stabbed him like a sheep.

7. She threw him in a deep, cold well
Where it was deep and cold.

. . . .

. . . .

No. 8. *Sir Hugh ; or the Jew's Daughter.* Child 155.

This ballad is interesting not for its antiquity alone, but for the story that lies behind it. In most of the European countries as well as in Great Britain, it has been thought for nearly a thousand years that Jews crucified children for ritualistic purposes in contempt of Christ, enticing them into their homes for that purpose.

The deep draw well of stanza 7 is in Child (A) *Our Lady's Well*. Here the boy's mother finds her son, Sir Hugh, who asks her to prepare his winding-sheet and appoints to meet her at the back of the town. Bells are rung without man's hands,

" And a' the books of merry Lincoln
Were read without man's tongue."

Bishop Percy says the ballad was probably built upon some Italian legend, and notes the great resemblance to Chaucer's *Prioresses Tale.* Both he and Child discredit absolutely the legend that Jews ever crucified Christian children, but consider these tales to excuse cruelties to these wretched people. Summers, *The History of Witchcraft and Demonology*, p. 195, associates the legend with black magic.

The ballad seems to be quite universal. It is a pity Mrs. McNab could not recall the rest of the words, for as far as it goes this is a particularly interesting and valuable variant.

Newell, No. 18, has found it sung by children on the streets of New York, and Scarborough, *On the Trail of the Negro Folk-Songs*, pp. 52–53, among the American negroes.

17

9.

Farmer's Curst Wife

1. THERE was an old farmer lived on a hill,
      (whistle second line)
   There was an old farmer lived on a hill,
   And if he's not dead he lives there still.

   Chorus.
   To me chorl a lido, chorl a lido, fall the diddle I dey.

2. The old devil he came to the man at the plow,
   He says, " I am after your scolding wife now."   Cho.

3. " Take her, old devil, with all of my heart,
   I hope you and her will never part."

4. The old devil he slounced her on his back,
   And like an old peddler when carrying his pack.   Cho.

5. He carried her till he came in sight of home,
   She tickled the skin off the devil's backbone.   Cho.

6. The devil he opened a big iron door
   And he slammed her in among ten thousand more.   Cho.

7. The little devils they all hung on chains,
   She up with her foot and she kicked out their brains. Cho.

8. Some of them they hung on wire,
   She up with her foot and kicked nine in the fire. Cho.

9. Three little devils peeped over the wall,
   Saying, " Take her away, master, or she'll kill us all." Cho.

10. Oh, the old devil he slounced her on his back,
    And like an old fool he carried her back. Cho.

11. " Oh, here's your wife, she's not worth a curse,
    She's been all through hell and she's ten devils worse." Cho.

12. And then she went whistling over the hill,
    " If the devil won't have me I don't know who will." Cho.

All verses are arranged in the same formation as the first. Sung by Mr. Faulkner, Devil's Island, with the assistance of Mr. Ben Henneberry and others.

No. 9. *The Farmer's Curst Wife.* Child 278.

The legend of a curst wife who was a terror to demons is widely spread in Europe and the Orient as well as in Great Britain. Child gives a variant with the chorus of whistlers, and Bell, pp. 204–205, gives the ballad as a Sussex countryman's whistling song. He writes that the effect when the singer is accompanied by the chorus of the strong whistles of a group of lusty countrymen is very striking. Burns is said to have founded his *Carle of Killyburn Braes* on this ballad.

For American texts see Barry, pp. 325–333 ; Lomax, 110–111 ; Davis, No. 46 ; J.A.F.L., 19, 298–299 ; 24, 348–349 ; 27, p. 68 ; 30, 329–330 ; Cox, No. 30 ; EFSSA, pp. 39–40. Nova Scotia text, Mackenzie, No. 15.

10.

Sweet Trinity: or The Golden Vanity

Sung by Mr. Richard Hartlan, South-East Passage.

GOLDEN VALLADY. (Singer's title.)

1. I HAD a ship in the northern counteree,
    She goes by the name of the *Golden Vallady.*
    I'm afraid she'll be taken by some bold Roosian crew
    As she lies on the lowlands, on the lowlands,
    As she lies on the lowlands low.

2. I will give you gold and silver,
    Likewise my daughter Jane,
    If you'll sink her in the lowlands, in the lowlands,
    If you'll sink her in the lowlands low.

3. Oh, the boy took his auger, and overboard jumped he,
    He swam till he came to the bold Russian crew.
    Oh, the boy took his auger, and he bore two holes in twice
    While some were playing chess and the others were playing dice,
    And he sank her in the lowlands, in the lowlands,
    And he sank her in the lowlands low.

4. Now the water came in, which dazzled all their eyes,
   And he sank her in the lowlands, in the lowlands,
   And they sank her in the lowlands low.

5. Oh, the boy took his auger, and back swam he,
   He swam till he came to the *Golden Vallady.*
   He called, " Captain, pick me up,
   For I'm sinking in the lowlands, in the lowlands,
   For I'm sinking in the lowlands low."

6. " I could kill you, I could stab you,
   I could sink you as you lie,
   I could sink you in the lowlands, in the lowlands,
   I could sink you in the lowlands low."

7. Oh, the boy swam around, around the starboard side,
   When his strength began to fail, and bitterly he cries,
   He cried, " Friends, pick me up, else I surely will be drowned,
   For I'm sinking in the lowlands, in the lowlands,
   For I'm sinking in the lowlands low."

8. Oh, his shipmates picked him up, and it's on the deck he died,
   They sewed him in his hammock which was so long and wide,
   They sewed him in his hammock, and it's overboard him threw,
   And they sank him in the lowlands, in the lowlands,
   And they sank him in the lowlands low.

No. 10. *The "Sweet Trinity"; or the "Golden Vanity."* Child 286.

Compare this variant of the Pepys ballad, *Sir Walter Raleigh Sailing on the Lowlands*, to the Child variant C to which this bears a close relationship. The bold Roosian crew is rather singular, for the enemy is usually Turkish, Spanish or French. This may be an echo of the Crimean War. The ship has a variety of names, as *The Goulden Vanitie, The French Galley, The French Gallolee, The Turkish Galley*, etc. Variant C agrees that the boy took his auger and bore two holes at twice, although in some cases it reads thirty holes at twice and fifteen at once. Between stanzas one and two of the Nova Scotia text there should be a line telling how the little cabin boy asked his master what reward he would be given for sinking the enemy ship. The ballad is widely current in Great Britain and on this continent. Compare stanza 3 of *The Louisiana Lowlands* in this volume.

11.

Katharine Jaffray

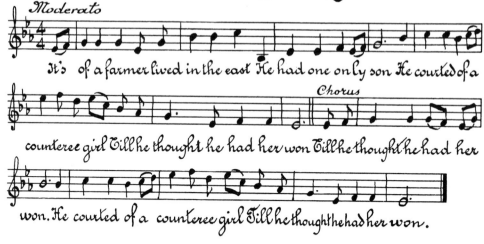

Sung by Mr. Ben Henneberry, Devil's Island.

1. It's of a farmer lived in the east,
   He had one only son,
   He courted of a counteree girl
   Till he thought he had her won.   Till he thought he had her won
   He courted of a counteree girl till he thought he had her won.

2. He got consent from her father and mother
   And the two young men likewise,
   And then she cried, " I am undone,"
   And the tears rolled from her eyes, etc.

3. She sent her love a love-letter,
   Gave him to understand
   This very night I am going to be wed
   To a rich gentleman, etc.

4. He sent her back an answer
   And sealed it with a ring,
   " The suit that you wear at your wedding,
   Be sure and put on green, etc.

5. " A suit of the same I will put on,
        To your wedding I'll prepare,
    And I'll wed you, my dearest, dear,
        In spite of all that's there," etc.

6. Then he looked to the east and he looked to the west,
        He espied far over the land,
    He espied fourscore of his best young men
        All under his command, etc.

7. Then he mounted them double on a milk-white steed,
        And a single man rode he ;
    He rode till he came to the wedding house
        Where the wedding was to be, etc.

8. She invited them all, both great and small,
        " Have you been out all day ?
    Or have you seen those foreign troops
        That have passed along this way ? " etc.

9. He laughed at her, and he scoffed at her,
        And then he seemed to say,
    " There might have been some gentlemen
        That have passed along this way," etc.

10. And he filled up a glass of the best port wine,
        He drank to the company round,
    Saying, " Here's a health to thee, young man,
        The man they call the groom.

11. " But ten times happier is the man
        That will enjoy the bride,
    For another might love her as well as he
        And take her from his side."

12. Then up spoke the intended groom,
        And a rough spoken man was he,
    " If it is for to fight that you came here
        I am just the man for thee."

23

13. " Oh, it is not to fight that I came here,
    But kind friendship for to show,
    Grant me one kiss from your bonny, bonny bride,
    And away from you I'll go."

14. He took her round the middle so small,
    And a hold of her grass-green sleeve,
    And he led her out of the wedding house,
    Of the company asked no leave.

15. Where the drums did beat and the fife did play
    And they did so merrily sing,
    Now she's conveyed to fair Edinborough Castle
    With her company dressed in green.

16. Now come all young fellows that are going to be wed,
    A warning take by me,
    Never be served as I've been served
    All on my wedding day.
    All on my wedding day,
    At catching fish instead of flesh
    I always had foul play.

No. 11. *Katharine Jaffray.* Child 221.

It is doubtful whether this ballad should be included in the first group, for it is undoubtedly a much later variant of that old ballad of *Katharine Jaffray* which Scott used in the first edition of his *Minstrelsy* and also used as the basis for his poem, *Young Lochinvar*.

The Nova Scotia text bears close resemblance to one which Child mentions as being "a copy from the recitation of a young Irishwoman living in Taunton, Massachusetts (learned from print, I suppose, and in parts imperfectly remembered), [which] puts the scene of the story at Edenborough town." There is much similarity between this Nova Scotia variant and that of A in Barry's collection from Maine, pp. 400–406, where it is listed among the secondary ballads. In Barry as in the Nova Scotia text the message is sealed with a ring and the bride is requested to wear green, which may point to an Irish rather than to a Scottish source, for, according to Child, no Scots girl would wear green for fear of ill-luck.

12.

Song of a Soldier

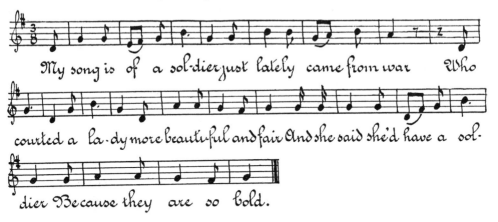

My song is of a sol-dier just lately came from war Who courted a la-dy more beautiful and fair And she said she'd have a sol-dier Because they are so bold.

Sung by Mr. Allan Hartlan, South-East Passage.

1. My song is of a soldier just lately came from war,
   Who courted a lady more beautiful and fair,
   And she said she'd have a soldier
   Because they are so bold.

2. He buckled his pistol and sword together
   Which made them for to frattle,
   He laid them by his side, and said that he would marry her
   If she would be his bride.

3. So off they went together.   On returning home
   They met her cruel father and seven armed men.
   " Since you are so mean to be a soldier's wife,
   Down in this lonesome valley I will quickly end your life."

4. " Aye, aye," said the soldier, " I do not like your father,
   For I am your bridesmaid and just prepared for battle."
   The lady held the horse
   Till the soldier fought the battle.

5. The first one he came to, he run him through the main,
   Next one he came to, he served him the same,

"Stay your hand," cries the old man, " you make my blood run cold,
You shall have my daughter and £500 in gold."

6. " Fight on, fight on," said the lady, " my fortune is too small."
" Stay your hand," cries the old man,
" And you shall have it all,
You shall have my daughter and £50000 in gold."

7. He took him to his house and called him his own,
And never no more would he let the soldier roam,
For they are husky lads, the brisky lads a-free,
They will fight for the pretty girls, the right property.

No. 12. *Song of a Soldier.* Cf. Child 7.

This is an interesting modern variant of the old ballad of *Earl Brand*, where the father and
seven brothers are slain by the lover they pursue. It is printed by Barry as *The Soldier's Wooing*,
pp. 377—382. See J.A.F.L., 23, 447-449 ; 30, p. 363 ; and Davis, No. 4, where it is given as
an Appendix to *Earl Brand*.

13.

Sung by Mr. Ben Henneberry, Devil's Island.

1. You pretty virgins, I pray draw near,
A pretty story you shall hear,
It's of a Turkish young lady gay
Who fell in love with an English slave.

2. A merchant ship at Bristol lay
   As we were sailing o'er the sea,
   By a Turkish rover took were we
   And all of us made slaves to be.

3. They bound us down in iron strong,
   They whipped and lashed us all along;
   No tongue can tell, I'm certain sure,
   What we poor seamen did endure.

4 Come sit you down and list awhile,
   I'll tell how fortune did on me smile,
   But it was my fortune all for to be
   A slave unto a rich lady.

5. She dressed herself in rich array
   And went to view her slaves one day.
   Hearing the moan this young man made
   She went to him and this she said :

6. " What countryman, young man, are you ? "
   " I am an Englishman, that's true."
   " I wish you was a Turk," says she,
   I'd ease you of your misery.

7. " I'll ease you of your slavish work
   If you'll consent and turn a Turk,
   And own myself to be your wife
   For I do love you as my life."

8, " Oh, no," then said he,
   " Your constant slave, madame, I'll be,
   I'd rather be burnt lashed on a stake,
   Before that I'll my God forsake."

9. To her chamber she then went,
   And spent that night in discontent,
   Like Cupid with his piercing dart
   Had deeply wounded her tender heart.

10. And she resolved the next day
    To ease him of his misery,
    And own herself to be his wife,
    For she did love him as her life.

11. She dressed herself in rich array,
    And with this young man sailed away,
    And to her parents she bid adieu,
    By this you see what love can do.

12. She is now turned a Christian brave,
    And is wed to one of her own slaves,
    That was in chains and in bondage too,
    So now you see what love can do.

No. 13. *Turkish Rover.* Cf. Child 53.

This is probably an inferior re-writing of *Young Beichan*. According to Mackenzie, Logan, *A Pedlar's Pack*, p. 11, conjectures that it was composed about the middle of the seventeenth century and compares it with *The Spanish Lady's Love to an Englishman*. See Mackenzie, No. 17 and J.A.F.L., 23, pp. 449–450, a variant like the Nova Scotia text.

14.

Well Sold the Cow

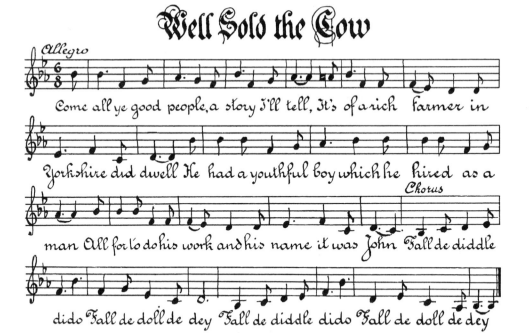

Come all ye good people, a story I'll tell, It's of a rich farmer in Yorkshire did dwell He had a youthful boy which he hired as a man All for to do his work and his name it was John Fall de diddle dido Fall de doll de dey Fall de diddle dido Fall de doll de dey

Sung by Mr. Ben Henneberry, Devil's Island.

1. COME all ye good people, a story I'll tell,
    It's of a rich farmer in Yorkshire did dwell.
    He had a youthful boy which he hired as a man
    All for to do his work, and his name it was John.

    Chorus.

    Fall de diddle dido, fall de doll de dey,
    Fall de diddle dido, fall de doll de dey.

2. Early one morning John's master arose,
    Into Jack's room he instantly goes,
    " Jack, my dear fellow, drive this cow to the fair,
    For she is in good order, and her we can spare."   Cho.

3. Jack took the cow, drove her out of the farm ;
    He had not gone far when he met with three men,

29

He had not gone far when he met with three men,
And he sold the cow for £5 10.   Cho.

4. They went to an ale-house all for to get a drink,
Those three men paid him right down in a jink,
" What will I do with my money, landlady ? " said he,
" In the lining of your coat I'll sew it," said she,
" For it's here upon the road it's robbed you might be."   Cho.

5. A robber in the room he sat drinking up his wine,
But thinking to himself, " That money shall be mine,"
Jack took his leave and started for home ;
The robber he followed him out of the room.   Cho.

6. The robber overtook him all on the highway,
" How far do you travel, young man ? " he did say.
" Three or four miles as near I know,"
And he jumped on behind and away they did go.   Cho.

7. They rode away together till they came to a narrow lane.
" Deliver up your money, young man," he did say ;
" Deliver up your money without fear or strike,
Or this very moment I'll take away your life."   Cho.

8. Jack jumped from the saddle without fear or doubt,
From the lining of his coat he pulled the money out,
From the lining of his coat he pulled the money out,
And along the green grass he scattered it about.   Cho.

9. The robber alighted down from his horse,
But little did he think it was to his loss ;
While a-gathering up the money which Jack threw on the grass,
Jack jumped on the saddle and rode off with the horse.   Cho.

10. One of the servants seen Jack coming home,
It's in to the master they instantly run.
He said, " Jack, my dear fellow, have you made a swap ?
Or did my cow turn into a horse ? "   Cho.

11. " No, my dear master, the truth I'll unfold,
    I was stopped on the way by a highwayman so bold,
    While gathering up the money which I threw upon the grass
    To prove myself a man I brought home the horse." Cho.

12. When the saddle-bags were opened, and in them were fold
    Five hundred bright guineas in silver and gold,
    A bright pair of pistols, the farmer did vow,
    " Jack, my dear fellow, you have well sold the cow." Cho.

No. 14. *Well Sold the Cow.* Cf. Child 283.

This interesting song of the thieved outwitting the thief is very similar in theme to *The Crafty Farmer*, Child 283. In Kidson's *Garland*, pp. 14–15, *The Highwayman Outwitted*, the intended victim is a girl. As *Saddle to Rags* it may be found in Dixon, vol. 17, pp. 126–130 ; as *The Silly Old Man* in Baring-Gould, No. 18 ; *The Lincolnshire Farmer*, Sharp, *English Folk-Songs of Norfolk*, pp. 42–43 ; *The Yorkshire Bite*, J.A.F.L., 23, 451–454 ; Barry, pp. 406–413 ; a Maine variant very like the Nova Scotia text ; *Down, Down Derry Down*, Sandburg, pp. 118–119. Yorkshire Bite means a shrewd trick played upon a person, such as Yorkshire people were supposed to think of.

15.

Annie

Every evening every evening as I go to my bed The
thoughts of you Annie still run through my head With a sobbing and a
sighing as I turn myself round When I think of you An-nie the
tears do run down

Sung by Mr. Richard Hartlan, South-East Passage.

1. EVERY evening, every evening as I go to my bed
   The thoughts of you, Annie, still run through my head,
   With a sobbing and a sighing as I turn myself round,
   When I think of you, Annie, the tears do run down.

2. I rise in the morning, my heart full of woe,
   I go to my shop my shutters to throw,
   There's no one that grieves me but the innocent dove,
   So I hope to gain pardon to the girl that I love.

3. Annie being listening and heard what was saying,
   She drew nigher and nigher to hear what he said.
   " Since you are the young man that I do adore,
   It's a trip I'll make with you to Lincolnham shores."

4. My friends and relations they do all they can
   For to part me and Annie, that's more than they can.

No. 15. *Annie.*

16.

Butcher Boy

In Jersey City where I once did dwell A butcher boy he loved me well He courted me my life away, And with me now He will not stay.

Sung by Mr. Edward Hartley, Dartmouth.

1. IN Jersey City where I once did dwell
   A butcher boy he loved me well,
   He courted me my life away
   And with me now he will not stay.

2. There is a place in that same town
   Where my love goes and he sits down,
   He takes a strange girl on his knee
   And tells her what he won't tell me.

3. Oh, mother dear, if you only knew
   What sorrow and pain my heart doth know,
   Give me a chair and sit me on
   And a pen and ink till I write it down.

4. And she wrote a letter, she wrote it long,
   She wrote it until she made a song,
   On every line she shed a tear
   And on every verse called Willie dear.

5. Her father came from work that night
   Enquiring for his heart's delight,
   He went upstairs, the door he broke,
   He found her hanging to a rope.

6. He took his knife and cut her down
   And in her bosom these lines he found,
   Saying, " What a foolish girl was I
   To hang myself for a butcher's boy.

7. " Dig me a grave and dig it deep,
    Place a marble stone at my head and feet,
    And on my breast place a turtle dove
    To tell the world I died for love."

No. 16. *The Butcher Boy.*

The Butcher Boy has been widely circulated in Great Britain and the United States, with the scene variously set in London City, New York or any of a number of places. Mackenzie, No. 59, gives two variants with a close affinity between his variant B and this of Mr. Hartley's.

The song is combined from several broadside ballads, namely (1) *Sheffield Park* (Catnach ; Jackson & Son, Birmingham) ; (2) *The Squire's Daughter*, also known as *The Cruel Father*, or *Deceived Maid*, and (3) *A Brisk Young Sailor* or its abbreviated version *There is an Alehouse in Yonder Town*. Compare also stanza 4 (A) of *My Sailor Lad* in this volume with stanza 5 of this song.

17.

Diana and Sweet William

In London fine city, there lived you might hear A noble rich

lord had a daughter so fair Her name was Di·ana scarce sixteen years

old Her fortune twenty thousand bright guineas in gold

Sung by Mr. Ben Henneberry, Devil's Island.

1. In London fine city, there lived, you might hear,
    A noble rich lord had a daughter so fair,
    Her name was Diana, scarce sixteen years old,
    Her fortune twenty thousand bright guineas in gold.

34

2. Besides an estate when her father did die,
   Which brought many a courter to this lady,
   And among the whole number sweet William was one
   Who thought for to make the fair lady his own.

3. It was early one morning her father did say,
   " Come dress yourself, Diana, both gallant and gay,
   I have a knight worth ten thousand a year,
   And he says he will make you his wife and his heir."

4. " Go onward, father, I pray now be kind,
   To marry, this lady, I do not feel inclined,
   Besides, honored father, I beg you therefore
   Pray let me live single for a few years more."

5. " Oh, stubborn daughter, it's what do you mean ?
   I say you must wed or else no more be seen,
   Considering ten thousand a year you shall have."
   " Oh, father, I'd rather go to my grave."

6. It was late in the evening Diana walked out,
   She came to the grave and she marched all about,
   She came to the spot where her true love and she
   Had oftentimes met and so sweet did agree.

7. " Ten thousand times, Willie, I bid you farewell,
   The love I have for you no mortal can tell,
   I wish you much joy, and more when I'm gone
   To a handsome rich lady, both charming and young."

8. She fell on her knees ; no more did she say,
   With a dose of strong poison took her own life away,
   She had not been laying half a hour on the ground
   When Willie came searching the grove all around.
   He found her lying dead and a note lying by
   Which gave an account how Diana did die.

9. He fell on his knees and he kissed her cold lips,
   And the joys of all breathing, I'm deprived of this.
   He leaned on his sword like a true lover so brave,
   Diana and her sweetheart were laid in one grave.

No. 17. *Diana and Sweet William.* See note No. 18.

35

18.

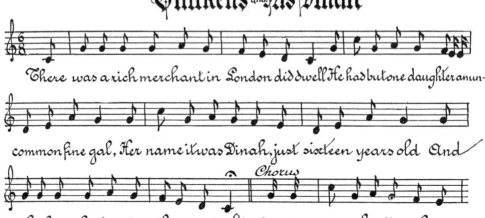

There was a rich merchant in London did dwell He had but one daughter an un-
common fine gal, Her name it was Dinah, just sixteen years old And
of a large fortune in silver and gold Singing tor-rol-i to rol-i
oo-rol-i-a, Tor-rol i tor-ror-i-i- oo rol-i-a

Sung by Marion Henneberry, aged 12, and Audrey Henneberry, aged 9.

1. THERE was a rich merchant in London did dwell,
    He had but one daughter an uncommon fine gal,
    Her name it was Dinah just sixteen years old,
    And of a large fortune in silver and gold.

    #### Chorus.
    Singing tor rol i to rol i oo rol i a,
    Tor rol i tor ror i i oo rol i a.

2. As Dinah was walking the garden one day
    Her father came to her and thusly did say,
    " Go dress yourself, Dinah, in gorgeous array
    And take yourself a husband both gallant and gay."   Cho.

3. " Oh, papa, oh, papa, I've not made up my mind,
    To marry just yet I do not feel inclined,
    But to you my large fortune I'd gladly give o'er
    If you'll let me live single a year or two more."   Cho.

36

4. " Go, go, boldest daughter," her parent replied,
   " If thou don't consent to be this young man's bride
   I will leave my large fortune to the nearest of kin
   And you shan't have a cent of my tin tin."   Cho.

5. As Villikens was walking the garden around
   He spied his dear Dinah lying dead on the ground,
   And a cup of cold poison it lay by her side
   And Villa dex station * 'twas poison she died.   Cho.

6. He kissed her cold corpus a thousand times o'er
   And called her his Dinah though she was no more,
   And taking the poison like a lover so brave
   And Villikens and his Dinah lie both in one grave.   Cho.

* These words are given phonetically, so it is little wonder the children could not tell what they meant.   They should read, " billet-doux, stating."

No. 18. *Villikens and His Dinah.*

This song and the foregoing are coupled together because *Villikens and His Dinah*, so well known, is a humorous parody on the much older ballad of *Diana and Sweet William.*   They may be found together in J.A.F.L., vol. 35, 418–420.   See also Spaeth, *Read 'Em and Weep*, pp. 59–60 ; J.A.F.L., 29, 190–191 ; 39, 112–113 ; Cox, No. 105, where the merchant meets the ghosts of Villikens and His Dinah in the garden as he goes walking.

19.

Green Bushes

All early, all early, all into the spring You hear the birds whistle and nightingales sing I spied a fair damsel, and sweetly sang she Down by some green bushes or chance to meet me

Sung by Mr. Richard Hartlan, South-East Passage.

1. ALL early, all early, all into the spring
   You hear the birds whistle and nightingales sing,
   I spied a fair damsel, and sweetly sang she
   Down by some green bushes, or chance to meet me.

2. Oh, it's " Where are you going, my pretty fair maid ? "
   " I'm in search of my true love, kind sir," and she said,
   " But if you'll be my true love, and we can agree,
   I'll leave my own Jimmie and follow with thee."

3. " I will buy you rich jewels, fine silks and fine gowns,
   I will buy you rich dresses all flounced to the ground,
   I will buy you rich dresses all flounced to the knee
   If you'll leave your own Jimmie and follow with me."

4. " I want none of your jewels, fine silks or fine house,
   Do you think I'm so poor as to marry for clothes ?
   But if you'll be my true love, and we can agree,
   I'll leave my own Jimmie and follow with thee.

5. " It is time to be going, young man, if you please,
    It is time to be leaving from under these trees,
    But my true love is coming, in yonder I see,
    A-whispering and a-singing all joys to meet me."

6. Oh, when he got there he found she was gone,
    He looked like a lambkin and cried out forlorn,
    " She is gone with some other and forsaken me,
    It's adieu to green bushes wherever you be."

No. 19. *Green Bushes.*

I can give no more interesting note than this sent very kindly by Mrs. M. E. Hobbs of the English Folk-Song Society, and taken from the Cecil Sharp notes.

" Two versions of this ballad recovered by Baring-Gould in Devon are printed in *Songs of the West*, No. 43, and *English County Songs*, p. 170. See also Kidson's T.T., p. 47 and Joyce, *Ancient Irish Music*, pp. 25–26. The words which are on the broadsides by Such have some affinity with the old Northumbrian ballad, *Sir Arthur and Charming Mollie* (Bell's *Songs of the Peasantry of England*, p. 236).

Buckstone's play *The Green Bushes* was produced in 1845, and this song, described as a popular Irish ballad, was given. It is sung freely throughout England. See *Journal*, vol. I, pp. 66–90.

Ord, p. 147, also gives it reprinted from an old chapbook similar to those sold at Feeing Markets half a century ago. The first stanza of the Nova Scotia variant is similar to *The Sign of the Bonny Blue Bell*, Sharp, No. 40.

20.

I Wrote My Love A Letter

Sung by Muriel Henneberry, aged 12, Devil's Island.

1. I WROTE my love a letter in red, rosy line,
    She wrote me another all twisted and torn,
    Saying, " You keep your love letters and I will keep mine,
    As you write to your love and I write to mine."

    Chorus.

    Green grows the laurel, soft falls the dew,
    And sad is my heart as I parted from you,

And it's at the next meeting I hope you'll pull through,
And change the green laurel for the red, white and blue.

2.   I pass my love's window both early and late,
    And the look that she gave me would make your heart ache,
    And the look that she gave me ten thousand would kill,
    I love another one far better still.   Chorus.

Chorus.

You drink the sherry and I'll drink the wine,
As you write to your love and I'll write to mine,
And it's at the next meeting I hope you'll pull through
And change the green laurel to the red, white and blue.

No. 20. *I Wrote My Love a Letter.*

This song, as little Muriel has sung it, is rather confused. The first stanza is like v. 3 in A and B of Cox, No. 139. My first chorus is similar to his two choruses, and my verse 2 is like verse 2 of his B variant. For the second chorus compare v. 3, Ord, p. 187, in *The Rose and the Thyme.* See also Ord, p. 182; J.A.F.L., 39, 147. Other titles are *The Green Laurels* and *The Orange and Blue.*

21.

James McDonald

Come all good people old and young I pray you lend an ear It is of a true stor-y As ever you did hear Young James he courted a comely maid Until her he had beguiled And for to take her precious life He planned his scheme in time

Sung by Mr. Allan Henneberry, Devil's Island.

1. COME, all good people, old and young,
     I pray you lend an ear,
   It is of a true story
     As ever you did hear,
   Young James he courted a comely maid
     Until her he had beguiled,
   And for to take her precious life
     He planned his scheme in time.

2. He wrote to her a letter,
     These words to her did say,
   " Now, Annie, if you give your consent
     To Lonsport we will go,
   And there we will get married,
     So don't let no one know."

3. The night being dark the day shut out
    To cross the counteree,
It would bring the tears down from your eyes
    To hear what he did say,
And before he went to murder her
    He made her this reply,
" Now, Annie, you will go no further,
    For here's your doom to die."

4. " Oh, James, think on your infant young
    And don't give me a fright,
And don't you think on murdering me
    This dark and stormy night.
I will pray to God here on my knees
    If you'll spare me my life,
I did not come to trouble you
    Nor want to be your wife."

5. All her pleadings they were in vain
    When he struck her right sore,
With a heavy loaded weapon
    He laid her in her gore.
The blood that flowed that stained the ground,
    Her cries would pierce your heart,
And when he had her murdered
    From her he did depart.

6. She being alive the next morning
    Just at the break of day,
When he found his only daughter,
    But chance I came that way.
He saw her bleeding on the ground
    And ran to her release,
She told him of her guilty one
    And sent her for the priest.

7. The priest and doctors was sent for
    And policemen too likewise,
And when they got information
    They dressed up in disguise.

They quickly surrounded me
    And put me on my drill,
And I was taken to Longford
    To lodge in bonds for jail.

8.   There I laid with a troubled mind
      Until my trial day.
   The judge he passed his sentence,
      Those words to me did say,
   " For the murder of young Annie O'Brien
      A country boy will see,
   On the twenty-fifth day of December
      You will die on the gallows tree."

9.   My name is James McDonald,
      Of life I now must part,
   For the murder of young Annie O'Brien
      I'm sorry to the heart,
   I hope that God will pardon me
      On my great judgment day,
   And when I am on the gallows tree
      Good Christians for me pray.

No. 21. *James McDonald.*

Mr. Sharp has included this in his *Folk-Songs from Somerset* with a note saying that the air which he found there seemed to him more Irish than English. Ord, pp. 477–479, describes it as an Irish song introduced into Scotland at the beginning of the last century by harvesters, and the name which is given in v. 2 here as Lonsport is in the Ord variant Longford.

22

Jocky Said to Jinnie

Croon slowly and softly

Jock he says to Jinnie "Oh Jinnie will ye hae me And if ye will na
hae me, ye aye can let me be, be I fall the diddle ol de dol de dey

Sung by Mrs. William McNab, Halifax.

> JOCK he says to Jinnie, "Oh Jinnie will ye hae me?
> And if ye will na hae me, ye aye can let me be, be,
> I fall the diddle ol, de dol de dey."
> I hae seven oxen, a gangin' by the pleuchie.*

* Plow.

No. 22. *Jocky Said to Jinnie.*

This is a fragment of a Scottish song found in Ramsey's *Miscellany*, p. 68, with the letter Z which signifies great age. It is more commonly known as *For the Love of Jean.* See Herd, *Ancient and Modern Scottish Songs and Heroic Ballads*, vol. 2, pp. 195–196; Johnson, *Scots Musical Museum*, vol. 1, p. 62; Dixon, *Edinburgh Book of Scottish Verse*, No. 141; Whitelaw, *Book of Scottish Songs*, p. 145.

It is a curious and interesting fact that Mrs. McNab, who learned this crooning lullaby from her mother, should later have two maids in her employ who knew this song. One from Cape Breton sang in Gaelic. The other from Chezzetcook, N.S., sang in French. Neither would sing it if she thought her mistress listening, and neither would interpret the words. The music was the same in all three cases.

23.

Quaker's Courtship

Sung by Mr. Ben Henneberry, Devil's Island.

1. " MADAME, I have come a-courting, Oh dear,
   Not for pleasure, not for sporting, Oh dear."
   " You may sit and court the fire,
   Tee diddle ding dum ding dum dey,
   To go to bed is my desire,
   Tee diddle ding dum ding dum dey."

2. " I've a ring and forty shillings, Oh dear,
   You may have them if you're willing, Oh dear."
   " I don't want your ring and money,
   Tee diddle ding dum ding dum dey,
   I want a young man to call me honey
   Tee diddle ding dum ding dum dey."

3. " Madame, you are young and tender, Oh dear,
   And your waist is small and slender, Oh dear."
   " But you know the way to flatter,
   Tee diddle ding dum ding dum dey,
   But I do despise a Quaker,
   Tee diddle ding dum ding dum dey."

4. " I'll go home and tell my daddy, Oh dear,
   That you're not disposed to marry, Oh dear."

46

" You go home and tell your daddy,
Tee diddle ding dum ding dum dey,
Find a Quaker girl to marry,
Tee diddle ding dum ding dum dey."

No. 23. *The Quaker's Courtship.*

This song of the hapless Quaker's wooing has been imported from England.

For American texts see Pound, No. 108 ; Sandburg, p. 71 ; Newell, No. 31 ; J.A.F.L., 18, 55–56 ; 24, 343 ; 29 ; 198–199.   From Nova Scotia, Mackenzie, No. 158.

24.

Sung by Mr. Ben Henneberry, Devil's Island.

1. IT's of a rich counsellor here I write
    Who had one only daughter,
    She was his dearest beauty bright,
    But mark what followed after.

Her uncle dear, I do declare,
  He left her a large fortune,
And her father dear was to take care,
  For fear of her discretion.*

2. She had £12,000
      In gold and silver ready,
    Courted she was by many's the lord
      But none could gain this lady.
    At length the squire's youngest son
      In private came a-wooing,
    When he had her favour won,
      Saying, " I fear you're at your ruin."

3. The damsel she made this reply,
      " I must confess I love thee,
    Lords, dukes and knights I have denied,
      But none I praise above thee.
    The art of jewel in thine eye." †
      She said, " You are the fairest,
    I'm afraid you were condemned to die
      For stealing of an heiress."

4. " Your father he is a rich counsellor,
      I will tell him my condition,
    And to your father I will go
      And give him a commission.
    Ten guineas, love, shall be his fee,
      He'll think I am a stranger,
    And with this gold he'll counsel me,
      And keep me clear from danger."

5. Unto the counsellor he goes
      The very next day after,
    But did not let the old man know
      The lady was his daughter.
    When the old man beheld the gold
      Thinking he was the gainer,
    A pleasant rate to him he told
      In safety to obtain her.

* Of her at his discretion.   † Thou art a jewel in mine eye.

6. " Let her prepare a horse to ride,
      And bring you up behind her,
   And to a parson's house may ride
      Before her parents find her.
   Then she stole you, you may complain,
      And so divide the theory,*
   Oh, those are laws I will maintain
      Before a judge and jury.

7. " Here take my right and hand and seal †
      Which I cannot deny thee,
   And if you any trouble feel
      In court I will stand by thee."
   " Oh, I give thee thanks," the young man cried,
      " By you I am befriended,
   Unto your house I'll bring my bride
      Soon as the work is ended."

8. Early the next morning ‡
      The news to him was carried,
   How she her father's counsel kept
      Till they were kindly married.
   After all night they took their ease,
      Their joys beyond expression,
   She fell upon her bended knees
      And begged her father's blessing.

9. When the old man beheld them both
      He looked like one distracted,
   Rough and revenge he swore he'd have
      For what they had transacted.
   Up spoke the new-made son,
      " There can't be no inditing,
   For those is laws which you have made,
      Here is your own handwriting."

* And so avoid their theory.
† Now take my writing and my seal.
‡ Next morning e'er the day did break.

49

10. Then up spoke the old man,
      " Was there e'er a man so ill-fitted ! *
    My hand and seal I gave to you,
      By you I am outwitted.
    Lords, dukes and knights she might have had,
      From royal lines descended,
    But since you are her heart's delight
      On you I'm not offended.

11. " She has £12,000 in gold
      Left by my brother,
    And when I die there'll be as much more,
      For child I have no other,
    Now you and I will ne'er depart,
      We have plenty out of measure,"
    And joined they were, both hearts and hands,
      With plenty, peace and pleasure.

              * Was ever man so fitted.

No. 24. *Rich Counsellor*.

This song of the lover who wins a wife by the ingenious use of his wits is given in *A Collection of Old Ballads* printed for J. Roberts and D. Leach, 1723, vol. 2, pp. 234-236, almost word for word like the Nova Scotia text. Bell, pp. 110-113, gives it as *The Crafty Lover*, or *The Lawyer Outwitted*. Variant lines from these have been appended where the sense of the Nova Scotia variant seems obscure.

25.

Silvy

Oh Silvy Silvy all on one day She dressed herself in

men's array With a sword and pistol hung by her side To

meet her true love a-way did ride

Sung by Mr. Ben Henneberry, Devil's Island.

1. OH, Silvy, Silvy, all on one day
   She dressed herself in men's array,
   With a sword and pistol hung by her side
   To meet her true love away did ride.

2. She had not travelled far o'er the main
   She met her true love upon the plain.
   " Stand and deliver, young man," she said,
   " Or the cold clay it will be your bed."

3. When he had delivered all his store
   He says, " Kind sir, there is one thing more,
   That gold diamond ring that I see you wear,
   Deliver that and your life I'll spare."

4. " That gold diamond that you see me wear
   My life you'll take before that I'll spare."
   She being tender hearted, just like a dove,
   She rode away from her own true love.

5. Next day unto the garden green
    Those two young lovers there were seen,
    He saw his watch hanging by her clothes
    Which made him blush like any rose.

6. " Why do you blush at such a silly thing ?
    I fain would have that gold diamond ring.
    It was me that robbed you all on the plain,
    Here, take your watch and your gold again."

7. " If I'd have had my pistol shot
    I'd have shot my true love dead on the spot,
    I'd have killed my true love dead on the plain,
    I'd ne'er forgive my own self again."

No. 25. *Silvy*.

See *The Female Highwayman*, Kidson G, pp. 4–5, which is very like the Nova Scotia variant with the exception of the last stanza in which " Sylva " says her motive was to prove his love. Mackenzie, No. 129, gives two variants from Pictou County, N.S., under the caption *Zillah*.

26.

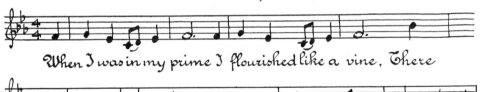

Sung by Mr. Enos Hartlan, South-East Passage.

1. WHEN I was in my prime
    I flourished like a vine,
    There came along a false young man
    Came stole away my thyme, thyme,
    Came stole away my thyme.

2. My thyme it is all gone,
    And that's what makes me mourn,
    The garnet * standing by
    Three offers he gave to me,
    The pink, the violet and red rose
    Which I refuse all three, three,
    Which I refuse all three.

3. Now pink's no flower at all,
    For they fade away too soon,
    And the violets are too pale a blue,
    I thought I'd wait till June, June,
    I thought I'd wait till June.

* Gardener.

53

4. In June the red rose blooms
   And that's no flower for me,
   For then I'll pluck up a red rose, boys,
   And plant a willow tree, tree,
   And plant a willow tree.

5. The willow tree shall twist
   And the willow tree shall twine,
   I wish I was in the young man's arms,
   The one the love of mine, mine,
   The one the love of mine.

6. There is a glorious plant
   That grows all over the land,
   And everybody my plant shall see
   I love that false young man, man,
   I love that false young man.

7. If I am spared for one year more
   And God shall grant me grace,
   I'll buy a barrel of crystal tears
   For to wash his deceitful face, face,
   For to wash his deceitful face.

No. 26. *When I Was in My Prime.*

This song of blighted love is known as *The Sprig of Thyme*, or in the older variant, *The Seeds of Love*. Bell, pp. 220–221, gives the author as Mrs. Fleetwood Habergham, of Habergham in the county of Lancaster, who expressed the thoughts of her unhappy married life in this way. Mrs. Habergham died in 1703. Harland, pp. 271–275, has published three songs, *Love's Evil Choice*, and *The Sprig of Thyme*, following the former with a traditional version which " as far as it goes is superior to the broadside copy." The Nova Scotia variant embraces all three.

See Johnson, *The Book of British Ballads*, p. 201 ; Sharp, *English Folk-Songs*, vol. 1, No. 17 and No. 18 ; Hullah, *The Song Book*, No. 32 ; Dixon, vol. xvii, pp. 222–223 ; Kidson TT., p. 69 ; Hammond, *English Folk-Songs from Dorset*, pp. 10–11 ; Joyce, *Ancient Irish Music*, No. 74 ; Kidson G., pp. 116–117 ; Baring-Gould, No. 7 ; Cox, No. 138.

27.

Broken Ring Song Fragment

Sung by Mr. Edward Hartley, Dartmouth.

> A SAILOR's life is a merry life,
> They rob young women of their heart's delight
> And leave them behind for to sigh and mourn,
> And never know when they will return.

No. 27. *Broken Ring Song Fragment.*

The ancient theme of the returned lover is one of the oldest as well as most widespread of motifs in folk-ballad and folk-epic. Variations of the theme are well-nigh innumerable, and this and the three following songs are examples. In English ballads the theme occurs in *Hind Horn*, *The Kitchie Boy*, *Katharine Jaffray*, etc. Classic examples are the myths of Odysseus, Agamemnon and Diomedes. This is but a fragment of a song, but my singer tells me it belongs to one of this type. See note accompanying *My Sailor Lad* in this volume.

55

28.

As I was sitting by my window A fair young man he passed me by—He looked at me as if he knew me And he said "Young girl, will you fancy I"

Sung by Mrs. Agnes Gorham, Eastern Passage.

1. As I was sitting by my window
   A fair young man he passed me by,
   He looked at me as if he knew me,
   And he said, " Young girl, will you fancy I ? "

2. " Fancy you, a man of honour,
   A maid of honour I'll never be,
   For I've been waiting for a sailor
   Whose home is far across the sea.

3. " Seven years I loved a sailor,
   And seven years he's been at sea,
   And seven more I'll wait for him
   Till he returns for to marry me."

4. " Why, young girl, you are so foolish
   To wait upon that lad so long,
   Perhaps he's sick, perhaps he's married,
   Or perhaps he's dead in some foreign land."

5. " Well, if he's sick I wish him better,
   And if he's married I wish him joy,
   And if he's dead I wish him heaven,
   Oh, Lord, protect my sailor boy."

6. When he saw she was contented,
   And when he saw she was so true
   He put his hand in his vest pocket,
   Pulled out a ring that was broke in two.

7. " The other part of that dear ring,
   It lies beneath the sea,
   And if you ever wish to marry
   Please kindly turn your thoughts to me."

No. 28. *Broken Ring.*

This is widely current in Great Britain and this continent, and has been printed repeatedly in broadsides. It is known as *Pretty Fair Maid*, and *The Broken Token*, etc.

See EFSSA, No. 98; Ord, pp. 326-327; Reed-Smith, *South Carolina Ballads*, No. 15; Mackenzie, No. 63; Cox, No. 92; J.A.F.L., 22, 67–68, and p. 379; 39, 145–146.

In most of the songs which come under this heading the lover returns in disguise to test the fidelity of his sweetheart, producing at last the half of the ring she has given him.

29

It was of a comely young lady fair Who was walking out for to

take the air, She met a sailor up-on her way So I paid attention, I

paid attention To hear what they might say

Sung by Mrs. Thomas Osborne, South-East Passage. Mrs. Osborne
learned this song as a child on Devil's Island.

1. IT was of a comely young lady fair
   Who was walking out for to take the air,
   She met a sailor upon her way
   So I paid attention, I paid attention
   To hear what they might say.

2. Says he, " Fair maid, why roam alone
   When night is coming and the day's far gone ? "
   Says she, while tears from her eyes did fall,
   " 'Tis my dark-eyed sailor, 'tis my dark-eyed sailor
   That is proving my downfall.

3. " It is two long years since he left this land,
   A ring he took from off my hand,
   He broke the token, here is half with me,
   While the other lies rolling, while the other lies rolling
   At the bottom of the sea."

4. Says William, " Drive him off your mind,
   As good a sailor as him you'll find,
   Love turns aside and cold does grow
   Like a winter's morning, like a winter's morning
   When the hills are clad in snow."

5. These words did Phoebe's heart inflame,
   She cries, " On me you'll play no game."
   She drew a dagger and thus did cry,
   " For my dark-eyed sailor, for my dark-eyed sailor
   A maid I'll live and die.

6. " But a dark-eyed sailor I will ne'er disdain,
   But I will always treat the same,
   To drink his health here's a piece of coin
   But my dark-eyed sailor, but my dark-eyed sailor
   Still claims this heart of mine."

7. When William did the ring unfold
   She seemed distracted midst joy and woe,
   Saying, " You are welcome, William.   I have lands and gold
   For my dark-eyed sailor, for my dark-eyed sailor
   So manly, true and bold."

8. In a cottage down by the river side
   In happiness and peace they now reside,
   So girls be true while your lover is away
   For a cloudy morning, for a cloudy morning
   Oft brings a pleasant day.

No. 29. *The Dark-Eyed Sailor.*

More commonly known as *Fair Phoebe and Her Dark-Eyed Sailor*, this song has been popular in Great Britain and America.   I remember how it appealed to me as being particularly tuneful when Mrs. Osborne sang it.

See Ord, pp. 323–324; Kidson G., pp. 120–121; Baring-Gould, No. 44; Mackenzie, No. 64; Cox, No. 93.   For text and further references see Gray, pp. 108–110.

30.

Mantle So Green

Andante

As I went a-walking one evening in spring To view the fine fields and the meadows so green I es-pied a fair damsel, she appeared like a queen With her costly fine robes and her mantle so green.

Sung by Mr. Ben Henneberry, Devil's Island.

1. As I went a-walking one evening in spring
   To view the fine fields and the meadows so green,
   I espied a fair damsel, she appeared like a queen.
   With her costly fine robes and her mantle so green.

2. I stood in amaze, I was struck with surprise,
   I thought her a damsel had fell from the skies,
   Her eyes like a diamond, her cheeks like the rose,
   She was one of the fairest that nature composed.

3. Says I, " Pretty fair maid, if you'll come with me
   We will join hands in sweet wedlock and sweet unity,
   I'll dress you in rich attire, you'll appear like a queen,
   With your costly fine robes and your mantle so green."

4. She answered me, " Young man, I must you refuse,
   Oh, I'll wed with no man, you must me excuse,
   To the green hills I'll wander and forsake all men's view,
   For the lad that I love lies in famed Waterloo."

5.   " Since you are not married, tell me your love's name,
     I have been in battle, I might know the same."
     " Draw near to my garment, and there you will see
     His name all embroidered on my mantle so green."

6.   In the raising of her mantle there I did behold
     His name and his surname in letters of gold,
     Young William O'Reilley he appeared to my view,
     " He was my chief comrade in famed Waterloo.

7.   " He fought so victorious where bullets did fly,
     On the field of Morgan your true love does lie,
     He fought for three days till the fourth afternoon,
     And received his death summons on the eighteenth of June.

8.   " As he was a-dying I heard his last cry,
     ' Were you here, lovely Nancy, contented I'd die,'
     Now peace is proclaimed, the truth I'll declare,
     Here is your love-token, this ring, love, I wear."

9.   She stood in amaze and the paler she grew,
     She flew from my arms with her heart full of woe,
     " Through the green woods I'll wander for the lad that I love."
     " Rise up, lovely Nancy, your grief I'll remove.

10. " Nancy, lovely Nancy, 'twas I won your heart,
     In your father's garden that day we did part,
     In your father's garden by a green shade tree,
     I rolled you in my arms in your mantle so green."

11. This couple got married, I heard people say,
     They had nobles to attend them on their wedding day,
     Now peace is proclaimed and war is all o'er,
     " You are welcome to my arms, lovely Nancy, once more."

No. 30. *Mantle So Green.*

Mackenzie gives a song *Waterloo*, No. 69, from Colchester County, N.S., which he thinks must be from the same source as this. His notes are very interesting. The *Mantle So Green* may also be found in O'Conor, p. 38 ; Ord, pp. 155-156 ; Joyce, *Old Irish Folk-Music*, No. 325.

31

Bessie Beauty so bright and fair Who lately came from Derbyshire, A

serving maid she proved to be To a rich lady of high degree

Sung by Mr. Al Coolen, Fox Point, Halifax County.

1. BESSIE BEAUTY so bright and fair,
   Who lately came from Derbyshire,
   A serving-maid she proved to be
   To a rich lady of high degree.

2. This lady had but one only son
   Whose heart by woman had never been won,
   But Bessie Beauty so bright and fair,
   Drew Johnny's heart into a snare.

3. He went one night, as you soon shall find,
   And thus began to relieve his mind,
   Saying, " Bessie, I love you as I love my life,
   And do intend to make you my wife."

4. His mother in the next room did lay,
   And hearing what her son did say,
   Resolved she was in her own mind
   To flusterate her own son's designs.

5. Early next morning his mother arose,
   Saying, " Get up, Bessie, put on your clothes,
   Out of this town you now must go
   To wait on me one day or two."

62

6. Now Bessie arose, put on her clothes,
   And away with her mistress she did drive,
   Saying, " There's a ship lies in this town
   And to Virginia, Bessie, you're bound."

7. Quite late that night his mother returned,
   " Bright well returned, dear mother," said he.
   " Bright well returned, dear mother," he said,
   " But where is Bessie your waiting-maid ? "

8. " Oh, son, dear son, it is plain to see
   That all your love is for Bessie,
   Your love for Bessie is all in vain,
   She is now crossing the raging main.

9. " Oh, son, dear son, I would rather see
   You in your grave than to wed Bessie.
   To equal Bessie along with me
   'Tis a sore disgrace I don't wish to see."

10. " Oh, mother dear, you are most unkind,
    You have ruined the soul and body of mine.
    And your desire you soon shall have
    When I am in my silent grave."

11. Now Johnny took to his love-sick bed
    The thoughts of Bessie ran in his head,
    In slumbering dreams he would sigh and say,
    " Oh, charming Bessie, so far away."

12. They sent for doctors both far and near,
    But no relief could he find there,
    In slumbering dreams he would sigh and cry,
    " Oh, charming Bessie, for you I'll die."

13. When his mother saw her son was dead,
    She wrung her hands and these words did say.
    " If love could bring life back again
    I would send for Bessie far o'er the main."

No. 31. *Bessie Beauty.*

See *Johnny and Betsy*, Pound, No. 26 ; Firth, *An American Garland*, pp. 69–71 ; J.A.F.L.,
12, 245–246 ; 19, 131–132, from California ; EFSSA, No. 74.

32.

Billy Taylor

Moderato

Billy Taylor was a smart young feller Full of mirth and full of glee
And he did his mind diskiver To a lady fair to see Fol de rol de rol de
ri do Fol de ray Fol de rol de rol de ri do

Sung by Mrs. William McNab, Halifax.

1. BILLY TAYLOR was a smart young feller,
   Full of mirth and full of glee,
   And he did his mind diskiver
   To a lady fair to see.

   Chorus.
   Fol de rol de rol de rido, fol de ray,
   Fol de rol, de rol, de rido.

2. Four and twenty smart young fellers,
   Dressed were they in blue array,
   They came and took poor Billy Taylor
   Whom they pressed and sent away.   Cho.

3. Soon his true love followed after,
   She went by the name of Richard Carr,
   And she smeared her lily-white fingers
   With the nasty pitch and tar.   Cho.

4. . . . .
   She went up aloft with the rest,
   Her sailor's jacket being unbuttoned
   There they diskivered her lily-white breast.   Cho.

64

5. When the captain came for to know it,
   Says he, " What wind did blow you here ? "
   " Sir, I've come to seek my true love
   Whom you've pressed and sent to sea."   Cho.

6. " If his name is Billy Taylor
   He is both cruel and severe,
   If you rise up early in the morning
   You will see him with his lady dear."   Cho.

7. Early, early in the morning,
   Early at the break of day,
   Who did she see but Billy Taylor
   Walking with his lady gay.   Cho.

8. Sword and pistols she called out for,
   And they came at her command,
   And she shot her Billy Taylor
   With his lady by the hand.   Cho.

9. When the Captain he came for to know it
   He very much applauded her for what she had done,
   And immediately he made her his first Lieutenant
   Aboard the gallant *Thunderbrun*.   Cho.

No. 32. *Billy Taylor*.

This is such a bright song, and possessed of so much action, that it is little wonder it should have enjoyed wide currency in Great Britain. One of the English magazines, *The Illustrated London News*, I think, published a copy some years ago, adding to its interest by the fascinating pictures that accompanied it.

See Sharp, *English Folk-Songs*, vol. 1, No. 50 ; *Journal of the Folk-Lore Society*, 7, p. 30 ; Ord, pp. 315–316 ; Joyce, *Old Irish Music*, No. 424 ; J.A.F.L., 22, 380–382 ; and 28, 162–163, given with a sad ending, where she throws herself into the sea and is drowned ; Mackenzie, No. 46 ; EFSSA, No. 51 ; Sharp, No. 71.

33.

Caroline and Her Young Sailor Bold

There lived a rich noble man's daughter So comely and
father pos-sessed a great for-tune Full thirty five

handsome and fair Her She being his on-ly
thousand a year

daughter Ca-ro-line is her name we are told One

day from her drawing room window She es-pied there a

young sailor bold

Sung by Mrs. Thomas Osborne, Eastern Passage.

1. THERE lived a rich nobleman's daughter,
      So comely and handsome and fair,
    Her father possessed a great fortune,
      Full thirty-five thousand a year.
    She being his only daughter,
      Caroline is her name we are told,
    One day from her drawing-room window
      She espied there a young sailor bold.

2. His cheeks they appeared like the roses,
   His hair was as black as the jet,
   This lady she watched his departure,
   Walked round and young William she met.
   " Oh," she cried, " I'm a nobleman's daughter,
   My income's five thousand in gold,
   I'll forsake both my friends and my fortune
   To wed with a young sailor bold."

3. Says William, " Fair lady, remember,
   Your parents you are bound for to mind,
   In sailors there are no dependence,
   When their true love is left far behind.
   Be advised, stay at home with your parents,
   And do by them as you are told,
   And never let anyone persuade you
   To wed with a young sailor bold."

4. " There is no one shall ever persuade me
   One moment to alter my mind,
   In the ships I'll proceed with my sailor
   And he never shall leave me behind."
   So she dressed like a jolly young sailor,
   Forsook both her friends and her gold,
   Three years and a half on the ocean
   She plied with her young sailor bold.

5. Three times with her love she was shipwrecked,
   Though she always moved constant and true,
   Her duty she done like a sailor,
   Went aloft in her jacket so blue.
   Her duty she done like a sailor,
   Could hand reef and steer we are told.
   At last they arrived in New England,
   Caroline and her young sailor bold.

67

6. Then straightway she went to her father
   In her trousers and jacket so blue,
   He sees her and instantly fainted
   When first she appeared to his view.
   But she cried, " Dearest father, forgive me,
   Deprive me for ever of gold,
   Grant me one request if contented
   To wed with a young sailor bold."

7. Her father embraces young William
   In honour and sweet unity,
   " If life shall be spared until morning
   It is married this couple shall be."
   They were married and Caroline's fortune
   Is thirty-five thousand in gold.
   And now they live happy together
   Caroline and her young sailor bold.

No. 33. *Caroline and Her Young Sailor Bold.*

34.

Female Sailor Bold

Come all ye good people and listen to my song While I relate a
circumstance that does to love belong Concerning a pretty maid who
ventured we are told A·cross the briny ocean as a female sailor
bold

Sung by Mr. Ben Henneberry, Devil's Island.

1. COME, all ye good people, and listen to my song,
   While I relate a circumstance that does to love belong,
   Concerning a pretty maid who ventured we are told
   Across the briny ocean as a female sailor bold.

2. Her name was Jane Thornton, so quickly you shall hear,
   And as we are informed was born in Gloucester,
   Her father lived in Ireland, respected we are told,
   But never thought his daughter was a female sailor bold.

3. She was courted by a captain when scarce fifteen years of age,
   And to be bound in wedlock this couple did engage.
   The captain had to leave the land as I will now unfold,
   And she ventured o'er the ocean as a female sailor bold.

4. She dressed herself in sailor's clothes, and overcome with joy,
   And with the captain did engage to serve as cabin boy.
   When in New York in America this fair maid did behold,
   She ran to seek her lover did this female sailor bold.

5. And to her true love's fate she listened with speed,
   And enquired for employment, but dreadful news indeed,
   Her true love had some time been dead this pretty maid was told ;
   In agony and sorrow wept the female sailor bold.

6. Some thousand miles she was from home, from parents far away,
   She travelled seventeen miles through the wood in North Americay ;
   She left her friends and kindred, no parents to behold,
   " My true love's gone," in anguish cried the female sailor bold.

7. Then she shipped on board the *Adelaide* to cross the briny wave,
   Through wind and hail and storm and gale she did attempt this brave ;
   She served as cook and steward in the *Adelaide* we're told,
   Then sailed on board the *Rover* did that female sailor bold.

8. From St. Andrews in Americay this fair maid did set sail,
   In a vessel called the *Sarah*, through tempest, storm and gale,
   She done her duty like a man, did reef and steer we are told,
   And respected by the captain was the female sailor bold.

9. With pitch and tar her hands were hard, though once like velvet soft,
   She weighed the anchor, heaved the lead, and boldly went aloft,
   Just one and thirty-six months she braved the tempest we are told,
   And always done her duty, did the female sailor bold.

10. Was in the month of February, eighteen sixty-five,
    She took a port of London, this *Sarah* did arrive,
    Her sex was then discovered, her secret did unfold,
    And the captain gazed with wonder on the female sailor bold.

11. This female was examined of course by the Lord Mayor,
    And in the public paper all reason did appear,
    Why did she leave her parents and her native land she told
    Across the briny ocean was the female sailor bold.

12. It was to seek her lover she sailed across the main
    True love she did encounter through tempest, wind and rain,
    Was love caused all her trouble and hardships we are told,
    May she rest at home contented now, the female sailor bold.

No. 34. *Female Sailor Bold.*

Here is another song in which the intrepid female follows her lover to sea, only to learn unhappily in this case that he has died. A closely related story is that of *Pretty Polly Oliver*, in which the girl follows her lover to war.

35.

The Gay Spanish Maid

'Twas a gay Spanish maid at the age of sixteen Through the valley she roamed far and wide Be-neath a beech tree she sat down for to rest With her gay, gallant youth by her side

Contributed by Mrs. Grantmyre, Halifax.

1. 'Twas a gay Spanish maid, at the age of sixteen
   Through the valley she roamed far and wide,
   Beneath a beech tree she sat down for a rest
   With her gay, gallant youth by her side.

2. " My ship sails to-morrow, my darling," he cried,
   " And together we ramble no more,
   So to-night when your parents retire to rest
   Will you meet me to-night, love, on shore ? "

3. That night when her parents retired to rest
   Lovely Annie stepped out the hall door,
   With her hat in her hand she ran down to the sand
   And she sat on a rock by the shore.

71

4. The moon had just risen from over the deep
Where the sea and the sky seemed to meet,
Naught came from the deep but a murm'ring wave
And it broke on the sand at her feet.

5. With her hat in her hand straight home she did go,
And her father he met her half way,
He took her in his arms, and he gave her a kiss
Saying, " He's left you and gone far away."

6. That night it arose to a terrible storm
And the good ship went down in the storm,
He swam to a plank that escaped from the wreck,
While the rest met a watery grave.

7. He returned to his love he had left on the shore.
How she thought of her boy in the storm !
She died like a rose that is called by the frost,
And she left him in sorrow to mourn.

No. 35. *Gay Spanish Maid.*

Mackenzie, No. 33, gives a slightly longer variant of this song, while Cox, No. 115, gives one of the same length as my text, although there are a number of changes in the wording. In the former the lovers meet and make their farewells before the storm comes on. There is an intimation in the Cox text too that they have met. Here one would judge the lover had been unable to keep his tryst.

36.

Gallant Brigantine

Andante

As I strayed ashore one Sunday My gallant brigan-tine, In the Island of Ja-maica where I have lately been; Being tired of my rambling I sat myself down to rest I sang a song of my native home The song that I love best

Sung by Mr. Tom Henneberry and Mr. Ben Henneberry, Devil's Island.

1. As I strayed ashore one Sunday, my gallant brigantine,
   In the island of Jamaica where I have lately been,
   Being tired of my rambling I sat myself down to rest,
   I sang a song of my native home, the song that I love best.

2. Oh, my sonnet being ended, my mind was more at ease,
   I rose to pick some oranges that hung down from the trees,
   When I espied a pretty maid, she filled me with delight,
   She wore the robe of innocence, her robe was snowy white.

3. Her dress was snowy white, my boys, and spencer of the green,
   A silken shawl hung round her neck her shoulder for to screen,
   Her hair hung down in ringlets, and that as black as coal,
   Her teeth were like the ivory white, and her cheeks were like the rose.

73

4. " Good morning to you, fair maiden." " Good morning, sir," says she,
   " I think you are a sailor just lately in from sea."
   " Oh yes, I am a sailor just lately in from sea,
   I do belong to that lofty ship lies anchored in the Bay."

5. Oh, we both sat down together and we chatted for awhile,
   I told her of some curious facts which caused her for to smile,
   And when she rose to leave me she gave me her address,
   Saying, " Call in and see my husband, he'll treat you of the best."

6. " Oh, there's one more reception I'll give you to understand,
   My name is Harry Rysall, I am a married man,
   Three weeks before I left the shore my troubles they begun,
   By the powers above, the wife I love, she brought me forth a fine young
      son."

7. Oh, it was hand in hand together we strolled across the farm,
   And there she introduced me to a noble looking man,
   The bottle stood on the table, the dinner was served up soon
   And we both sat down together, then a pleasant afternoon.

No. 36. *Gallant Brigantine.*

37

Homeward Bound

With a slow swing

We're homeward bound to Halifax town, Good-bye, fare you well, Good

bye, fare you well We're homeward bound to Halifax town, Good-

bye my boys we're homeward bound

Sung by Mr. Ben Henneberry, Devil's Island.

1. WE'RE homeward bound to Halifax town,
    Good-bye, fare you well,
    Good-bye, fare you well,
    We're homeward bound to Halifax town,
    Good-bye, my boys, we're homeward bound.

2. We'll heave our anchor up from the bows,
    Good-bye, fare you well,
    Good-bye, fare you well,
    We'll heave our anchor up from the bows,
    Hurray, my boys, we're homeward bound.

3. We're homeward bound with our nine months' pay,
    Good-bye, fare you well,
    Good-bye, fare you well,
    Our sails all set and we're all under way,
    Hurray, my boys, we're homeward bound.

4. The pretty young girls will come down and say,
   Good-bye, fare you well,
   Good-bye, fare you well,
   You're welcome back, Jack, with your nine months' pay,
   Hurray, my boys, we're homeward bound.

5. We'll drink and dance when we get on shore,
   Good-bye, fare you well,
   Good-bye, fare you well,
   When our money's all gone we will go get more,
   Hurray, my boys, we're homeward bound.

No. 37. *Homeward Bound.*

This is one of the most popular of all chanties, and can be found in almost any chanty collection. The home port is usually given in the first stanza to give the song a local application.

38.

It is of a Rich Lady

It is of a rich lady in fair London town Possessed of great beauty, both rich and renown Until a rich warrior came courting that way And many the rich present was offered the same.

Sung by Mr. Richard Hartlan, South-East Passage.

1. IT is of a rich lady in fair London town,
   Possessed of great beauty, both rich and renown,
   Until a rich warrior came courting that way,
   And many the rich present was offered the same.

76

2. Until one fine summer's evening, one fine summer day,
   'Till a jolly young sailor came a-straying that way,
   Being brave, brisk and jolly as he was passing by,
   She waved unto him and bid him draw nigh.

3. Oh it's, " Where are you going ? " and, " From whence did you came ? "
   And, " What is your occupation, pray tell me your name ? "
   " My name it is Willie, I'm a sailor by trade,
   In all parts of America I've already surveyed.
   In a seaport called Boston where I make my abode,
   And I hope it's no harm, love, I'm walking this road."

4. " All in this country, love, I'd have you tarry,
   And to some rich lady I would have you marry,
   We can gather up riches and lay them in store,
   Be advised, lovely William, don't ramble no more."

5. " No, I would not leave off rambling for a fortune or more,
   I've silver in my pocket, and gold likewise."
   Like an innocent lover tears fell from her eyes.

6. Oh, it's, " Willie, lovely Willie, consent and marry me,
   For it's men and maidservants you will have to wait on thee,
   With coach and six horses at your leisure may ride
   If you will consent, love, and make me your bride."

7. Oh, it's Willie consented to be the bridegroom,
   The parson was sent for all in the forenoon,
   And the jolliest wedding that ever was seen
   Was the handsome young sailor to his beautiful queen.

No. 38. *It Is of a Rich Lady.*

   The theme of the lady of wealth offering to be the wife of a sailor seems to have been very
popular in broadsides. Compare *The Turkish Rover* in this volume.

39.

Jack the Sailor

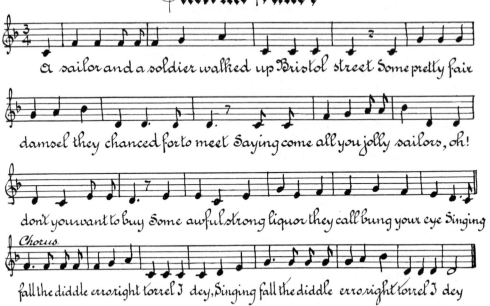

A SAILOR and a soldier walked up Bristol Street,
Some pretty fair damsel they chanced for to meet,
Saying, " Come, all you jolly sailors, oh, don't you want to buy
Some awful strong liquor they call bung your eye ? "

Chorus.

Singing fall the diddle erro, right torrel I dey,
Singing fall the diddle erro, right torrel I dey.

No. 39. *Jack the Sailor.*

40.

Jack Robson

My voyage is over and home at last My good ship in Portsmith ar-

rived at last The sails all furled and the anchor cast The

happiest of the crew was Jack Rob-son

Sung by Mr. Ben Henneberry, Devil's Island.

1. My voyage is over, and home at last
   My good ship in Portsmith arrived at last,
   The sails all furled and the anchor cast,
       The happiest of the crew was Jack Robson.

2. In the fob he had trinkets and gold galore
   Besides prize money he had quite a store,
   Along with the crew he was on shore,
       The coxswain in the boat was Jack Robson.

3. He met a man and to him he did say,
   " Perhaps you know one, Polly Day,
   She lives about here."   But the man he said, " Nay,
       Indeed I do not know," to Jack Robson.

4. Into an ale-house they sat themselves down
   And talked of admirals of high renown,
   And drank as much grog as came to half a crown,
       This clever young fellow, Jack Robson.

5. Jack he calls out the reckoning to pay,
   The landlady came dressed in fine array.
   " Blest my eye," said Jack, " isn't that Polly Grey ?
   Who thought I'd meet her ? " said Jack Robson.

6. The landlady staggered back against the wall,
   She says at first, " I don't know you at all."
   " Dang my eyes," said Jack, " isn't that a pretty squall ?
   The devil you don't know me," said Jack Robson.

7. " Don't you mind one handkerchief that you gave to me
   When I was in agony, four years to sea ?
   Whenever I look on it I'd always think of thee,
   'Pon my soul, I have got it," said Jack Robson.

8. " Somebody came to me and said
   Somebody else somewhere had read
   In somebody's paper that you were dead."
   " Oh, I wasn't dead at all," said Jack Robson.

9. " Oh," said the lady, " I have changed my state."
   " You don't mean," said I, " you have taken a mate ?
   The promise that you made to me ? "   " I could no longer wait,
   For no tidings could I gain of you, Jack Robson."

10. Jack turned up his cud and he swallowed his glass,
    He hitched up his trousers, " Alas, alas,
    The devil I should live to be made such an ass
    To be baulked by a woman," said Jack Robson.

11. " But to fret and to stew it is all in vain,
    I'll take a ship go to England, Holland, France and Spain,
    No matter that to Portsmith I'll never come again,"
    And he was off before you could say Jack Robson.

No. 40. *Jack Robson.*

This is a privateering song in which the prize money the hero brings back with him is insufficient balm to soothe his disappointment with regard to Polly Grey. See also Stone, No. 36.

41.

Jimmie and Nancy

Lovers I crave lend an ear to my story Take an example by
this constant pair It is of a young couple who love out of measure
Beautiful Nancy from Yarmouth we hear

Sung by Mr. Ben Henneberry, Devil's Island.

1. LOVERS, I crave, lend an ear to my story,
    Take an example by this constant pair,
    It is of a young couple who love out of measure,
    Beautiful Nancy from Yarmouth we hear.

2. She was a merchant's comely fair daughter,
    Heiress of fifteen thousand a year,
    A young man he courted her to be his jewel,
    The son of a gentleman who lived near.

3. Many long years this couple did court,
    When they were children in love did agree,
    When to an age this couple arrived
    Cupid his arrow between them displayed.

4. When they were promised for to be married,
    But when her father the same came to hear,
    He took his charming, beautiful daughter,
    Acted a part that was cruel and severe.

5. " Daughter," he said, " give o'er thy proceedings,
   That if you consent to be wed,
For evermore we resolve to disown you
   If you with one that so meanly wed.

6. " Besides, dear child, you are of great fortune,
   Likewise you are beautiful, handsome and young,
You are a match, dear child, that is fitted
   For any lord in great Christendom."

7. Then did reply this pretty damsel,
   " Riches and honour I both do deny
If I'm deprived of my dearest lover,
   And good-bye to this world which is all vanity."

8. Then did reply her cruel parent,
   " To sea Jimmie shall go in a ship of my own,
And I swear he shall have my daughter
   When to fair Yarmouth again he returns."

The rest of the song is only known to the singer in part.

According to the story Jimmie went away, and while in a foreign country a girl fell in love with him and asked him to marry her. This Jimmie refused, being constant to Nancy at home, and the love-sick girl " put a knife in herself." Jimmie went back then, but on the way word came from Nancy's father to kill him, saying, " A handsome reward I will give you." The result was that Jimmie was thrown overboard, but the songs say that the next day,

His cruel ghost to his love did appear,
   Her fond amours .   .   .   .

Her nightgown embroidered in gold and silver
   Carelessly around her body she throws,
With her own maidens indeed to attend her
   To meet her true love she instantly goes.

The maidens they heard her sad lamentations,
   But the apparition indeed could not see,
Thinking the maiden had fell in distraction
   They strove to persuade her contented to be.

Still she cried, " I am coming,
　　Now on your bosom I'll still fall asleep."
Just she had spoke, this unfortunate lady
　　Suddenly plunged herself into the deep.

When to her father the maids told the story,
　　Crying, " Cruel monster, oh, what have you done ? "
　.　.　.　.　.　.　.　.　.　.　.
" I have killed the flower of fair Yarmouth town."

The boatswain he confessed the murder,
　　To the yardarm he was hung for the same,
And the parents broke the heart of their daughter
　　Before the ship to the fair harbour came.

No. 41. *Jimmie and Nancy.*

Mr. Henneberry regrets that much of this interesting story of love, tragedy and the ghostly revelation of the murdered hero has escaped his memory. J.A.F.L., 26, 178, gives one verse only, but alludes to a manuscript copy of fifty-six stanzas. Other references given are *Forget-Me-Not Songster*, pp. 86–92 ; Glyde, *The Norfolk Garland*, pp. 266–273. Cf. Journal, 11, 113–114 ; 11, 103, 272 ; Christie, *Traditional Ballad Airs*, 11, 282. The Harvard College Library has several copies in garlands and broadsides, etc.

See also EFSSA, No. 53, under caption *Pretty Nancy of Yarmouth.*

42.

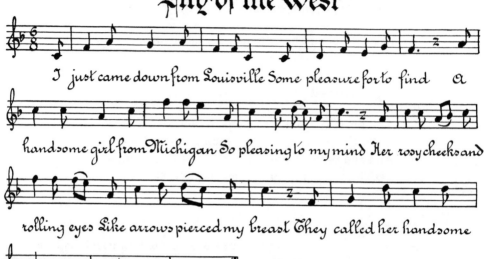

I just came down from Louisville Some pleasure for to find A handsome girl from Michigan So pleasing to my mind Her rosy cheeks and rolling eyes Like arrows pierced my breast They called her handsome Flora The Lily of the West.

Sung by Ruth Purdy, Devil's Island.

1. I JUST came down from Louisville
     Some pleasure for to find,
   A handsome girl from Michigan
     So pleasing to my mind,
   Her rosy cheeks and rolling eyes
     Like arrows pierced my breast,
   They called her handsome Flora,
     The Lily of the West.

2. Her hair hung down in ringlets,
     Her dress was spangled o'er,
   A ring on every finger,
     Came from a foreign shore,
   And to entice some lord or knight
     So modestly she dressed,
   And began I once loved Flora,
     The Lily of the West.

3. I courted her for many a day,
    Her love I thought to gain,
 Too soon, too soon she slighted me,
    Which caused me grief and pain;
 She robbed me of my liberty,
    And deprived me of my rest,
 They called her handsome Flora,
    The Lily of the West.

4. One evening as I rambled
    Down by yon shady grove,
 I met a lord of high degree
    Conversing with my love,
 He sang, he sang so merrily,
    While I was sore oppressed,
 He sang for handsome Flora,
    The Lily of the West.

5. I rushed upon my rival,
    My dagger in my hand,
 I tore him from my true love,
    And badly made him stand,
 Being made to desperation
    My dagger pierced his breast,
 I was betrayed by Flora,
    The Lily of the West.

6. Now my trial has come on
    And sentenced soon I'll be,
 They put me in the criminal box
    And there convicted me,
 She who spoke to the jury
    So modestly she dressed,
 She far outshone bright Venus,
    The Lily of the West.

7. Since then I've gained my liberty,
    I throve the country through,
 I'll travel the city all over
    To find my loved one true,

Although she stole my liberty
And deprived me of my rest,
Yet still I love my Flora,
The Lily of the West.

No. 42. *Lily of the West.*

Although the scene of this song is given in America, it is evidently an old country song. Baring-Gould, No. 58, gives a variant beginning, " 'Twas when I came to England." A note accompanying it says the ballad had clearly an Irish origin. It used to be sung at the Revel at St. Breward's on the Bodmin Moors, and can be traced back there to 1839.

43.

Lion's Den

Sung by Mr. Ben Henneberry, Devil's Island.

1. A FAIR maid was courted by many's the noble,
   But none of them her heart could win,
   There came two lovers and they were brothers,
   And one of them she wished for to win.

One was the captain on board of the *Lively*,
  The *Lively* ship the seas do draw,
And the other was a bold lieutenant
  On board of the *Tigress* man-of-war.

2. As they were a-sitting at the dinner-table
  This fair one made reply,
" We will take a walk to the lakes for pleasure
  Our unconstant hearts all for to try."
They walked till they came to the mulberry bushes,
  They walked till they came to the lion's den.
In her hand she held her fan,
  Into the den she threw it in.

3. " Is there a man here wishes to gain my favour ?
  Is there a man my heart wish to win ?
I dropped my fan in the den of lions
  And the man that shall bring it my heart shall win."
Then up spoke the bold sea captain,
  Unto her he thus did say,
" Madame, there is not a man in Greenwood
  Into the den his life would brave."

4. Then up spoke the bold lieutenant,
  Unto her made this reply,
" Madame, here is one man in Greenwood,
  Will bring to you your fan or die."
Into the den he boldly ventured,
  The lions were thick, and fierce did grin,
With his sword in hand he picked up her fan
  And out of the den he returned again.

5. When she saw her true lover coming,
  And no harm to him was done,
She fell into his arms a-saying,
  " Pick up the prize you have nobly won."
Then up spoke the bold sea captain,
  Unto her made this reply,
" Madame, I will go to a foreign country,
  And for your love I will pine and die."

No. 43. *The Lion's Den.*

Ord, pp. 393–394 gives a variant of this song in which the brave lieutenant not only wins the lady but is made an admiral as well.   The ship *Lively* is not mentioned, but the *Tigress* is there as the *Tiger*.   From Pictou County, N.S., comes a variant from Mackenzie, No. 22, who notes that Kittredge points to Bishop Percy's broadsides for the earliest text.   See also Christie's *Traditional Ballad Airs*, 11, 126.

The story has been known and recorded through Europe since the sixteenth century and localized in the court of Francis 1st of France.   It has been made familiar through Schiller's *Der Handschuh*, Leigh Hunt's *The Glove and the Lions*, and Browning's *The Glove*, in all of which the lover returns the glove but deserts the lady, saying that it was vanity that prompted her request, not love.   It is typical of folk-songs that the singers should see nothing incongruous in the request.

44. (1)

Oh! build me up some little boat That on the o - cean I may float and every ship I chance to spy I will require for my sailor bold.

Sung by Muriel Henneberry, aged 12, Devil's Island.

1. " Oh ! build me up some little boat
    That on the ocean I may float,
    And every ship I chance to spy
    I will require for my sailor bold."

2. She sailed not far o'er the deep
    When a big ship she chanced to meet,
    Saying, " Bold captain, oh, tell me true,
    Is my sailor lad here among your crew ? "

3. " Oh, no, fair maid, he is not here,
    He is drowned in the deep I fear."
    She wrang her hands and tore her hair
    Just like a fair maiden would do.

89

4. " I'll go home and write a song,
   I'll write it true, I'll write it long,
   And every line I'll shed a tear
   To be to you, my lover dear.

5. " The blue jacket he used to wear,
   His light blue eyes, his coal black hair,
   His lips were of the velvet fine
   And often used to meet at mine.

6. " Dig my grave both long and deep,
   A marble stone at my head and feet,
   On my heart a turtle dove
   To show the world I died for love."

44. (2)

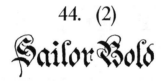

Pa-pa, papa build me a boat That I may on the o-cean float To

hail all ships as they pass by And to enquire for my

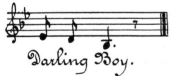

Darling Boy.

Sung by Mrs. Chas. Kelley, Yarmouth, who has often
heard this sung as a chanty by the men of sailing vessels
which used to frequent this port.

PAPA, papa, build me a boat
That I may on the ocean float,
To hail all ships as they pass by
And to enquire for my Darling Boy.

What colour was your Willie's hair?
What kind of clothes did Willie wear?
A little round jacket of Royal blue
And light curly hair had my Willie too.

As we were out on the Eastern Isle
We lost four men and your Darling Boy,

   .   .   .   .

   .   .   .   .

Come, all you Sailors, dress alike,
Come, all you Sailors, dress in white,
And hoist your colours at half-mast high
To help me mourn for my Darling Boy.

O lay me out when I am dead
With a marble slab at my foot and head,
And on my breast place a turtle dove
To show the World I died for love.

No. 44. *My Sailor Lad.*

Note from Mrs. M. E. Hobbs of the English Folk-Song Society gives this as Sharp's *Sweet William.*

Other versions are in *Journal*, 1, p. 90; *English County Songs*, p. 74; Christie's *Traditional Ballad Airs*, vol. 1, p. 248. The song is a very common one, and I have noted several variants.

Cecil Sharp, *One Hundred English Folk-Songs* (Oliver Ditson). It begins,

> A Sailor's life is a merry life,
> He'll rob young girls of their hearts' delight,
> Then go and leave them to sigh and moan,
> No tongue can tell when he will return.
> Oh, father, father, build me a boat, etc.

Sung to C. Sharp by Mr. William F. Wells at Swannanoa, N.C., U.S.A. See EFSSA, No. 106.

The above verse given by Mr. Sharp is in this volume as *Broken Ring Song Fragment.*

45

Prentice Boy

Andante

As down in Cupid's garden for pleasure I did walk I
heard two loyal lovers most sweetly for to talk It was a brisk young
lady And her prentice boy And in private they were courting for he was all her joy

Sung by Mr. Ben Henneberry, Devil's Island.

1. As down in Cupid's garden for pleasure I did walk,
   I heard two loyal lovers most sweetly for to talk.
   It was a brisk young lady and her prentice boy,
   And in private they were courting, for he was all her joy.

2. He said, " My honoured lady, I am your prentice boy ;
   However can I think a fair lady to enjoy ? "
   His cheeks as red as roses, his honour kind and free,
   She said, " Dear youth, if e'er I wed I'll surely marry thee."

3. But when that her parents they came to understand,
   They did this young man banish to some foreign land.
   While she lay broken-hearted, lamenting she did cry,
   " For my honest, charming prentice a maid I'll live and die."

4. This young man to a merchant a waiting-man was bound,
   And by his good behaviour great fortune there he found.
   He soon became a butler, which prompted him to fame,
   And for his careful conduct a steward he became.

5. For a ticket in a lottery his money he put down
   And there he gained a prize of thirty thousand pounds.
   With store of gold and silver, he packed up his clothes indeed,
   And to England returned to his true love with speed.

6. He offered kind embraces, but she flew from his arms ;
   " No lord, duke or nobleman shall e'er enjoy my charms.
   The love of gold is cursèd, great riches I decry ;
   For my honest, charming prentice a maid I'll live and die ! "

7. He said, " My honoured lady, I have been in your arms.
   This is the ring you gave me when toying in your charms.
   You vowed if e'er you married your love I should enjoy.
   Your father did me banish ; I was your prentice boy."

8. When she beheld his features she flew into his arms,
   With kisses out of measure she did enjoy his charms.
   And then through Cupid's garden a road to church they found,
   And there in virtuous pleasure in Hymen's chains were bound.

No. 45. *The Prentice Boy.* (*As down in Cupid's garden.*)

Compare *The Lady and the Prentice*, Baring-Gould, No. 107, which, he says, is almost identical with the broadside by Pitts 1790–1801. See Pound, No. 31 ; J.A.F.L., 26, pp. 363–364. For further references, Mackenzie, No. 25.

46.

Pretty Polly

Sung by Mrs. William McNab, Halifax.

If I were a fisherman down by the waterside
And Polly a salmon swimming close by my side,
I'd cast down my net, and I'd catch her in a snare,
I'd bring down pretty Polly, I vow and declare.

46. *Pretty Polly.*

47.

Rambling Rover

Ye rambling boys of pleasure Give ear to these few lines I write It is true I am a rov-er And in roving I take great delight.

Sung by Mr. Ben Henneberry, Devil's Island.

1. YE rambling boys of pleasure,
   Give ear to these few lines I write,
   It is true I am a rover,
   And in roving I take great delight.

2. I placed my mind on a fair maid,
   Though oftentimes she does me slight,
   My mind is never easy
   Only when my darling is in sight.

3. The second time I saw my love
   I really thought she would be mine,
   But as the weather alters,
   The fair maid she did change her mind.

4. Gold is the root of all evil,
   Although it shines with a glittering hue,
   Causes many the lad and lass to part
   Let the hearts and minds be ever true.

5. There is one thing I have to relate
   Before that I do go away,
   In my young counteree where I was born
   Cupid would not let me free.

95

6. To leave my girl behind me,
    My dear, alas, what must I do ?
    Must I become a rover
    And court some girl I never knew ?

47. *Rambling Rover.*

All I have found related to this song is *When I Became a Rover*, J.A.F.L., 28, 161–162.

48.

Sung by Mr. Ben Henneberry, Devil's Island.

1. ATTENTION give both high and low
    And quickly you shall hear,
    I love a damsel true and kind
    Who lived in Lincolnshire.

Her cheeks like blooming roses were
    And her face appeared to smile,
This damsel's name was lovely Jane,
    She's the rose of Britain's Isle.

2. She was her father's only child
        And her mother's only joy,
    But when eighteen she fell in love
        With her father's prentice boy,
    Young Edmund lived contentedly
        Till Jane his heart beguiled,
    " By all above," he cries, " I love
        The Rose of Britain's Isle."

3. But when her father came to hear
        That courting this couple were,
    Her father in a passion flew
        How he did rage and swear.
    He said, " If you bring disgrace on me
        I will banish you many's the mile,
    All in disdain across the Main
        From the Rose of Britain's Isle."

4. The day it was appointed
        That he had to cross the main,
    Young Jane at home did weep and mourn,
        Her bosom swelled with pain,
    She dressed herself in men's attire
        All in a little while,
    And shipped on board with Edmund,
        Did the Rose of Britain's Isle.

5. They scarce had been a week at sea
        When a storm it did arise,
    Young Edmund climbed the mast so high,
        Jane wept with watery eye ;
    But little did young Edmund think
        When Jane did on him smile
    That by his side there stood his bride,
        The Rose of Britain's Isle.

6. They scarce had been a month at sea
       When an enemy gave the alarm
   That by a ball young Jane did fall
       That shattered her right arm.
   The crew all went to lend their aid
       When Jane did on them smile.
   " Behold my bride," young Edmund cried.
       " She's the Rose of Britain's Isle."

7. Now this young couple are returning home
       Most joyfully to relate,
   Her parents are both dead and gone
       And leave a large estate.
   They married were, and bells did ring
       And the villagers did smile,
   Now happy is young Edmund with
       The Rose of Britain's Isle.

No. 48. *Rose of Britain's Isle.*

The same song with somewhat different wording and construction is given by Mackenzie, No. 37. Here again we have the lover followed by his sweetheart to sea, but unlike the luckless *Female Sailor Bold*, this song has a happy ending. For further references see Mackenzie.

49.

A Sailor Courted

A sailor courted a farmer's daughter He lived convenient to the Isle of Man But mark, good people what followed after, A long time courting 'bout little won A long time courting and yet discoursing Of things concerning the ocean wide He says my dearest At our next meeting If you'll consent I'll make you my bride.

Sung by Mr. Ben Henneberry, Devil's Island.

1. A SAILOR courted a farmer's daughter,
    He lived convenient to the Isle of Man,
But mark, good people, what followed after,
    A long time courting but little won.
A long time courting, and yet discoursing
    Of things concerning the ocean wide,
He says, " My dearest, at our next meeting
    If you'll consent I'll make you my bride."

99

2. " Oh, sailors' promises are soon forgotten,
   They sail to many and foreign parts,
The more we love them the worse we're slighted,
   And leave us behind with broken hearts."
" Oh no, my dear, that is not my fancy,
   I never intend to leave you so,
Just one more trip across the ocean
   So now, my dear, I must go."

3. The news was carried unto his mother
   Before he put his foot on board,
She says, " My son, if this be your proceeding
   Not a penny portion will I afford.
Not a penny portion bound across the ocean,"
   His mother quite distracted run,
Saying, " My son, forsake her ; your bride not make her,
   Or I'll disown you to be my son."

4. " O mother dear, don't get in a passion,
   I'm sorry you have spoke so late,
Don't you remember in your first proceeding
   My father married you, a servant maid ?
So don't dispraise her, I mean to raise her,
   Just as my father by you have done.
My bride I'll make her, to the seas I'll take her,
   My scolding mother may hold her tongue.

5. " Money or not she is my lot,
   She has my heart and affection still,
My bride I'll make her, to the seas I'll take her,
   My scolding mother may say what she will."

No. 49. *A Sailor Courted.*

50.

When I Was A Young Man

When I was a young man I took delight in love I
gave my heart unto a girl Who did inconstant prove She
promised for to be My own true love Which makes me sigh and
say But now I find she has changed her mind to a quite contrary
way

Sung by Mr. Enos Hartlan, of South-East Passage.

1. WHEN I was a young man
   I took delight in love,
   I gave my heart unto a girl
   Who did inconstant prove.
   She promised for to be
   My own true love,
   Which makes me sigh and say,
   But now I find she has changed her mind
   To a quite contrary way.

2. I went unto my love one day
   And this to her did say,
   " As we have loved each other
   This long and many a day,

But now I've come
To let you know
That married we should be,"
So then said he, " Let us agree
And point a wedding day."

3. " Oh no," replied this fair maid,
" I think you are in haste,
For I never knew a young man
To spend his days in waste.
For the time is gone
Since you might 'a' had
All opportunity ;
For now you see you shan't have me,
Some other you may go and try.

4. " You may go tell your mother dear
That love you have not crossed,
And if you went the right way to work
Your love you ne'er would have lost.
You ne'er would 'a' lost, my boy,
The truth I do intone,
Or in the spring had you cropped my wing
From you I never would have flown."

5. Now come, my boys, fill up your bowls,
Don't let it be said we die.
If she proves false I will do so,
And some other I will go and try.
I will go try, my boy,
We'll sail the ocean o'er,
For the loss of one is a gain of two
And a choice of twenty more.

No. 50. *When I Was a Young Man.*

This song may be of no value from a literary or musical point of view, and I have found it
in no other collection. But to me it holds much sentimental value. It was the first song I
collected. See story in Introduction.

51.

Young Indian Lass

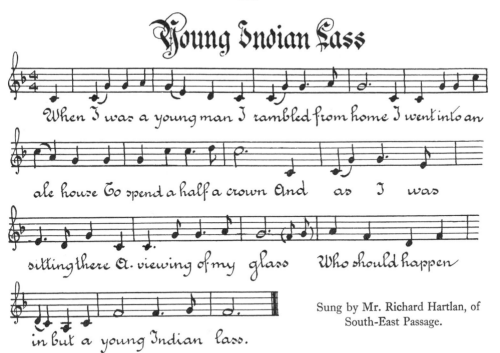

When I was a young man I rambled from home I went into an ale house To spend a half a crown And as I was sitting there A. viewing of my glass Who should happen in but a young Indian lass.

Sung by Mr. Richard Hartlan, of
South-East Passage.

1. WHEN I was a young man
   I rambled from home,
   I went into an ale-house
   To spend a half a crown ;
   And as I was sitting there
   A-viewing of my glass,
   Who should happen in but
   A young Indian lass.

2. She sat down beside me
   And squeezèd my hand,
   She said, " You're a stranger
   From some foreign land."
   And with joy and pleasure
   We passed the time away,
   And I never thought of leaving
   Till nine the next day.

3. I viewed this comely Indian,
    I found that she was good,
I viewed this comely Indian
    On the ground that she stood.
She was tall, lean and handsome,
    Her age was sweet sixteen,
She was born and brought up in
    The sweet New Orleans.

4. Oh, early the next morning
    Away from her I flew,
And with her pocket-handkerchief
    She bid me adieu,
And with her pocket-handkerchief
    She bid me adieu,
A sweet and pleasant gale
    Took me out of her view.

5. Now I'm safe landed
    On my native shore,
My friends and relations
    Come to see me once more.
There's none that comes round me,
    There's none that goes past
That's fit to be compared
    To the young Indian lass.

No. 51. *Young Indian Lass.*

This song and *The Lass of Mohee*, which Kittredge remarks is a chastened American remaking of the well-known English broadside, *The Indian Lass*, are very closely related. Mackenzie, No. 57, has a song very similar to mine, and he also gives *The Lass of Mohee*, No. 58, where stanza 8 is very like stanza 5 of my variant. A variant very like that sung by Mr. Hartlan is in Kidson T.T., pp. 109–111. For *The Lass of Mohee* see also Pound, No. 91; Dean, p. 17; Eckstorm, pp. 230–233; Cox, No. 116; Botsford, *Folk-Songs of Many Peoples*, 11, pp. 24–25; J.A.F.L., 39, 132–134; 42, 282–285.

52.

Bay of Biscay Oh

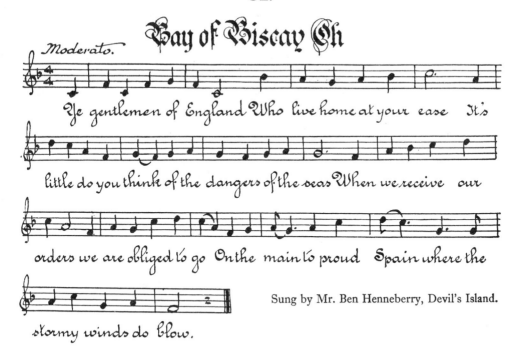

Moderato.

Ye gentlemen of England Who live home at your ease It's
little do you think of the dangers of the seas When we receive our
orders we are obliged to go On the main to proud Spain where the

Sung by Mr. Ben Henneberry, Devil's Island.

stormy winds do blow.

1. YE gentlemen of England who live home at your ease,
   It's little do you think of the dangers of the seas,
   When we receive our orders we are obliged to go
   On the main to proud Spain where the stormy winds do blow.

2. Was on the fourth of August from Spithead we set sail
   With *Rameley* and Company blest with a pleasant gale,
   We sailed along together in the Bay of Biscay Oh,
   Where a dreadful storm it did arise and the stormy wind did blow.

3. The *Rameley* she left us, she could no longer stay,
   And by distress of weather from us she bore away,
   When she arrived at Gibraltar they told the people so,
   How they thought we were all lost at the Bay of Biscay Oh.

4. Kind heaven did protect her, it was not quite so bad,
   First we lost our foremast and then we lost our flag,
   And then we lost our mainmast, one of our guns also,
   And the men we lost ten on the Bay of Biscay Oh.

5. When the mainmast started it gave a dreadful stroke,
   In our starboard quarter a large hole did it broke,
   Then the seas came battering in, our guns soon overflow,
   So boldly she ploughed it on the Bay of Biscay Oh.

6. The night being dark and dreary, at twelve o'clock that night
   Our captain in the forecastle he was killed then outright,
   The ring upon his finger in pieces burst in two,
   There he laid till next day when we overboard him threw.

7. The storm it being abated we rigged up jury mast
   And steered for Gibraltar, where we arrived at last,
   They said it was a dismal sight as ever they did know,
   We forced to drink wine and drowned all our woe.

No. 52. *Bay of Biscay Oh.*

This is not to be confused with its better-known namesake by Andrew Cherry. This is a very different song, and begins in much the same way as *Neptune's Raging Fury*, or *The Gallant Seaman's Suffering*, of Martin Parker, *circa* 1635, Stone, No. 14, which tells of the sailors and their perils and dangers, of the extraordinary hazards they undergo and so on in a general way, while Mr. Henneberry's song describes a specific case. There may be no relation between the two, but it is interesting to compare them.

53.

Bold Princess Royal

Allegro

On the eighth of October As we left the land On the bold Princess Royal bound to Newfoundland We sailed to the eastward to the eastward sailed we With forty brave seamen our ship's compan-y.

Sung by Mr. William Faulkner, Devil's Island.

1. ON the eighth of October
   As we left the land
   On the bold *Princess Royal*
   Bound to Newfoundland,
   We sailed to the eastward,
   To the eastward sailed we,
   With forty brave seamen
   Our ship's company.

2. We had not been sailing
   Scarce two days or three,
   When a man from our masthead
   A vessel did see.
   It came bearing down on us
   With sail set so high,
   And from under her mizzen
   Black colours let fly.

107

3. " If this is a pirate
        He'll soon put us through.
    Oh, Lord," said our captain,
        " Oh, what will we do ? "
    " Oh no," said our chief mate,
        " That ne'er shall be so,
    We'll shake out our reef, boys,
        And from her we'll go."

4. At length this bold pirate
        Came bearing with pride,
    With his loud-speaking trumpet
        Said, " I'll be at your side,"
    When out spoke our captain
        And answered him so,
    " We're just from America
        Bound down to Bordeaux."

5. " Back your maintopsail
        And heave your ship to,
    I have plenty of letters
        In my locker for you."
    " When I've backed my maintopsail
        And heaved my ship to,
    It'll be in some harbour
        Not alongside of you.

6. " It's hoist your maintopsail,
        Your staysail also,
    Your royal and skysail
        And from her we'll go."
    He fired a shot after us
        Thinking to prevail,
    When the bold *Princess Royal*
        Soon showed them her tail.

7. He chased us to windward
        All that livelong day,
    He chased us to windward
        We beat him fair play,

He chased us to windward
    We beat him fair play,
Till he clued up his spanker
    And kept her away.

8. " Thank God," said our captain,
        " The pirate is gone,
    Here's a glass of good liquor
        To every man.
    Come down and get your dinner, boys,
        And be of good cheer,
    For while we have sea room
        There's nothing to fear."

No. 53. *The Bold Princess Royal.*

My singer gives this as a " true song " of a ship which carried passengers between Halifax and Newfoundland. Stanza 5 has undoubtedly been borrowed from *The Coasts of High Barbary,* which in turn seems to have been influenced by *The George Aloe and the Sweepstake,* Child 285.

See also Eckstorm, pp. 256–257; Sharp, *English Folk-Songs from Norfolk,* pp. 40–41; Kidson G., pp. 34–35; Sharp, *English Folk-Songs,* vol. 1, p. 32; Barry, pp. 413–415; Shay, pp. 98–99.

54.

Captain Burke

Sung by Richard Hartlan of South-East Passage, Nova Scotia.

1. I SAILED on a ship called the *Caroline,*
        Burke was the captain's name,
    Bound out on the coast of Africa
        On a sweet and pleasant gale.

2. We had on board four hundred slaves
       In our ship's hole below,
    We did not know what moment would turn on us
       And prove our overthrow.

3. Oh, we had not been sailing long
       When a storm it did arise,
    And dark and dismal was the night
       And cloudy looked the skies.

4. The captain called, " All hands on deck,
       Come bear a hand aloft,
    Be quick and reef out foretopsails,
       Our ship is fore and aft."

5. As up aloft like tars we mounted
       Our canvas to take in,
    When the heavy clap of thunder came
       And the lightning first began.

6. Likewise the mate and cabin boy
       Fell from the maintop yard,
    And then we were eight in number
       Our ship and lives to guard.

7. Oh, it was after a long time sailing
       Our ship in port arrived,
    Then it was off to the hospital we were marched
       Four seamen lame and blind.

8. Oh, the doctors there tried all their skill
       But it was all in vain,
    It's in a state of darkness
       We all have to remain.

9. Oh, if it is to be God's will
       That only we could see,
    We'd earn our bread as we always did
       By sailing the rough salt sea.

No. 54. *Captain Burke.*

55.

Captain Glen

There was a ship, and a ship of fame Launched off the stocks bound a-
cross the main A hundred and fifty brisk young men Were picked and choosen

every one

Sung by Mr. Ben Henneberry, Devil's Island.

1. THERE was a ship, and a ship of fame
   Launched off the stocks bound across the main,
   A hundred and fifty brisk young men
   Were picked and choosen every one.

2. William Glen was our captain's name.
   He was a tall and a nice young man,
   As fine a sailor as ever went to sea,
   And we were bound for New Barbee.

3. One night our captain on his pillow did lay,
   A voice came to him, those words did say,
   " Prepare yourself and ship's company
   To-morrow night you must lay with me."

4. Then he awoke in a terrible fright,
   It being the hour of twelve at night,
   And for his boatswain he did call
   And told to him his secrets all.

5. " Boatswain," he says, " it grieves me to the heart,
   To think I've acted a villain's part,
   To take what was not my lawful due
   And starve my passengers and crew.

6. " There's one thing more I have to rehearse
    Which I shall mention in this verse,
    A squire I slew in Stratfordshire
    All for the sake of a lady fair.

7. " And on my servant I lay the blame
    And he was hung and all for the same."

8. " O dearest captain, if that be so
    Don't let none of our ship's crew know,
    Keep that secret within your breast
    And pray to God to give you rest."

9. Next morning early the storm did rise,
    Which give our seamen much surprise,
    The sea broke over us fore and aft,
    Till scarce a man on deck was left.

10. Then our boatswain he did declare
    That our captain was a murderer.
    It soon enraged our whole ship's crew
    And overboard our captain threw.

11. When this was done the calm was there,
    Our goodly ship onward did steer,
    The wind abated and calmed the sea
    And we got safe to New Barbee.

12. And when we did arrive out there
    Our goodly ship for to repair,
    The people all were amazed to see
    What a poor distressed ship's crew were we.

No. 55. *Captain Glen.*

The belief embodied in the anger of the sea until the murderer is removed is at least as old
as the story of Jonah. See *Folk-Lore Record*, London, 2, 120; Kidson G., pp. 110–111, with
music. For text and references, Mackenzie, No. 90. Stone, No. 56, gives a variant of 22
verses with a warning at the end to others not to sail with a murderer. Another song in this
volume based upon the supernatural is the *Ghostly Sailors.*

56.

Chanty Song

Sung by Mr. Richard Hartlan, South-East Passage.

1. So, it's pass around the grog, my boys,
    And never mind the scores,
    But give to me the girl I love,
    I'll never ask for more.
    Oh, here's to him that merry be
    And never taste of joy,
    Sing, sing the merry, merry song,
    March onward, my brave boys.

2. Oh, here's to Queen Victoria,
    Oh, long may she reign,
    Here's to her jolly tars
    That plough the raging main,
    For here's to him that merry be
    And never taste of joy,
    Sing, sing the merry, merry song,
    March onward, my brave boys.

3. Oh, it's pass around the grog, my boys,
     And never mind the scores,
   And when our money is all gone
     We'll go to sea for more.
   Oh, here's to him that merry be
     And never taste of joy,
   Sing, sing the merry, merry song,
     March onward, my brave boys.

No. 56. *Chanty Song.* (*So, it's pass.*)

Although Mr. Hartland has sung this as a chanty it looks more like a sailor's adaptation of a soldier's song. It is a merry piece, and one can imagine either sailor or soldier singing it with the greatest gusto.

57.

Chanty Song

Soon we'll be in England town Heave me lads, heave ho To see the King with a golden crown Heave me lads, heave ho Heave ho, on we go Heave me, lads, heave ho Little powder monkey Jim handing up the powder from the magazine below When he got stuck with a ball That laid him so low heave ho, on we go Heave me lads, heave ho

Sung by Mr. Richard Hartlan, South-East Passage.

Chorus.

SOON we'll be in England town,
Heave, me lads, heave ho,
To see the king with a golden crown,
Heave, me lads, heave ho,
Heave ho, on we go,
Heave, me lads, heave ho.

1. Little powder monkey Jim handing up the powder
   From the magazine below,
   When he got struck with a ball
   That laid him so low,
   Heave ho, on we go,
   Heave, me lads, heave ho.   Cho.

No. 57. *Chanty Song.*   (*Soon we'll be.*)

This is one of the few chanties heard in Nova Scotia which I have not found published in any other collection, though Stephen Adams in his well-known *The Powder Monkey* shows some acquaintance with it.   Chanties are sung only when there is a definite piece of work to be done, and as far as I can learn from long talks with retired sea captains, there are standard chanties which are sung by all English-speaking countries alike.   It seems unlikely that I shall ever find any which are peculiar to Nova Scotia.

58.

City of Baltimore

Moderato

I am a true born Irishman Mc Carthy is my name And if you want to know any more From Liverpool I came Down by the northern docks one day I happened for to stray On board of an ocean going boat He stowed himself a way

Sung by Mr. Ben Henneberry, Devil's Island.

1. I AM a true born Irishman,
    McCarthy is my name,
   And if you want to know any more
    From Liverpool I came.
   Down by the northern docks one day
    I happened for to stray,
   On board of an ocean-going boat
    He stowed himself away.

2. A-sailing down the river,
    To New York we were bound,
   This Irish boy being bound away
    To leave his native home.
   This Irish boy being borne away
    To leave his native shore,
   On board of a western-going boat
    Called the *City of Baltimore*.

117

3. When he came out from his hiding-place
     The captain he did say,
   " What brought you here ? come tell to me
     Or else you'll rue the day.
   What brought you here ? come tell to me
     Or else I'll ask no more.
   You'll curse the day that you stole away
     On board of the *Baltimore*."

4. Very early every morning
     The mate would turn him to,
   As early every morning
     The mate would put him through.
   " Where is that ugly Irish dog ? "
     The mate would loudly roar,
   " He'll curse the day he stole away
     On board of the *Baltimore*."

5. " I am a true-born Irishman,
     The same I'll never deny,
   Before I'll be cowed down by you
     I'll fight until I die.
   If you're a man of courage
     It's you I'll stand before,
   I'll fight you fair upon the deck
     Of the *City of Baltimore*."

6. The mate he being a cowardly man
     Before him would not stand,
   But with an iron b'laying pin
     Towards McCarthy ran.
   McCarthy being a smart young man
     He soon did lay him o'er,
   And laid him senseless on the deck
     Of the *City of Baltimore*.

7. The second mate and boatswain
     Came to the first mate's relief,
   McCarthy with the b'laying pin
     He soon made them retreat.

His Irish blood it was boiling,
  Like a lion he did roar,
The blood it began to flow in streams
  On the deck of the *Baltimore*.

8. The captain being a Scotchman,
     McDonald was his name,
   Was when he saw what McCarthy done
     He unto him did came.
   " Since you're a man of courage,
     A man of courage score,
   You are the very best man I have
     On board of the *Baltimore*.

9. " Come down into my cabin,
     Come down along with me,
   Come down into my cabin,
     With me you will agree.
   Since you're a man of courage,
     A man of courage score,
   I'll make you mate this very day
     On board of the *Baltimore*."

No. 58. "*City of Baltimore*."

It is probable that this song was written on this side of the Atlantic, but as I have no reference to give I am putting it in the general group of songs of the sea.

59.

Come All Ye Old Comrades

Sung by Patrick Williams, Devil's Island.

1. COME, all ye old comrades,
      Come now let us join,
    Come and join your sweet voices
      In chorus with mine,
    For we'll laugh and be jolly
      While sorrow refrain,
    For we may and, may never
      All meet here again.

2. Fare ye well, I had a sweetheart
      Which I dearly loved well,
    Without, or with beauty,
      There is none to excel ;
    She would laugh at my folly
      As she'd sit on my knee,
    There were few in this wide world
      More happier than we.

120

3. Fare ye well, I had a mother
   By the great powers above,
May she always be honoured,
   Respected with love.
May she always be honoured
   On land or on sea,
I will never forget
   Her kindness to me.

4. Fare ye well, my old comrades,
   For I must away,
And now I will leave you
   For many a long day.
To leave my old comrades
   So kind and so dear,
And away for old England
   My barque for to steer.

5. Here's adieu, my old comrades,
   Here's adieu and farewell,
If ever I return again
   There is no tongue can tell.
But we'll trust to His mercy
   Who can sink or can save
Or carry us over
   The wide swelling wave.

No. 59. *Come, All Ye Old Comrades.*

See Ord, pp. 350–351, where, as *The Emigrant's Farewell to Donside,* it is given with the same haunting melody.

60.

Crocodile Song

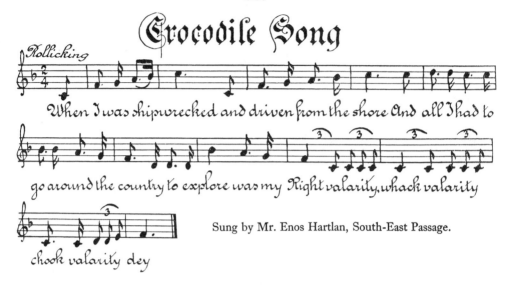

When I was shipwrecked and driven from the shore And all I had to go around the country to explore was my Right valarity, whack valarity chook valarity dey

Sung by Mr. Enos Hartlan, South-East Passage.

1. WHEN I was shipwrecked and driven from the shore
   And all I had to go around the country to explore, was my
   Chorus.
   Right valarity, whack valarity, chook valarity dey.

2. And steering up the other side I found the crocodile,
   From the tip of his nose to the end of his tail he was 10,000 miles, with a
   Chorus.

3. The crocodile, you see, was not of the common race,
   For I had to get up a very tall pine for to look into his face, with a
   Chorus.

4. I bore away from his head one day with every stitch of sail,
   And going nine knots by the log in ten months reached his tail, with a
   Chorus.

5. The wind was blowing hard, and blowing from the south,
   The tree broke down and I saw right in the crocodile's mouth, with a
   Chorus.

122

6. The crocodile he set his mouth and thought he had his victim,
   But I went down his throat you see, and that is how I tricked him,
   with a
   > Chorus.

7. I roamed about his throat until I found his maw,
   And there was bullock's heads and horses laid up there by the score,
   with a
   > Chorus.

8. This crocodile was getting old and surely had a hide,
   It took me six months and forty-two days to work a hole through his
   side, with a
   > Chorus.

9. Come, all you gentlemen, listen to me, if ever you travel the Nile
   Somewhere you will find the shell of this wonderful crocodile, with a
   Right valarity, whack valarity, chook valarity dey.

No. 60. *Crocodile Song.*

This is the sea-going man's counterpart to the *Darby Ram*, exaggerating to the nth degree the characteristics of the animal described. There is an interesting ballad in the *Pepysian Garland*, Rollins, pp. 439–442, giving " a description of a strange (and miraculous) Fish, cast upon the sands in the meads, in the Hundred of Worwell, in the county Palatine of Chester (or Chesshiere). The certainty whereof is here related concerning the said most monstrous Fish." Date 1595–1639. Here is stanza 5 :

> His lower jaw bone's five yards long,
> The upper thrice so much.
> Twelve yolk of oxen stout and strong
> (the weight of it is such)
> Could not stir it out o' the sands
> Thus works the All-creating hands.

A variant of this song is to be found in *English County Songs*, taken down from a native of Dorset.

61.

Donald Munro

Moderato

Ye sons of North Britain, you that used to range In search of foreign countries and lands that was strange Amongst that great number was Donald Munro A way to America he likewise did go

Sung by Mr. Ben Henneberry, Devil's Island.

1. YE sons of North Britain, you that used to range
   In search of foreign countries, and lands that was strange,
   Amongst that great number was Donald Munro,
   Away to America he likewise did go.

2. Two sons with his brother he caused them to stay,
   On account of their passage he could not well pay.
   When seven long winters were ended and gone
   They went to their uncle one day alone,

3. To beg his consent to cross o'er the main
   In hopes their dear parents to meet with again.
   Their uncle replied then, and answered them, " No,
   Thou hast no money wherewith thou canst go."

4. And when they were landed in that country wild,
   Surrounded by rebels on every side,
   There being two rebels that lurked in the wood
   They pointed their pistols where the two brothers stood,

5. And lodging a bullet in each brother's breast
   They ran for their prey like two ravenous beasts,
   " You cruellest monsters, you blood-thirsty hounds,
   How could you have killed us until we hath found,

6. " Found out our dear parents whom we sought with much care?
   I'm sure when they'll hear us they'll die in despair,
   For they left us in Scotland some twelve months ago,
   Perhaps you might know them—their names were Munro."

7. " Oh, who is that young man lies dead by your side ? "
   " Oh, it's my elder brother," the younger replied.
   " It's my elder brother and your eldest son,
   The crime would not be so bad had there only been one."

8. " Oh, curse to my hands !   Oh, what have I done ?
   Oh, curse to my hands, I have murdered my sons ! "
   " Is that you, dear father ?   How did you come by ?
   And since I have seen you, contented I'll die."

9. " I'll sink into sorrow until life it is o'er
   In hopes for to meet you on a far brighter shore,
   In hopes for to meet you on a far brighter shore
   Where I'll not be able to kill you no more."

No. 61. *Donald Munro.*

Although this is not a sea song in the truest sense, yet it is given in this group for want of a more suitable place to put it.   See Rickaby, No. 51 ; Logan, *A Pedlar's Pack*, pp. 413–415 (from a Scottish chapbook of about 1778) ; Mackenzie, No. 131 ; *Adventure Magazine*, July 30, 1925, p. 191, contributed from a singer in Washington who probably learned it in Ontario.

62.

Flying Cloud

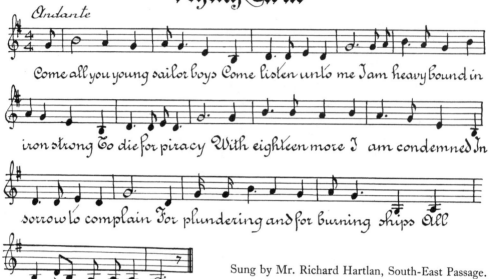

Come all you young sailor boys Come listen unto me I am heavy bound in iron strong To die for piracy With eighteen more I am condemned In sorrow to complain For plundering and for burning ships All on the Spanish Main

Sung by Mr. Richard Hartlan, South-East Passage.

1. COME, all you young sailor boys,
    Come listen unto me,
  I am heavy bound in iron strong
    To die for piracy.
  With eighteen more I am condemned
    In sorrow to complain
  For plundering and for burning ships
    All on the Spanish Main.

2. My name is Edward Anderson
    As you may understand,
  I was born in the county of Waterford
    Near Erin's happy land.
  Oh, I was reared most tenderly
    Until I went to sea,
  The whisky and bad company
    Has made a wretch of me.

126

3. My father bound me to a trader
     In Waterford fair town,
   He bound me to a cooper
     Whose name was William Brown.
   I served my master faithfully
     For eighteen months or more,
   When I shipped on board of the *Ocean Queen*
     Bound down to Valparaiso shore.

4. Now when we arrived in Valparaiso
     I fell in with Captain Moore,
   He commanded the clipper *Flying Cloud*
     Sailing out of Baltimore.
   He asked me to sign up with him
     On a slavery voyage to go
   To the burning shores of Africa
     Where sugar cane does grow.

5. We sailed away the raging Main
     Till we came to Africa's shore,
   Five hundred of those poor souls
     From the native shores we tore ;
   We drugged the bodies cross the deck
     And put them down below,
   It was eighteen inches to a man
     That's all we did allow.

6. We sailed away on the raging Main
     With a cargo of black slaves,
   It would have been better if those poor souls
     Had been going to their graves,
   For the plague and fever came on board,
     Took half of them away,
   We dragged their bodies on the deck
     And threw them in the sea.

7. We sailed away the Spanish Main
     Till we came to Cubia shores,
   We sold them to the planters there,
     They were slaves for ever more,

To work in the rice and the sugar fields
　　All under the burning sun,
To drag along a wretched life
　　Till their career was done.

8.　Though after our money was all gone
　　　We came on board again,
　　Oh, Captain Moore called us on deck
　　　And said to us his men,
　　" There's gold and silver to be had
　　　Down on the Spanish Main,
　　If you'll agree, my bully boys,
　　　I'll tell you how it's gained.

9.　" We'll run aloft a pirate flag
　　　And plough the Spanish Main."
　　We all agreed but five brave youths
　　　Told us them to land.
　　Oh, two of them was Boston boys
　　　And two from Newfoundland,
　　The other was an Irish chap
　　　Belonging to Trimore,
　　I wish to God I had joined them two
　　　And landed safe on shore.

10.　We have a fast a sailing ship
　　　That ever scun the sea,
　　Or ever spread a main topsail
　　　Before a lively breeze.
　　We have an iron chest and magazine
　　　All safely stowed below,
　　And between our spars a Long Tom
　　　On a swivel it does go.

11.　The *Flying Cloud* is a clipper ship
　　　Eight hundred tons or more,
　　She can easily sail around anything
　　　Sailing out of Baltimore.

I offtimes saw that goodly ship
  With the wind be after beam,
With her royals and her sternsails set
  Taking fourteen from the reel.

12. We robbed and burnt there's many's the ship
       Down on the Spanish Main,
   Left many a widow and orphan child
       In sorrows to complain ;
   We made the crew to walk the plank
       As it hung out from our rail,
   For the saying of our captain,
       " The dead man tells no tales."

13. We were offtimes chased by man of wars,
       Privateers and liners too,
   But to overtake our goodly ship
       That's a thing they never could do
   Until the Spanish man o' war
       The *Dungeon* hove in view.

14. She fired a shot across our bow,
       A signal to heave to,
   We gave them to answer
       But steered before the wind,
   Till a chain shot took our mizzenmast,
       Of course we fell behind.

15. We cleared our decks for action
       As she came up alongside,
   And soon upon our quarterdeck
       There ran a crimson tide.
   We fought till Captain Moore was killed
       And thirty of our men,
   When a bombshell shot our ship on fire,
       We were forced to surrender then.

16. We were all taken prisoners
       And into prison cast,
   We were tried and found guilty
       To be hung at last ;

129

So now you see what I have come to
    By my unhappy hand,
It's on the gallows I must die
    By the laws of the Spanish land.

17. Here's adieu unto my country
    And the girl I love so dear,
Her voice like music to my ears
    I never more shall hear;
I'll never kiss her ruby lips
    Or squeeze her lily-white hands,
For on the gallows I must die
    By the laws of the Spanish land.

No. 62. "*Flying Cloud.*"

This interesting song of piracy in which Negro slaves were forced to cross the ocean with an allowance of eighteen inches to a man, gives a vivid picture of the cruel days of the black flag. The name of the hero varies in almost every copy found, but the story remains the same. See Rickaby, No. 41; Colcord, pp. 73–75; J.A.F.L., 35, 370–372; Dean, pp. 1–2; Eckstorm, pp. 214–216; Mackenzie, No. 111; Gray, pp. 116–123, who notes another variant from Scotland in Greig's *Folk-Songs of the North-East*, cxiii. Colcord gives the date as probably between 1819–1825.

63

Van Diemen's Land

Sung by Mr. Ben Henneberry, Devil's Island.

1. COME, all ye lads of learning, and rambling boys beware,
   It's when you go a-hunting with your dog, your gun, your snare,
   In search of hare and widgeon, keep them at your command,
   And think on the tedious journey going to Van Diemen's Land.

2. We had on board two Irish lads, Pat Murphy and Paul Jones,
   As two a loyal comrades in this country are well known,
   Those two poor boys were taken by the Keeper of the strand,
   And for seven long years transported to plough Van Diemen's Land.

3. We had on board an Irish girl, Jane Summers was her name,
   And she was sent to Dublin for playing of the game.
   Our captain fell in love with her and married her off the hand,
   And the best usage she gave us going to Van Diemen's Land.

4. O when we were safe landed upon the fatal shore
   The Negroes gathered round us, about five hundred score,
   They yoked us in like horses and sold us off the hand,
   And they put us in the trace, my boys, to plough Van Diemen's Land.

5. The bed they gave us to lie upon was built of moss and hay,
   And there we lay the whole night long, one word we dare not say,
   With rattling fires all round us saying, " Slumber if you can,
   But think on the snakes and tigers that's in Van Diemen's Land."

6. O, one night as I lay rousing all in a silent dream,
   I dreamed that I was in Ireland down by a purling stream,
   With my true love all by my side, and her at my command,
   I woke a broken-hearted being in Van Diemen's Land.

No. 63. *Van Diemen's Land.*

Mackenzie, No. 122, says this has been sung extensively in England, Scotland and Ireland, with the names and scenes varied so as to domesticate the song wherever it happens to be current. Consult Mackenzie for further references. Also a text from Minnesota, Dean, p. 95.

64.

Western Ocean

Sung by Mr. Richard Hartlan and family, South-East Passage.

1. OH, I only got one cap, and the crown of it's all gone
   And the peak is all tore to a slunder,
   And if I don't get no more, I'll put this cap in store
   And across the western ocean I shall wander.

   Chorus.

   Then hurrah for your grog,
   Your jolly, jolly grog,
   Hurrah for the rum and tobacco,
   For I've spent all my tin
   On a lassie drinking gin,
   And across the western ocean I shall wander.

2. Oh, I only got one shirt, and the neck of it's all gone
   And the back is all tore to a slunder,
   And if I don't get no more, I'll put that shirt in store
   And across the western ocean I shall wander.   Cho.

3. Oh, I only got one coat and the back of it's all gone
   And the sleeves is all tore to a slunder, etc.   Cho.

133

4. Oh, I only got one pair of pants, and the buttons they are gone
   And the legs is all tore to a slunder, etc.   Cho.

5. Oh, I only got one pair of shoes, and the heels they are gone
   And the toes is all tore to a slunder, etc.   Cho.

No. 64. *Western Ocean.*

It is quite possible that this song was composed for music-hall entertainment by one who had knowledge of the sea.   The chorus has probably been borrowed from a genuine sea song. Both in words and music this is faintly suggestive of *The Little Old Shanty*, and is sung to the same air as the verse.   Lomax, pp. 187, 189, which in its turn is a parody of *The Little old Log Cabin In the Lane.*

65.

Sung by Mr. Faulkner, Devil's Island.

1. I've been a wild rover these many long years,
   I have spent all my money in ale, wine and beers,
   But now I'm resolved for to lay it in store
   And I ne'er shall be called the wild rover no more.

134

Wild rover, wild rover, wild rover give o'er,
I ne'er shall be called the wild rover no more.

2. I went to an ale-house where I used to resort,
   I began for to tell them my money was short,
   I asked them to trust me but their answer was, " Nay,
   Such customers as you we can get every day."   Cho.

3. I put my hand in my pocket before I went out,
   And on to the counter bright guineas counted out.
   She said she had ale, wine and beer of the best,
   And all that she said that was only a jest.   Cho.

4. If I had all the money that I left in your care
   It would buy me a big house, my family to rear,
   It would buy me a big house, it would patch me a barn,
   It would buy me a new coat to keep my back warm.   Cho.

5. I'll go home to my father, tell him what I've done,
   In hopes that he'll pardon his prodigal son ;
   I'll go home to my mother, and there I'll remain
   And I ne'er shall be called the wild rover again.   Cho.

6. Now I'm resolved to lead a new life,
   I'll settle me down and marry a wife,
   And to keep those wild, ravenous wolves from the door,
   I ne'er shall be called the wild rover no more.   Cho.

No. 65. *Wild Rover.*

The portion of this song where the sailor pretends to have no money and is given short shrift until he shows himself the possessor of a fortune is slightly reminiscent of the much older and widely diffused song, *The Green Beds*. Mr. Faulkner's comment here is rather naïve, for he says songs like this were composed in the forecastle of sailing-vessels, and in them he sees proof that in those days " people were smarter than they are now."

66

Ye Gentlemen of England

Andante

Ye gentlemen of England fair Who live at home free from all care It's little do you think or know What we, poor seamen undergo It's mild we toil a-long our way Worked like Turks or galley slaves

Sung by Mr. Ben Henneberry, Devil's Island.

1. YE gentlemen of England fair,
   Who live at home free from all care,
   It's little do you think or know
   What we poor seamen undergo,
   It's mild we toil along our way
   Worked like Turks or galley slaves.

2. Was from England the second day
   Our goodly ship she bore away,
   We bore away from our native shore,
   The wind east-south-east did roar,
   Attended by a dismal sky
   Rattling seas rolled mountains high.

3. The very first land we chanced to see
   Was the land of Plymouth it chanced to be,

Which caused our captain to stand and swear
Thinking to weather the old Ram's Head.
The wind and weather increasing more
Which drove nine sailors on the shore.

4. The first in came was *Northumberland*,
   The *Derby*, the *Dully* and the *Antelope*,
   The *Royal Gay* and the *Sandy* too.
   The *Elizabeth* she made them all to rue,
   She rowed so long till her cable broke,
   Sank was she at the very first stroke.

5. That was not the worst of all,
   The largest ship had the heaviest fall,
   For the *Queen's Crownation* and all her men
   They were all lost except nineteen,
   Which was the mate and eighteen more
   Into the longboat got ashore.

6. As I was a-walking Plymouth one day
   I heard two loving sisters say,
   " May God reward all jolly tars
   And keep them from a man of war.
   May God reward them for their deed
   Flogging poor sailors when there is no need."

No. 66. *Ye Gentlemen of England.*

67.

Battle of Alma

On September last the eighteenth day We landed safe at
big Crimea In spite of all the splashing spray To cheer our hearts for
Alma Then Britain's sons may long remember the glorious twentieth
of September We caused the Russians to surrender Upon the heights of

Sung by Mr. Ben Henneberry, Devil's Island.

Al·ma.

1. On September last the eighteenth day
   We landed safe at big Crimea,
   In spite of all the splashing spray
   To cheer our hearts for Alma.

   Chorus.

   Then Britain's sons may long remember
   The glorious twentieth of September,
   We caused the Russians to surrender
   Up on the heights of Alma.

2. That night we lay on the cold ground,
   No tent nor shelter to be found,
   And with the rain was almost drowned
   Upon the heights of Alma.   Cho.

138

3. Next morning a scorching sun did rise
   Beneath the eastern cloudy skies,
   Our noble chief Lord Raglan cries,
     " Prepare to march for Alma." Cho.

4. Oh, when the heights we hove in view
   The stoutest heart it could subdue
   To see the Russian warlike crew
     Upon the heights of Alma. Cho.

5. Their city was well fortified
   With batteries on every side,
   Our noble chief Lord Raglan cried,
     " We'll get hot work at Alma." Cho.

6. Their shot it flew like winter rain
   When we their batteries strove to gain,
   Fifteen hundred Frenchmen lie slain
     In the bloody gore at Alma. Cho.

7. Our Scottish lads with sword in hose
   Were not the last you may suppose,
   But daring faced their daring foes
     And gained the heights of Alma. Cho.

8. To Sebastopol the Russians fled,
   They left their wounded and the dead,
   The rivers there that they run red
     From the blood was spilled at Alma. Cho.

9. There was fifteen hundred Frenchman I heard say
   Had fell upon that fatal day,
   And eighteen hundred Russians lay
     In the bloody gore at Alma. Cho.

10. Now France and England hand in hand,
    What ne'er a foe could them withstand ?
    So let it run throughout the land,
      The victory won at Alma. Cho.

No. 67. *Battle of Alma.*

Mackenzie, No. 74, gives this as *The Heights of Alma*, accompanying it with what he describes as a rousing chorus, different in wording from the text which I present. Otherwise the songs are quite similar, although mine boasts an added stanza or two. The song was very popular after the Crimean War. See also Dean, pp. 40–41.

68.

Bonny Bunch of Roses O

On the borders of the ocean One morning in the month of
June For to hear the warlike songsters Their cheerful notes and
sweetly tune I o'erheard a female talking Who seemed to be in
grief and woe, Conversing with young Buonaparte Concerning the bonny bunch of Roses O.

Sung by Alexander Henneberry,
Eastern Passage.

1. ON the borders of the ocean
   One morning in the month of June,
   For to hear the warlike songsters
   Their cheerful notes and sweetly tune,
   I o'erheard a female talking
   Who seemed to be in grief and woe,
   Conversing with young Buonaparte
   Concerning the bonny bunch of roses O.

2. Then up steps young Napoleon
   And takes his mother by the hand,

Saying, " Mother dear, have patience
Until I am able to command ;
Then I will take an army,
Through tremendous dangers I will go ;
In spite of all the universe
I will conquer the bonny bunch of roses O."

3. The first time I saw young Buonaparte
    Down on his bended knees fell he ;
    He asked the pardon of his father,
    Who granted it most mournfully.
    " Dear son," he said, " I'll take an army,
    And on the frozen Alps will go ;
    Then I will conquer Moscow
    And return to the bonny bunch of roses O."

4. He took five hundred thousand men,
    With kings likewise to bear his train ;
    He was so well provided for
    That he could sweep this world alone.
    But when he came to Moscow
    He was overpowered by the driven snow
    When Moscow was a blazing,
    So he lost his bonny bunch of roses O.

5. " Oh, son, don't speak so venturesome,
    For in England are the hearts of oak ;
    There is England, Ireland, Scotland,
    Their unity was never broke.
    Oh, son, think of thy father—
    On the isle of St. Helena his body lies low,
    And you must soon follow after him,
    So beware of the bonny bunch of roses O."

6. " Now do believe me, dearest mother,
    Now I lie on my dying bed,
    If I had lived I would have been clever,
    But now I droop my youthful head.

But whilst our bodies lie mould'ring,
And weeping willows over our bodies grow,
The deeds of great Napoleon
Shall sing the bonny bunch of roses O."

No. 68. *Bonny Bunch of Roses O* .

See Hannaghan, *Songs of the Irish Gaels*, No. 8, where an interesting point is raised concerning the title of this song. The editor remarks that a version of this air is sung in the south of Ireland to *The Bonny Bunch of Roses*, and he goes on to quote a stanza from a Napoleonic song which seems to be a variant of this song given here. He explains that the Irish word *Beinsin* (little Bench) is frequently misinterpreted as " a Bunch."

Baring-Gould, No. 27, gives a variant like Mr. Henneberry's, noting it an anti-Jacobite production, adapted to Napoleon, with an additional verse relating to Moscow. In the broadside versions, he remarks, the song is given " to the tune of the *Bonny Bunch of Roses O !* " indicating that there was an earlier ballad of the same nature. Might this song of the Irish Gaels not be that earlier ballad ?

See also Mackenzie, No. 72, Ord, pp. 301–302; Yeats, No. 4, Third Year; Hayward, *Ulster Songs and Ballads*, pp. 17–18; O'Conor, p. 127; Christie Traditional Ballads, 11, 232–233.

69.

Bonny Light Horseman

Ye wise maids and widows I pray give at-tention Unto those few lines I'm now going to mention Our maid in distraction I'm now going to wander She relies upon George for the
Chorus
loss of her lover Broken hearted I'll wander for the
loss of my lover My bonny light horseman was slain in the
war

Sung by Mr. Ben Henneberry, Devil's Island.

1. YE wise maids and widows, I pray give attention
   Unto those few lines I'm now going to mention,
   Our maid in distraction, I'm now going to wander,
   She relies upon George for the loss of her lover.

   ### Chorus.
   Broken-hearted I'll wander for the loss of my lover,
   My bonny light horseman was slain in the war.

2.   Three years and six months since he left England's shore,
My bonny light horseman I'll never see more.
When he mounted on horseback so gallant and brave,
And among the whole regiment respected he was.   Cho.

3.   There does she lament for the loss of her mate,
" Oh, where will I wander, my true love ? " she said,
" There is no mortal breathing my favour shall gain
Since my bonny light horseman in war he was slain."   Cho.

4.   If I had wings of an eagle in the air I would fly,
1 would fly o'er the field where my true love does lie,
And with my fond wings I would bear on his grave,
And kiss the cold lips that lie cold in the clay.   Cho.

5.   When Boney commanded his men how to stand
And proud moved the banners all gayly and grand,
He fixed his cannon the victory to gain,
But my bonny light horseman in the war he was slain.   Cho.

No. 69. *Bonny Light Horseman.*

A broadside of Waterloo.

70.

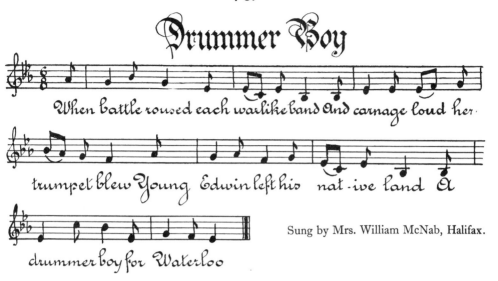

Drummer Boy

When battle roused each warlike band And carnage loud her trumpet blew Young Edwin left his native land A drummer boy for Waterloo

Sung by Mrs. William McNab, **Halifax**.

1. WHEN battle roused each warlike band
   And carnage loud her trumpet blew,
   Young Edwin left his native land,
   A drummer boy for Waterloo.

2. His mother, when his lips she pressed
   And bade her noble boy adieu,
   With wringing hands and aching breast
   Beheld him march for Waterloo.

3. But he who knew not infant fears
   His knapsack o'er his shoulder threw,
   He cried, " Dear mother, dry those tears
   Till I return from Waterloo."

4. He went, and e'er the setting sun
   Beheld the foe their arms subdue,
   The flash of death, the murderous gun
   Had laid him low at Waterloo.

5. " O comrades, comrades," Edwin cried,
   And proudly beamed his eye of blue,
   " Go tell my mother Edwin died
   A soldier's death at Waterloo."

6. They laid his head upon his drum
   Beneath the pale moon's mournful hue,
   When night had stilled the battle's hum
   They dug his grave at Waterloo.

No. 70. *The Drummer Boy.*

A broadside of Waterloo.   For references see Cox, No. 82.

71.

Erin Far Away

Sung by Mr. Ben Henneberry, Devil's Island.

1. THE sun was fast declining on India's fatal shore,
   There laid the dead and dying at the close of that sad war,
   But the saddest sight that I did see upon that field of gore
   Was a young and handsome Irishman who sailed from Erin's shore.

2. His face was like the lilies fair, his hair like threads of gold,
   They laid him down to slumber where India's waters roll,
   He cried, " Oh, give me water, and list to what I say,
   By to-morrow you'll be marching to old Erin far away."

3. His brother held him in his arms, tears down his cheeks did flow,
   Saying, " Brother, dearest brother, it is hard to let you go,
   Have you no kindly message for the parents you love dear,
   And for that young and tender girl in Erin's land so fair ? "

4. " Tell my parents that I nobly fell, my face towards the foe,
   I never thought of turning when on them we did go,
   But rebel soldiers dropped me down, and left me in the gore,
   And I long to see old Ireland with its green and holy shore.

5. " Tell them I thought about them in the thickest of the fray,
   The balls fell fast around me, I ne'er forgot to pray,
   It was one thing yet, my brother, I'll have you to do more,
   Will you mark my grave, my brother, on India's fatal shore ?

6. " For there is one thing yet, my brother, bring my love across the way,
   And bring with her a shamrock to plant upon my grave,
   Tell her it was my last request as I laid down to die,
   And kiss me now, my brother, once more, and then good-bye."

7. His brother laid him gently down, saying, " Your wish shall be done."
   He closed his eyes with one low moan, died at the set of sun.
   They dug for him a narrow grave, and marked it well with care,
   And then began their lonely march to Erin's land so fair.

No. 71. *Erin Far Away.*

72.

Napoleon's Farewell to Paris

They say the cause of my downfall was parting from my consort To wed the German lady it's wounded my heart sore But the female train I'll never blame, though they did me inflame They seen my sword in battle flame and did me a-dore

I AM Napoleon Buonaparte, the conqueror of nations,
I've conquered dukes and earls and pulled kings from their thrones,

They say the cause of my downfall was parting from my consort,
To wed the German lady, it's wounded my heart sore,
But the female train I'll never blame, though they did me inflame,
They seen my sword in battle flame and did me adore.

But I severely felt the rod for meddling the house of God,
Golden coins and images in thousands away I bore,
I stole Malta's golden gate and did the laws of God disgrace,
But if He gives me time and space back to Him I will restore.

Fragments of the song as remembered by Mr. Ben Henneberry, Devil's Island. Strangely, with all his large and varied repertoire Mr. Henneberry found this song beyond him, although he tried to learn it many times. His uncle sang it often, but the Devil's Island men are all doubtful whether anybody can be found who knows the whole song.

Another fragment says,

> They say my lover's gone and I'll never see him more,

(All of that verse.)

> They cause my subjects to eat herbs on the plain,
> Is he gone ? Will I never see him more ?

Mr. Clarence Henneberry gives a different rendering of the second line as remembered from his father's singing. Thus :

> I've conquered dukes and Dutch and Danes
> And surprised the grand seigneur.

No. 72. *Napoleon's Farewell to Paris.*

Having found a copy of this song, I can quite understand why Mr. Henneberry found it so difficult to memorise. The complete text is given as a broadside, Yeats, No. 3, Sixth Year. In quoting part of the first stanza you will appreciate Mr. Henneberry's difficulty.

> I visited the splendid city, the metropolis called Paris,
> Situated every morning by Sol's refulgent beams,
> Conjoined by bright Aurora advancing from the Orient,
> With radiant lights adorning in fire shining ray.
> Commanding Scethua to retire . . . etc.

The controversial line is given in the broadside : " I conquered Dutch and Danes and surprised the Grand Signor." Personally I prefer Mr. Henneberry's line where he " pulled kings from their thrones." The Devil's Island men are as one in agreeing that this is the best song of Napoleon they have ever heard.

73.
Casey's Whiskey

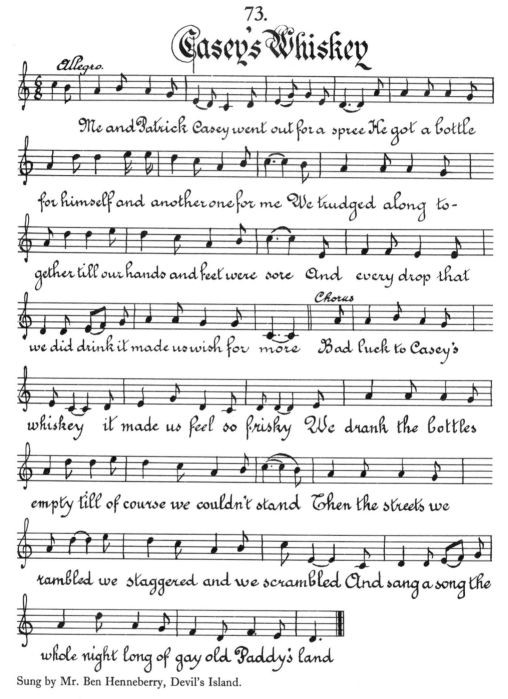

Me and Patrick Casey went out for a spree He got a bottle for himself and another one for me We trudged along together till our hands and feet were sore And every drop that we did drink it made us wish for more Bad luck to Casey's whiskey it made us feel so frisky We drank the bottles empty till of course we couldn't stand Then the streets we rambled we staggered and we scrambled And sang a song the whole night long of gay old Paddy's land

Sung by Mr. Ben Henneberry, Devil's Island.

150

1. ME and Patrick Casey went out for a spree,
   He got a bottle for himself and another one for me,
   We trudged along together till our hands and feet were sore
   And every drop that we did drink it made us wish for more.

Chorus.

Bad luck to Casey's whiskey, it made us feel so frisky,
We drank the bottles empty till of course we couldn't stand,
Then the streets we rambled, we staggered and we scrambled,
And sang a song the whole night long of gay old Paddy's land.

2. We met a big policeman who looked at us, says he,
   " What brings you out as late as this ? " Says I, " The country's free."
   " Come along," says Casey. " Devil a bit," says I,
   " I'll hit him if he says a word, the dirty, mean old spy." Cho.

3. He turned away and left us, for he was not to blame,
   I called him back and asked him if he'd please to tell his name.
   " Of course," said he ; " it's Flannigan, I'm from the county Clare."
   " Hurrah ! " said I, " me Irish by, old whiskey we must share." Cho.

4. Out came the empty bottle, as I put it in his paw,
   " Look out," said he, " upon the post, drinking's against the law."
   He put the bottle to his lips, but devil the sup was there,
   And whilst we laughed at Flannigan, shure he began to swear. Cho.

5. He riz his club above our heads, and swore he'd take us in.
   " For drinking on the highway ? " said Casey, " that's too thin."
   He lugged poor Casey off to jail, he tried to take me too,
   But to keep his hold on Casey was as much as he could do. Cho.

No. 73. *Casey's Whiskey.*

74.

Courtship of Willie Riley

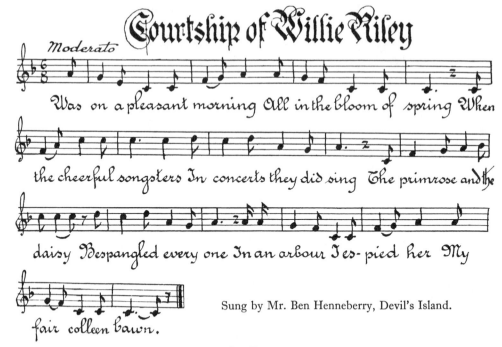

Was on a pleasant morning All in the bloom of spring When the cheerful songsters In concerts they did sing The primrose and the daisy Bespangled every one In an arbour I es-pied her My fair colleen bawn.

Sung by Mr. Ben Henneberry, Devil's Island.

RILEY'S COURTSHIP

1. Was on a pleasant morning
   All in the bloom of spring
   When the cheerful songsters
   In concerts they did sing.

2. The primrose and the daisy
   Bespangled every one,
   In an arbour I espied her,
   My fair colleen bawn.

3. I stared awhile amazed,
   Perched up with surprise,
   On her with rapture gazed,
   While from her bright eyes

4. She shot such killing glances
   My heart away was gone,
   She ravished all my senses,
   My fair colleen bawn.

152

5. Politely I addressed her,
      " Hail, matchless fair maid,
   You have with grief oppressed me
      And I am much afraid.

6. " Unless you cure my anguish
      That now is in its dawn,
   You'll cause my sad overthrow,
      My fair colleen bawn."

7. And with a gentle smile
      She replied unto me,
   " I cannot patronize
      Dear Willie over thee.

8. " My father he is wealthy
      And gives severe command,
   If you'll but gain his favour
      I'll be your colleen bawn."

9. In rapture I embraced her,
      We swore eternal love,
   And nought could separate us
      Except the powers above.

10. I hired with her father
      And left my friends on land,
   That in pleasure I might gaze on
      My fair colleen bawn.

11. I served in port twelve months
      Right faithfully and just,
   Although not used to labour
      Was true unto my trust.

12. I valued not my wages
      And would not it demand,
   Oh, I could live for ages
      With my fair colleen bawn.

13. One morning as her father
     And I walked out alone,
  I asked him for his daughter,
     Saying, " Sir, it is well known,

14. " I have a well-stocked farm,
     £500 in land,
  Which I'll share with your daughter
     My fair colleen bawn."

15. Her father full of anger
     Most scornfully did frown,
  Saying, " Here are your wages,
     Now, sir, depart this town."

16. Increasing still his anger
     He bid me quick begone,
  " Oh, none but a rich squire
     Shall wed my colleen bawn."

17. I went unto his daughter
     And told her my sad tale,
  Oppressed with grief and anguish
     We both did weep and wail.

18. She said, " My dearest Riley,
     The thought I can't withstand,
  That with sorrow you must leave
     Your dear colleen bawn."

19. A horse I did get ready
     All in the silent night,
  Having no other remedy
     We quickly took our flight.

20. The horse he chanced to stumble
     And threw us both along,
  Confused and sorely bruised me
     And my dear colleen bawn.

21.   Again we quickly mounted
      And swiftly rode away,
  O'er lofty hills and mountains
      We travelled night and day.

22.   Her father swift pursued us
      With his well-chosen band,
  And I was overtaken with
      My dear colleen bawn.

23.   Committed straight to prison
      There to lament and wail
  And utter my complaints to
      A dark and dismal jail,

24.   Loaded with heavy iron
      Till my trial does come on,
  But I'll bear the utmost malice
      For my dear colleen bawn.

25.   If it should please kind fortune
      Once more to set me free,
  For well I know my charmer
      Is constant unto me.

26.   In spite of her father's anger,
      His cruelty and scorn,
  I hope to win my heart's delight
      My fair colleen bawn.

Trial

27.   " Come, rise up, Willie Riley,
      Now come away with me,
  I mean for to go with you
      And leave this counteree.

28.   " I'll forsake my father's dwelling,
      His houses and rich land,
  And go along with you, my dear,
      To a fair colleen bawn."

29. O'er lofty hills and mountains
      Along the handsome dale,
   Through shady groves and mountains,
      Rich meadows and sweet vales,

30. We climbed the rugged woods and
      Went over silent lawns,
   But I was overtaken with
      My dear colleen bawn.

31. They hurried me to prison,
      My hands and feet they bound,
   Confined me like a murderer
      With chains unto the ground.

32. But this hard, cruel treatment
      Most cheerfully I'll stand,
   Ten thousand deaths I'll suffer for
      My dear colleen bawn.

33. In came the jailor's son
      And to Riley he did say,
   " Rise up, unhappy Riley,
      You must appear to-day

34. " Proud Squire Follard's anger
      And power to withstand,
   I'm afraid you'll suffer sorely
      For your dear colleen bawn.

35. " This is the news, young Riley,
      Last night I heard of you,
   The lady's oath will hang you
      Or else will set you free."

36. " If that be so," said Riley,
      Some hope began to dawn,
   " Oh, I never can be injured
      By my dear colleen bawn."

37. The lady she is sensible,
    And in her tender youth,
If Riley has deluded her
    She will declare the truth.

38. Then like a spotless angel
    Before them she did stand,
" You are welcome here," says Riley,
    " My dear colleen bawn."

39. About the noble Fox
    Who stood attentive by,
" Gentlemen of the jury,
    In justice we reply,

40. " To hang a man for love
    Is foul murder, you may see,
Oh, spare the life of Riley,
    And banished let him be."

41. " But stop, my lord, he stole her
    Bright jewels and nice ring,
Gold watch and diamond buckle,
    And many costly things.

42. " I gave them to my daughter,
    They cost £1000,
When Riley was first taken
    These things with him were found."

43. " Oh no, my lord, I gave them
    As a token of true love,
He never stole my jewels,
    I swear by all above.

44. " Oh, if you have them, Riley,
    Pray send them home to me."
" I will, my honoured lady,
    With many thanks to thee."

45. " There is one ring among them
    I wish for you to wear,
It is set with costly diamonds
    And plaited with my hair.

46. " In token of true friendship
    Wear it on your right hand,
Think on my broken heart, love,
    When in a foreign land."

Marriage

47. All tender-hearted lovers
    Attend unto my theme,
The hardships of young Riley
    I mean now to explain.

48. Who, for stealing of an heiress
    'Fore the court did stand,
Ordered for transportation
    Unto a foreign land.

49. The daughter of Squire Follard
    This lady proved to be,
Beautiful as an angel,
    And born of high degree.

50. For her young Willie Riley
    Both night and day doth wail,
Loaded with heavy irons
    Confined in Sligo jail.

51. Like a poor malefactor
    Transported he must be,
The lady cried, " Dear Riley,
    Your face I ne'er shall see.

52. " My cruel-hearted father,
    Thou weren't the only one
That banished Willie Riley
    From his poor colleen bawn."

158

53. Her father in a passion
       Unto his daughter said,
    " For your foul disobedience
       You shall be conveyed

54. " Unto a lonesome chamber,
       To there repent the deed,
    Twelve months on bread and water
       You shall be forced to feed."

55. Then unto a dark chamber
       His daughter he did hide,
    With nothing but coarse blankets
       And straw whereon to lie.

56. She says, " My dearest Riley,
       'Tis for my sake alone
    That you with grief and sorrow
       In Sligo jail doth mourn."

57. Three nights this lonely lady
       In grief and sorrow spent,
    Till overcome with anquish
       She quite distracted went.

58. She wrung her hands and tore her hair,
       Crying, " My only dear,
    My cruel-hearted father
       Hath used you most severe."

59. Unto a private madhouse
       They hurried her away,
    Where she was heard each morning
       For to weep and pray.

60. Her chains loud she'd rattle,
       And then would cry and rave,
    " For me poor Willie Riley
       Is treated like a slave.

61. " Alas, dear Billy Riley,
        If I could once more see,
    But for my father's anger
        I'd try to set you free.

62. " I could hold you in my arms,
        From you I'd never part,
    For though I'm here confined,
        Young Riley has my heart."

63. Now we will leave this fair one
        In sorrow for awhile,
    And speak of Willie Riley
        Confined in Sligo jail.

64. Who with twenty other criminals
        To Dublin marched away,
    Who went on board a transport,
        And straight to Botany Bay.

65. When in Dublin they arrived
        They were conveyed to jail,
    Until the transport ship
        Was ready for to sail.

66. Then Riley cried, " Squire Follard,
        You cruel-hearted man,
    In Bedlam lies your daughter
        My dear colleen bawn."

67. But fortune to poor Riley
        Happened to prove kind,
    While he lay in Ireland,
        A thought came in his mind.

68. A petition from the prison
        Unto the parson sent,
    Unto the Lord Lieutenant
        Whose heart it did relent.

69. The noble Lord Lieutenant
      Unto the prison haste,
   And here young Willie Riley
      He speedily released.

70. With him unto Bedlam
      Straightway he went anon
   Likewise released his jewel,
      His fair colleen bawn.

71. As soon as the lady
      Did her true love behold,
   She in her snowy arms
      Young Riley did enfold.

72. Her senses soon revived ;
      They for the parson sent,
   Who married this young couple
      Unto their heart's content.

73. A license from the Primate
      Was got immediately,
   And constant William Riley
      Was mated to his lady.

74. A feast was then prepared
      Which lasted four days long,
   Success attend young Riley
      And his young colleen bawn.

75. Soon as the old man heard it
      His old heart did relent,
   He cried, " For my offences
      I sorely do repent,

76. " But now you shall live happy
      With me in Sligo town,
   A fortune I will give thee
      Of £30,000.

77. " And as it is God's will
I have no child but thee,
I beg it as a blessing
That you will live with me.

78. " And at my death you shall possess
My horses and rich land,
My blessings on you, Riley,
And our dear colleen bawn."

No. 74. *Courtship of Willie Riley.*

What more tangible proof of Mr. Henneberry's remarkable memory can be given than this seventy-eight verse song ? sung from beginning to end without hesitation. I have not found the complete text in any other collection, but understand there should be some 95 verses. There seems to be " a hole in the ballad " here in the story of the trial.

Joyce, *Old Irish Folk Music and Songs*, notes that the event which prompted the writing of this song occurred towards the end of the eighteenth century with the scene near Baindoram, where the ruined home of Squire ffolliott can still be seen. The penal laws then in effect made it dangerous for a Catholic Irishman to run away with the daughter of a Protestant squire.

The song is sometimes given in three separate parts, each a distinct song. Occasionally it is in one part, terminating where the trial ends in this variant.

75.

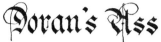

Sung by Mr. Ben Henneberry,
Devil's Island.

1. PADDY DOYLE lived in Killarney
   Courted a girl named Biddy Toole,
   Her tongue was tipped with a bit of blarney,
   The same was Pat with a golden rule.
   Both day and dawn she was his colleen
   And to her he'd often say,
   " 'Arrah, what's the use, you're my darling
   Coming to meet me on the way ? "

   Chorus.
   Whack fall de derro, derro, derro,
   Whack fall de derro, derro lay.

2. One heavenly night in last November
   Paddy walked out to meet his love,
   The night it was I don't remember
   But the moon shone bright above.
   That day the boys had got some whiskey
   Which made Pat's spirits light and gay,

" Oh, what's the use of walking quicker
When I know she'll meet me on the way ? "

3. As Pat walked on in gentle number
Merrily onward he did go,
Sleep and whiskey overcame him,
Pat laid down upon the sod.
He was not long without a comrade,
One that could kick up the hay,
A big jackass he smelled out Paddy
And lay down beside him on the way.

4. He hugged and snugged the fairy mesher
And flung his hat with worldy care,
" She's mine, and only heaven bless her,
But by my soul she's like a bear."
He put his hand on the donkey's nose,
With that the ass began to bray.
Pat jumps up and swore like thunder,
" Who served me in such a way ? "

5. Then Pat ran home as fast as he could,
At railway speed was fast I'm sure,
And never stopped a leg or foot
Until he arrived at Biddy's door.
By that time it was growing daylight,
Down on his knees he fell to pray,
" 'Arrah, let me in, my Biddy darlin',
I'm kilt, I'm murdered on the way."

6. He told his story mighty civil
While she prepared a whiskey glass,
How he hugged and snugged that hairy devil,
" Go along," said Biddy, " it was Doran's ass."
" I knew it was, my Biddy darling."
They both got married the very next day,
But he never got back his old straw hat
Which the donkey ate upon the way.

No. 75. *Doran's Ass.*

Mackenzie, No. 138, gives this with several references. See also Dean, pp. 38–39 ; O'Conor, p. 43.

76.

Down By the Can-Yard Side

Andante

I am a rambling hero With life I am ensnared. Near
to the town of Bonny Glas There dwells a comely maid. She is
fairer than Di-ana bright She is free from earthly pride She's a
lovely girl and her dwelling place Lies near the Can-Yard
side .

Sung by Patrick Williams, Devil's Island.

1. I AM a rambling hero,
       With life I am ensnared,
    Near to the town of Bonny Glas
       There dwells a comely maid.
    She is fairer than Diana bright,
       She is free from earthly pride,
    She's a lovely girl, and her dwelling-place
       Lies near the tan-yard side.

2. I stood in meditation,
       I viewed her o'er and o'er,
    I thought she was Aurora bright
       Descending down so low.

165

" Oh no, kind sir, I'm a country girl,"
    She modestly replied,
" I labour daily for my bread
    Down by the tan-yard side."

3. Her golden hair in ringlets rare
      Fell o'er her snowy neck,
   The killing glances of her eyes
      Would save a ship from wreck,
   Her two brown sparkling eyes
      And her teeth like the ivory white,
   It would make a man become her slave
      Down by the tan-yard side.

4. For twelve long months we courted
      Till at length we did agree,
   And for to acquaint her parents
      And married we would be,
   Until her cruel father
      To me he proved unkind,
   He made me sail across the sea
      And leave my love behind.

5. Fare ye well, my ancient parent,
      Farewell to you I bid adieu,
   I am crossing the main ocean
      All for the love of you,
   And if ever I return again
      I will make you my bride,
   I will enrol you in my arms, love,
      Down by the tan-yard side.

No. 76. *Down By the Tan-Yard Side.*

   O'Conor, p. 25, gives the town mentioned in v. 1 as Bollinglass. In the broadside, Yeats, No. 10, Sixth Year, it is Baltinglass.

77

The Green Mossy Banks of the Lea

When first to this country a stranger Curiosity caused me to roam Over Europe an exile I wandered Far a- way from my 'Merican home. Till at length I arrived in sweet E - rin The land which I long wished to see And my footsteps seemed guided by fai - ies On the green mossy banks of the lea.

Sung by Mr. Faulkner and Patrick Williams, Devil's Island.

1. WHEN first to this country a stranger
   Curiosity caused me to roam,
   Over Europe an exile I wandered
   Far away from my 'Merican home.
   Till at length I arrived in sweet Erin,
   The land which I long wished to see,
   And my footsteps seemed guided by fairies
   On the green mossy banks of the lea.

2. One morning of late as I rambled
   Where the sweet winds from heaven did blow,

'Twas down by a clear crystal river
    Where the sweet running waters did flow,
It was there I espied a fair damsel,
    Most modest appearing to me,
As she rose from her seat near the water
    On the green mossy banks of the lea.

3. I stepped up to bid her good-morning,
        Her fair cheeks they blushed like the rose,
    I said then, " Those meadows are charming,
        Your escort I'll be if you chose."
    She said, " Sir, I never need any escort,
        Kind sir, you're a stranger to me,
    But yonder my father is coming
        On the green mossy banks of the lea."

4. I waited till up came her father,
        I picked up my courage once more,
    I said then, " If this be your daughter
        She is truly the girl I adore,
    Ten thousand a year is my fortune,
        A lady your daughter shall be,
    She shall ride in a coach of six horses
        On the green mossy banks of the lea."

5. They welcomed me down to their cottage,
        Soon after in wedlock were joined,
    'Twas there that I rented the cottage
        In splendour and grandeur divine
    So now the American stranger
        Right pleasure and pastime to see,
    With his adorable, gentle Matilda
        From the green mossy banks of the lea.

6. Come, all pretty maidens, take warning
        No matter how poor you may be,
    There's many a poor girl that's handsome
        As those that has large property.
    By flattery let no man deceive you
        No matter how poor you may be

Be like adorable, gentle Matilda
On the green mossy banks of the lea.

No. 77. *Green Mossy Banks of the Lea.*

See Mackenzie, No. 47; *Journal*, 11, 150, and compare *Pretty Girl Milking Her Cow.* Cf. also Hannaghan, *The Book of Irish Gaels, The Old Bridge at Toor.*

78.

Sung by Mr. Ben Henneberry, Devil's Island.

1. ONE fine summer's evening as I was a-walking
   Down by Leicester market I chanced for to go,
   I spied a fair damsel, she attracted my attention,
   I'll tell you about her as far as I know.

   Chorus.
   Right fall de di dey, right fall de di daddy,
   I'll tell you about her as far as I know.

169

2. I said, " My fair lady, oh, where is your dwelling ?
   Oh, who is your father I'd fain like to know ? "
   " My father's a blacksmith, he lives down at Liscomb,
   And I am his daughter young Jessie Munroe.

Chorus.

Right fall de di dey, right fall de di daddy,
And I am his daughter young Jessie Munroe."

3. " Oh, I have fine buildings and lands of my own, love,
   And they are by the wayside as you go,
   And you, my dear darling, may lie in my arms
   Like a lamb in the bosom of Jessie Munroe.

Chorus.

Right fall de di dey, right fall de di daddy,
Like a lamb in the bosom of Jessie Munroe."

4. " Deceitful young Johnny, begone with such flattery
   Into your buildings I never will go,
   Your buildings are shattery, so begone with such flattery,
   There's a handsome a laddie for Jessie Munroe.

Chorus

Right fall de di dey, right fall de di daddy,
There's a handsome a laddie for Jessie Munroe."

5. " Begone now, young Jessie, since you are so saucy
   Back to my Betsy again I will go,
   She isn't so bonny, she's fitting for Johnny,
   So away to the devil young Jessie Munroe.

Chorus.

Right fall de di dey, right fall de di daddy,
So away to the devil young Jessie Munroe."

No. 78. *Jessie Munroe.*

79

The Mantle of Green

One evening of late as I rambled On the banks of a clear crystal stream I sat down on a bank of primroses And so gently fell into a dream I dreamt I beheld a fair damsel Her equal I ne'er saw before And she sighed for the woes of her country As she strayed along Erin's green shore

Sung by Mrs. Jane Henneberry,
aged 77, Devil's Island.

1. ONE evening of late as I rambled
      On the banks of a clear, crystal stream,
    I sat down on a bank of primroses
      And so gently fell into a dream,
    I dreamt I beheld a fair damsel,
      Her equal I ne'er saw before—
    And she sighed for the woes of her country
      As she strayed along Erin's green shore.

2. I quickly addressed the fair damsel,
      " My jewel, come tell me your name,
    For to this country I know you're a stranger
      Or I would not have asked you the same."

She resembled the goddess of liberty,
    And green was the mantle she wore,
And she sighed for the woes of her country
    As she strayed along Erin's green shore.

3. " I know you're a true son of Erin,
        And my secret to you I'll unfold,
    I am here in the midst of all dangers
        Not knowing my friends from my foes.
    I am daughter of Daniel O'Connell,
        And from England I lately came o'er ;
    I am come to awaken my brothers
        That slumber on Erin's green shore."

4. Her eyes were like two sparkling diamonds
        Or the stars of a cold, frosty night ;
    Her cheeks were like two blooming roses,
        And her teeth like the ivory so white.
    She resembled the goddess of liberty,
        And green was the mantle she wore,
    Bound round with the shamrock and roses
        That grow along Erin's green shore.

5. In transport of joy I awakened
        And found it had been but a dream,
    For the beautiful damsel had fled me
        And I longed then to slumber again ;
    Oh, may heaven above be her guardian
        For I know I shall see her no more,
    And may sunbeams of glory shine on her
        As she strays along Erin's green shore.

No. 79. *Mantle of Green.*

Four stanzas of this song appear in O'Conor, p. 38, as *Erin's Green Shore*, where line 1 stanza 3 reads " I know you're a true son of Granue."

80.

Mary Nail

Sung by Mr. Ben Henneberry, Devil's Island.

1. I AM a bold undaunted youth, my name is John McCann,
   I'm a native of sweet Denagogue, convenient to Scotland,
   Who was stealing of an heiress, and lying long in jail,
   Her father swears he'll have my life along with Mary Nail.

2. While in strong irons I lie bound my love sent word to me
   Not to dread her father's anger, she would try and set me free,
   Although her father gave consent to let me out on bail,
   I had to stand my trial for his daughter Mary Nail.

3. The day of my trial my prosecutor she was to be,
   The day of my trial she did try and set me free,
   But like a loyal lover to appear she did not fail,
   She cleared me from all danger did my charming Mary Nail.

4. My trial it being over I searched her garden round,
   My trial it being over the hedges I made round,
   My well-known voice soon reached her ears which covered hill and dale.
   " You are welcome here, my Johnny dear," cried charming Mary Nail.

5. Down on the flowery banks we sat, and did we chat awhile,
   " It's Mary dear, if you'll agree, I'll free you from exile,"
   " The *Charlie Stewart* is ready for Adara for to sail,
   And come along with me, my dear," cried charming Mary Nail.

6. I gave consent, straight home she went and stole her best of clothes,
   And to no one in the house she ne'er let know the news,
   Likewise £500 in ready gold from her father she did steal,
   And that was twice I did in love my charming Mary Nail.

7. The coach it was got ready for Adara for to go,
   She also bribed the coachman for to let no one know,
   He swore he'd keep our secret, his mind would ne'er avail,
   And off to Quebec I did go along with Mary Nail.

8. It was on our passage to Quebec my passage she did pay,
   It was on our passage to Quebec we under cover lay,
   We joined our hands in wedlock bands before we did set sail.
   Her father's wrath I value not, I have my Mary Nail.

9. It was on our passage to Quebec our ship did gently glide,
   It was on our passage to Quebec while on a matchless tide,
   Until we arrived on Woodland reef we had no cause to fail,
   In Guysboro' Bay I thought that day I'd lost my Mary Nail.

10. On the fourth of June in the afternoon the heavy fog came on.
    Our captain cried, " Look out, my boy, or surely we're undone."
    Our ship against the sandbanks came, she was driven by the gale,
    And forty-four washed overboard 'long with my Mary Nail.

11. Soon now I saw her yellow locks come floating by the gale,
    I jumped into the raging main and saved my Mary Nail.
    Her father wrote me a letter, gave me to understand
    That if I would come back he would give me half his land.

12. I wrote him back an answer, and that without avail.
    £5 a week I did receive with charming Mary Nail,
    £5 a week I did receive with charming Mary Nail,
    While ever I lived I'd ne'er deceive my charming Mary Nail.

No. 80. *Mary Nail.*

See *Charming Mary Neill*, Joyce, *Old Irish Folk Music and Songs*, No. 256.

81.

My Irish Polly

As I rowed out one May morning Down by the riv-er-side A-walking all a-round there An Irish girl I spied Red and rosy were her cheeks And yellow were her hair And costly were those robes of gold that Irish girl did wear Saying Jimmie dearest Jimmie From the marks of the bramble tree Are you going to leave me here alone For to thank your own Polly.

Sung by Muriel Henneberry, aged 12, Devil's Island.

1. As I rowed out one May morning
    Down by the riverside,
    A-walking all around there
    An Irish girl I spied.

2. Red and rosy were her cheeks
    And yellow were her hair,

And costly were those robes of gold
That Irish girl did wear.

3. Her shoes were made of Spanish leather
And neatly did they tie,
Her hair hung down in ringlets
And on her shoulders fell.

Chorus.

Saying, Jimmie, dearest Jimmie,
From the marks of the bramble tree,
Are you going to leave me here alone
For to thank your own Polly ?

4. And if I were a butterfly
I would light on my love's breath,
And if I were a linnet
I would sing my love to rest,

5. And if I were a nightingale
I would sing to the morning clear,
I would still sing to you, Polly,
For it's once I love you dear.   Cho.

6. And if I were in Dublin City
A-sporting on the green,
On each hip a bottle of wine
And on his knee a lass,

7. I'd call for liquor merrily
And pay before I go,
I would roll you in my arms, Polly,
Let the wind blow high or low.   Cho.

8. Let the wind blow high or low, brave lads,
Let the seas run mountains high,
For it is a seaman's duty
At the helm to stand by.

9. It takes two men to reef and steer
The chief of all our care,
And when our main decks are secured
No danger did we fear.   Cho.

No. 81. *My Irish Polly.*

As Muriel sings this, the song seems a bit confused. The first five stanzas are much the same as those of *The Irish Girl*, Sharp, *Songs from Hampshire*, p. 6; Joyce in *Old Irish Folk-Music and Songs*, p. 190, gives 4 verses somewhat similar. Davis, p. 274, gives a song in an appendix to *The Lass of Roch Royal*, in which the first two stanzas are like this text, and v. 5 is much like v. 7 in my N.S. text. The first stanza in O'Conor, p. 15, combines vv. 1, 2 and 3 of this variant.

82.

Sung by Richard Hartlan, South-East Passage.

1. ONE morning, one morning, one morning in May
    I saddled my horse for to ride all the way,
    My horse he stood still, threw me off in the dirt,
    He dabbed all my body and bruised all my shirt,

Chorus.
Singing fall diddle diddle I dey,
Singing fall diddle diddle I dey.

177

2. I had been a firm fellow I mounted again,
   On all my tip-toes for to ride on the plain,
   My horse he got lazy, he would not go down
   For to ride on again to far London town.   Cho.

3. Three years I was riding to far London town,
   But when I got there not a soul could I see,

   .   .   .   .

   For all the old women were gazing at me.   Cho.

4. But when I got there not a soul could I see,
   For all the old women were gazing at me,
   Such darnation gazing I ne'er saw before,
   My shoes were all bruised and my heels were all tore.   Cho.

5. I sat myself down on a hot frozen stone,
   Ten thousand around me but me all alone,
   I called for a glass to drive madness away
   To banish the dust that had rained all the day.   Cho.

6. As I was a-walking through St. James Park
   A moon had shone down although it was dark,
   I saw two pretty fair maids all raking in hay
   In the middle of winter one fine summer day.   Cho.

7. I stepped up to court one of them that was there,
   She was dark and no lass, I vow and declare,
   She was the prettiest creature that ever I seen,
   Her age it was red and her hair was nineteen.   Cho.

8. It is home to old England I'll carry my bride,
   My ship will sail over dry land and fair tide,
   And won't my old mother laugh and stare
   To see a coach and six horses pulled by the grey mare.

Chorus.
Singing fall diddle diddle I dey,
Singing fall diddle diddle I dey.

No. 82. *Paddy Backwards.*

This merry story is an early form of a theme which became very popular with the burnt-cork minstrels.   The best example is *Oh, Susanna.*

83.

Rambling Shoemaker

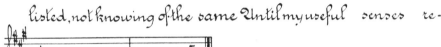

I am a rambling shoemaker From Ireland I came And

to my sad misfortune I enlisted in the train Being drunk when I en-

listed, not knowing of the same Until my useful senses re-

Sung by Mr. Ben Henneberry, Devil's Island.

turned to me again

1. I AM a rambling shoemaker, from Ireland I came,
   And to my sad misfortune I enlisted in the train,
   Being drunk when I enlisted, not knowing of the same,
   Until my useful senses returned to me again.

2. I had a loving sweetheart, Jane Wilson was her name,
   It grieved her to the very heart to see me in the train,
   She said that if I would desert and quickly let her know
   She'd dress me up in her own clothes where'er I'd choose to go.

3. We marched for Tipperary, my officers gave command,
   Me and my loyal comrades that night on guard to stand,
   The night being dark and very wet with me did not agree,
   I knocked down my loyal comrade and ran my liberty.

4. I ran all that livelong night, at length I lost my way,
   I jumped down a meadow and lie down on some hay,
   I had not long been lying there when I awoke again
   And looking all around me I 'spied nine of our train.

5. We had a bloody combat ; it's true I beat them all,
   I made those cowardly rascals for mercy loud to call,
   Saying, " Spare our lives, dear Irvin, and we will pray for thee,
   I will swear by all that's good, my boy, you fought for your liberty."

6. " Go home, you cowardly rascals, what more then can you say ?
   I care not for your officers, and with them I will not stay.
   Go home and tell your officers, likewise your sergeants three,
   I mean to fight till the day I die or gain my liberty."

7. There was John Brown from Galway town, a man both poor and mean,
   For the sake of twenty shillings he sent on me a train,
   He put me in a guardhouse, my sorrows to deplore,
   There were six to guard each window and as many to guard the door.

8. It's early the next morning I searched the guardroom round,
   I leapt out of the window and knocked three of them down.
   With their train and lighthorsemen they soon did follow me,
   But I had friends upon the road who fought for my liberty.

9. Now I am a rambling shoemaker, James Irvin is my name,
   I'll beat as many Orangemen as you have in your train,
   I'll beat as many Orangemen as stand in a row,
   And I'll make them fly before me like an arrow from a bow.

No. 83. *Rambling Shoemaker.*

See Yeats, No. 5, Third Year.

84.

Since Love Can Enter an Iron Door

It's of a damsel neat, tall and handsome Those lines are true as I've been told, On the banks of Shannon in a lofty mansion Her father claimed great stores of gold

Sung by Mr. William Faulkner, Devil's Island.

1. It's of a damsel neat, tall and handsome,
    Those lines are true as I've been told,
    On the banks of Shannon in a lofty mansion
    Her father claimed great stores of gold.

2. Her hair was as black as the raven's feathers,
    To form her features describe who can.
    Why does folly belong to nature ?
    She fell in love with her servant man.

3. As Mary Ann and her love were walking
    Her father saw them and near them drew,
    As Mary Ann and her love were talking
    Her father home in great anger flew.

4. To build a dungeon was his intention
    To part true lovers he contrived to plan,
    He swore an oath which is too wild to mention
    That he'd part his daughter from her servant man.

181

5. He built a dungeon with brick and mortar,
      Three flights of stairs all underground,
   And the food he gave her was bread and water,
      On nothing else was the poor girl found.

6. Three times a day he would cruelly beat her,
      Till at length she in anger began,
   Saying, " Father dear, if I am transgressèd
      I'll live and die for my servant man."

7. When Edmund found out her habitation
      Was well secured by an iron door,
   He vowed and swore that by all the nations
      He'd gain her releasement or be no more.

8. Then at his leisure he'd toil with pleasure
      To gain releasement of Mary Ann,
   He sought his object ; he gained her favour,
      She cried, " My faithful young servant man."

9. A suit of clothes he brought his lover,
      In men's attire for to disguise,
   Saying, " For your sake I will face your father,
      To see me here it will him surprise."

10. When her cruel father brought bread and water,
       Loud for his daughter he then did call,
    When Edmund answered, " I've cleared your daughter,
       The one in fault is your servant man."

11. When the old man saw that his daughter vanished
       He like a lion began to roar,
    He said, " From Ireland I'll have you banished,
       With my broadside * I will spill your gore."

12. " Agreed," said Edmund, " and at your leisure
       Since I have cleared her do all you can,
    But give your daughter to loyal pleasure,
       The one at fault is your servant man."

* Broadsword.

13. When the old man found him so tender-hearted
    He fell down on the dark dungeon floor.
    He said true lovers should ne'er be parted
    Since love can enter an iron door.

14. Now those young couple they are instead
    To roll in riches this couple can,
    Young Mary Ann at her royal pleasure
    Is blessed for ever with her servant man.

No. 84. *Since Love Can Enter an Iron Door.*

85.

Song of the Croppy Boy

Moderato

All early, early in the spring The small birds do warble and sweetly sing Changing their notes from tree to tree And the song they sing is old Ireland free.

Sung by Mr. Richard Hartlan of South-East Passage.

1. ALL early, early in the spring
    The small birds do warble and sweetly sing,
    Changing their notes from tree to tree
    And the song they sing is old Ireland free.

2. All early, early last Friday night
   The roving cavalry gave me great fright,
   The roving cavalry was my downfall,
   And I was taken by Lord Cornwall.

3. All in his guardroom where I was laid,
   All in his parlour where I was tried,
   My sentence passed and my courage low
   And to New Guinea I was forced to go.

4. I chosed the green and I chosed the blue,
   I chosed the red and I chosed orange too ;
   If all these colours I did deny
   I'll wear the green and for it I'll die.

5. As I was marching up Ashworts * street
   The drums and fifes they did play so sweet,
   The drums and fifes they did sweetly play
   When I was marching so far away.

6. As I was marching up Ashworts street
   My sister Mary I chanced to meet,
   That false young woman did me betray
   And for a guinea swore my life away.

7. As I was marching up Ashworts hill,
   And who could blame me to cry my fill,
   I looked behind and I looked before
   My tender mother could see no more.

8. As I was mounting the gallows high
   My aged father as he stood nigh
   My aged father it's me denied
   And the name he gave me was the Croppy Boy.

   * Wexford. Mr. Edward Hartley says this is Backsford.

No. 85. *Song of the Croppy Boy.*

It will be seen in the text that the name Ashworts Street is noted below as Wexford. When collecting I had difficulty in understanding the name as Mr. Hartlan sang it, and I doubt if he himself was very sure of it. Joyce, *Ancient Irish Music*, No. 61, says this song is a lament uttered by the Croppy Boy, one of the Wexford insurgents of 1798 who had been taken prisoner. Croppy Boy was a designation of Irish Catholic troopers.

See also Joyce O.I.M., No. 385 ; Dean, pp. 45–46 ; Colum, *Broad-Sheet Ballads*, pp. 52–53.

86.

Tim Finnigan's Wake

Tim Finnigan lived in Walker Street A gentleman Irishman

mighty odd—Had a beautiful brogue, so rich and sweet And to

rise in the world he carried a hod. He had a sort of

tippling way With a love for liquor poor Tim was born To

help him through his work each day Drop of the creature

Chorus

every morn Whack hurrah. Blood-hounds ye sol ye

Whack the floor, your trotters shake Now isn't this the

truth I've told ye Lots of fun at Finnigan's wake

Sung by Mr. Frank Faulkner, South-East Passage.

1. TIM FINNIGAN lived in Walker Street,
   A gentleman Irishman, mighty odd,
   Had a beautiful brogue, so rich and sweet,
   And to rise in the world he carried a hod.
   He had a sort of tippling way,
   With a love for liquor poor Tim was born,
   To help him through his work each day
   Drop of the creature every morn.

   Chorus.
   Whack hurrah. Blood-hounds ye sol ye,
   Whack the floor, your trotters shake,
   Now isn't this the truth I've told ye ?
   Lots of fun at Finnigan's wake.

2. One morning Tim was rather full,
   His head felt heavy, which made him shake,
   He fell from the ladder, broke his skull,
   They carried him home, his corpse for the wake.
   They rolled him up in a nice clean sheet,
   Laid him out upon the bed
   With fourteen candles around his feet
   And a couple of dozen round his head. Cho.

3. All the neighbours assembled at the wake,
   Mrs. Finnigan called out for the lunch ;
   First they brought in tray and cake,
   Pipes and tobacco, whisky punch.
   Miss Mary O'Connor began to cry,
   " What a pretty a corpse did ever you see ?
   Arrah, Tim avorney, why did ye die ? "
   " Och, none of your gab," says Judy McGee. Cho.

4. Miss Biddy O'Brian took up the job,
   Says, " Arrah, Judy, you're wrong there, I'm sure."
   Judy gave her a belt on the gob
   Which left her sprawling all on the floor.
   Each side in war did soon engage,
   Woman to woman and man to man,
   Shillelagh law was all the rage,
   And bloody ructions soon began. Cho.

5. Mickey Mulvaney raised his head
   When a gallon of whisky flew at him,
   It missed him hopping o'er the bed,
   Liquor was scattered over Tim.
   Bedad, he revives, see how he raises,
   And Timothy jumping from the bed
   Cried, while he lathered around like blazes,
   " Bad luck to your souls ; do you think I'm dead ? "   Cho.

No. 86. *Tim Finnigan's Wake.*

Irish Air.

87.

There was a widow lived in this place Who had three darling sons Their father died and left them When they were very young. A long time she endeavoured To maintain her darling sons Her youngest one became a man At the age of twenty-one

Sung by Mr. Ben Henneberry,
Devil's Island.

1. THERE was a widow lived in this place
   Who had three darling sons,
   Their father died and left them
   When they were very young.

187

A long time she endeavoured
To maintain her darling sons,
Her youngest one became a man
At the age of twenty-one.

2. He discoursed with his mother one night
   And unto her did say,
   " I think it will fall to one of our lots
   For to go far away ;
   Our land is too small to support us all
   And if you will agree,
   I am fully bent and well content
   A clergyman to be."

3. His mother being glad to hear
   Such thoughts come in his mind,
   Says she, " I will do all I can
   To help my darling child ; "
   She discoursèd with his brothers,
   And they did soon agree,
   And sent him off to college
   A clergyman to be.

4. He was not long in college
   When the Reverend Bishop Brown
   Came a-viewing those collegians,
   He viewed them all around.
   He espied this clever young man,
   Marked him above them all,
   He was the first he did discourse,
   And on him he did call.

5. He says, " Young man, where are you from ?
   Come, tell to me your name."
   " I am from the county of Armagh,
   They call me Tom O'Neil.
   My mother she's a widow
   And of a low degree,
   She has done her best endeavours
   To make a priest of me."

6. " Since Tom O'Neil it is your name,"
   The bishop he did say,
   " Go study hard both night and day,
   I'll soon have you ordained.
   To help your tender mother
   Who done so well for thee,
   I'll send you home a credit
   Your country boys to see."

7. When this young man came home ordained
   The neighbours were glad to see,
   And all that came to welcome him
   They came by twos and three,
   Especially his own dear friends
   To welcome him did run,
   And you never saw such a welcome
   As there was for the widow's son.

8. There was a man lived in that place
   Was as rich as a duke or knight,
   He had one only daughter,
   She was a beauty bright.
   She says unto her father,
   " This young man I'll go see,
   Before he went to college
   He was a schoolboy along with me."

9. She was brought unto a parlour
   Where she drank ale and wine,
   She says, " You are a clever young man,
   I would have you resign.
   What made you be a clergyman ?
   You know you are astray,
   A clergyman must ride by night
   And travel hard by day.

10. " Come, take some noble lady
    Whose fortune it is grand,
    You may have men to wait on you
    And be a gentleman.

Come take myself just as I stand,
You know my fortune's great,
I have £10,000 a year,
At death the whole estate."

11. He says, " My honoured lady,
Do not explain your mind,
If you were to offer ten times more
I would not resign ;
For in this holy station
I mean to lead my life,
So say no more, my dearest child,
I'll never take a wife."

12. When he did deny her
This villain she went home,
And into eight weeks after
The secret she made known.
She swore before the magistrate
That he had her beguiled,
And for eight long weeks before she came
By him she proved with child.

13. The morning of this trial
Would grieve your heart full sore,
To see his tender mother
Would grieve you ten times more,
To see her son a clergyman
His age about twenty-three,
To be cut down all in his prime
By cruel perjury.

14. " Now, Tom, what is the reason
You don't marry this fair ?
I think she is a companion
For a duke I do declare.
And what are you but a widow's son,
A man both poor and mean ?
You ought to think it a great honour
Such a lady to obtain."

15. Then Father Tom stood up and said,
    " I have no witness here,
    I'll call on the Almighty
    And He will set me clear.
    I never said I'd marry her
    Or yet make her my wife,
    For I never knew a female
    From a male all in my life."

16. " Now, Tom, since you won't marry her
    I'll give you to understand
    Seven long years transportation
    Unto a foreign land."
    " O that is bad, but it might be worse,"
    Father Tom did say,
    " Our Saviour suffered worse than that
    When He died on Calvary."

17. Those words were hardly spoken
    When a horse came as swift as wind,
    And on him came a rider
    Saying, " I was not here in time ;
    I call that trial o'er again,
    I'm here and can reply,
    She wants two fathers for her child,
    That is Father Tom and I.

18. " I can tell to the very moment
    Likewise to the very spot,
    A thousand pounds she gave me
    The night the child was got,
    And a thousand more she offered me
    Never to let on,
    She thought to make a husband
    Of Right Reverend Father Tom."

19. Then Father Tom put on his hat
    And he began to smile,
    He says unto his mother,
    " You see God assists your child."

They looked at one another
And they found it perjury,
The villain was found guilty
And the Right Reverend came home free.

No. 87. *Tom O' Neil.*
 O'Conor, pp. 8, 9.

88.

Whiskey in the Jar

As I rode over Kilkenny mountain I met Captain
Irwin and his money he was counting First I drew my dagger
Then I drew my weapon Saying, "Stand and deliver For I am a
Chorus
bold deceiver" My cheering de ding de dey right fall de daddy oh
Right fall de daddy oh, there's whiskey in the jar.

Sung by Mr. Ben Henneberry, Devil's Island.

1. As I rode over Kilkenny mountain
   I met Captain Irwin and his money he was counting,
   First I drew my dagger then I drew my weapon,
   Saying, " Stand and deliver, for I am a bold deceiver."

Chorus.

My cheering de ding de dey, right fall de daddy oh,
Right fall de daddy oh, there's whiskey in the jar.

2. I counted my money, I had a pretty penny,
   I put it in my pocket and carried it home to Molly O,
   She swore in her heart that she never would deceive me,
   But the devil's in the women for they never can be easy.   Cho.

3. I went to Molly's chamber to get a little slumber,
   I laid my head upon the bed and it began to wonder, oh,
   I had not been lying there before I was awakened
   And press gang overtook me and among them was Captain Irwin.   Cho.

4. I reached for my pistol, but I was much mistaken,
   I snapped them off and a prisoner I was taken,
   She discharged my pistol, then she filled them with water,
   A prisoner I was taken like a lamb upon a slaughter.   Cho.

5. I had two brothers, they both live in the army,
   One is in Cork and the other in Killarney,
   And if I had them here to-night I would be brisk and jolly,
   I'd rather have them here to-night than you, my sporting Molly.   Cho.

6. My brother Pat he is a brisk young soldier,
   He carries his firelock all over his left shoulder,
   And on the field of battle, by me soul he's ne'er undaunted,
   For he'll fight like the devil or some fairy that is haunted.   Cho.

7. Some take delight in fishing and farming,
   Others take delight in carriage rolling, oh,
   But I take delight in being brisk and jolly,
   A-pouring out good whiskey stout for you my sporting Molly.   Cho.

No. 88. *Whiskey in the Jar.*

See J.A.F.L., 25, 152 ; Ord, pp. 368–369.

89.

It Was a Mouse

Sung by Mr. Richard Hartlan,
South-East Passage.

1. It was a mouse lived in a well-a-hum,
   There was a mouse lived in a well
   And there he lived there very well,

   Chorus.

   And lickedy too de fall de dey,
   Whack fall de dum.

2. Next come in it was a flea-a-hum,
   Next come in it was a flea
   And he fetched in a load of tea.   Cho.

3. Next come in it was a fly-a-hum,
   Next come in it was a fly
   He eat so much it made him die.   Cho.

4. Next come in it was a tick-a-hum,
   Next come in it was a tick
   He eat so much it made him sick.   Cho.

194

5. Next come in it was a frog-a-hum,
   Next come in it was a frog
   And he fetched in a load of grog.   Cho.

6. Next come in it was a snail-a-hum,
   Next come in it was a snail
   He had the bagpipes on his tail.   Cho.

7. Next come in it was a bee-a-hum,
   Next come in it was a bee
   He brought the fiddle on his knee.   Cho.

8. Next come in it was a snake-a-hum,
   Next come in it was a snake
   And he fetched in a load of cake.   Cho.

9. The big black snake he swamped the land-a-hum,
   The big black snake he swamped the land
   And he was killed by an overgrown man.   Cho.

10. This overgrown man he went to France-a-hum
    This overgrown man he went to France
    To learn the ladies how to dance.   Cho.

No. 89. *It Was a Mouse.*

This vies with the ballad of *Lord Thomas and Fair Ellinor* for being the most widely current of the songs in my collection.   In J.A.F.L., 35, 392–399, there is an extensive note which reads : The oldest record of *The Frog and the Mouse* is the mention of " The frog cam to the myl dur " in *The Complaint of Scotland* (1549, ed. Murray), p. 64.   On Nov. 21, 1580, a " ballad " entitled *A Moste Strange Weddinge of the ffroge and the mowse* was entered to Edward White in the Stationers' Register (Collier, 11, 132 ; Arber, 11, 382).   It is found in songbooks of the Elizabethan age, and was arranged to meet the demands of the comic stage when the frog appeared with his opera hat.   In this variant of Mr. Hartlan's the singer has skipped the wooing and gone right on to the wedding.

The last stanza is not unlike v. 15 of *Rob Roy*, Child, 225, A:

" I'm gauin (I'm gauin)
I'm gauin to France, lady ;
Whan I come back
I'll learn ye a dance, lady."

90.

Me One Man

Sung by Mr. Richard Hartlan, South-East Passage.

1. ME one man, me two men
   They mow me down a meadow.
   Me three men, me four men
   They mow me hay away.
   Me four and me three and me two and me one
   And it's aye lots more,
   They mow me hay and they take it away
   On a beautiful midsummer's day.

2. Me five men, me six men
   They mow me down the meadow.
   Me seven men, me eight men
   They mow me hay away.
   Me eight and me seven and me six and me five
   And it's aye lots more,

They mow me hay and they take it away
On a beautiful midsummer's day.

Repeat, adding numbers up to thirty-four.

No. 90. *Me One Man.*

See Sharp, No. 100.   The song is better known in this country as *One Man Went to Mow.*

91.

Sung by Mr. Richard Hartlan, South-East Passage.

1. OLD King Coul was a merry old soul
     And a merry old soul was he,
   He called for his wife and he called for his pipe
     And he called for his fiddlers three.

Chorus.

" Teedle teedle dee," said the fiddler,
   " And happy we shall be."

197

2. Old King Coul was a merry old soul
   And a merry old soul was he,
He called for his wife and he called for his pipe
   And he called for his drummers three.

Chorus.

" Boom, boom, boom," went the drummer,
" Teedle teedle dee," said the fiddler,
   " And happy we shall be."

3. Old King Coul was a merry old soul
   And a merry old soul was he,
He called for his wife and he called for his tailor
   And he called for his needles three.

Chorus.

" Stick it in now," said the tailor,
" Boom, boom, boom," said the drummer,
" Teedle teedle dee," said the fiddler,
   " And happy we shall be."

4. Old King Coul was a merry old soul
   And a merry old soul was he,
He called for his wife and he called for his cobbler
   And he called for his hammers three.

Chorus.

" Rap a tap a tap," said the cobbler, etc.

5. Old King Coul was a merry old soul
   And a merry old soul was he,
He called for his wife and he called for his painter
   And he called for his brushes three.

Chorus.

" Slap it up against the wall," said the painter,
" Rap a tap a tap," said the cobbler, etc.

6. Old King Coul was a merry old soul
    And a merry old soul was he,
    He called for his pipe and he called for his wife
    And he called for his carpenters three.

Chorus.

" Nail the boards," said the carpenter,
" Slap it up against the wall," said the painter, etc.

No. 91. *Old King Coul.*

Old King Coul was a king who flourished in either the third or the fifth century. A note in Johnson's *Scots' Musical Museum*, 5, 473 reads, " It is said that Fyn MacCoule, the sonne of Coelus, *Scottisman*, was in thir days (of King Eugenius, fifth century) ane man of huge stature, of seventeen cubits hycht. He was ane great hunter, rycht terrybill for his huge quantitie to the pepyll, of quhom *ar mony vulgar fabyllis amang us*, nocht unlike to thir fabyllis that *ar rehersit* of Kyng Arthure." See also Whitelaw, *Book of Scottish Songs*, p. 19; Halliwell, *Nursery Rhymes of England* for Percy Society, 5, No. 77.

92.

Sung by Mr. Chas. Hartlan, South-East Passage.

1. OH, on this hill there was a tree,
    The prettiest tree you ever did see,
    The tree on the hill,
    And if it's not gone, oh I'm sure it's there still.

199

2. On this tree there was a branch,
   The prettiest branch you ever did see,
   The branch on the tree and the tree on the hill,
   And if it's not gone, oh I'm sure it's there still.

3. On this branch there was a nest,
   The prettiest nest you ever did see,
   The nest on the branch and the branch on the tree and the tree on the hill,
   And if it's not gone, oh I'm sure it's there still.

4. And on this nest there were four eggs,
   The prettiest eggs you ever did see,
   The eggs on the nest and the nest on the branch and the branch on the tree
      and the tree on the hill,
   And if it's not gone, oh I'm sure it's there still.

No. 92. *On This Hill.*

See Sharp, No. 98; Newell, No. 46; EFSSA, No. 110.

93.

Three Men Went A-Hunting.

Ah three men went a-hunting, but nothing could they find Until they came to a haystack and that they left behind The Englishman said "Haystack", the Scottish he said: "Nay" – "Oh bedad," said Pat, "It's the end of the world", And the whole three ran away And it's only look at that now What do you think of that now? Only look at that now Father um diddle um dey

Sung by Richard Hartlan, South-East Passage.

1. Ah, three men went a-hunting, but nothing could they find
   Until they came to a haystack, and that they left behind.
   The Englishman said, " Haystack," the Scottish he said, " Nay,"
   " Oh, bedad," said Pat, " it's the end of the world,"
   And the whole three ran away.

And it's only look at that now,
What do you think of that now ?
Only look at that now,
Father um diddle um dey.

2. Those three men went a-hunting, but nothing could they find
    Until they came to a milestone, and that they left behind.
    The Englishman said, " Milestone," the Scottish he said, " Nay,"
    " Ah, bedad," said Pat, " it's a plum-pudding tree
        And the currants was blowed away." Cho.

3. There were three men went hunting, but nothing could they find
    Until they came to a monkey, and that they left behind.
    The Englishman said, " Monkey," the Scottish he said, " Nay,"
    " Oh, bedad," said Pat, " he's your grandfather
        And his whiskers is turning grey." Cho.

4. There were three men went hunting, but nothing could they find,
    Until they came to a donkey, and that they left behind.
    The Englishman said, " Donkey," the Scottish he said, " Nay,"
    " Ah, bedad," said Pat, " it's an elephant,
        And his trunk is on the wrong way." Cho.

5. There were three men went hunting, but nothing could they find
    Until they came to a ship in full sail, and that they left behind.
    The Englishman said, " Ship in full sail," the Scottish he said, " Nay,"
    " Ah, bedad," said Pat, " it's a washing-tub
        And the clothes hung out to dry." Cho.

6. All those three men went hunting, but nothing could they find
    Until they came to a black man, and that they left behind.
    The Englishman said, " Black man," the Scottish he said, " Nay,"
    " Oh, bedad," said Pat, " it's the devil,
        And he's come to take us away." Cho.

7. Oh, three men went a-hunting, but nothing could they find
    Until they came to a toll gate, and that they left behind.
    The Englishman said," Toll gate," the Scottish he said, " Nay,"
    " Ah, bedad," said Pat, " it's the end of the world,"
        And the rest of them ran away. Cho.

Other titles for this are *The Three Farmers*; or *Three Jovial Welshmen*. It is probably a very old song, for in the Roxburghe collection there is a ballad giving a verse like this where the first man makes a comment and the second answers "Nay." See Baring-Gould, No. 75; Halliwell, *Nursery Rhymes of England*, No. 208; J.A.F.L., 3, 242–243; 10, 134; Newell, No. 34; and for extensive references Cox, No. 165.

94.

The Miller

Sung by Mrs. William McNab, Halifax.

1. THERE was a miller in Derbyshire,
    He had three sons as you shall hear,
    And to these three he made a will,
    Saying, " Which of you will take the mill ? "

    Chorus.
    Fol lol li lay—
    Fol the diddle i day.

2. He called to him his eldest son,
    Saying, " My glass it is almost run,
    And if I should you the miller make
    Come tell to me what toll you'd take ? "   Cho.

3. " Father," said he, " my name is Jack,
   Of every bushel I'd take a peck
   Of every bushel that I should grind,
   So that I may a good living find." Cho.

4. Says the old man, " You're a silly blade !
   You have not learned your old father's trade,
   And by such terms no man could live,
   So the mill unto thee I'll not give." Cho.

5. He called to him his second son,
   Saying, " My glass it is almost run,
   And if I would you the miller make
   Come tell to me what toll you'd take." Cho.

6. " Father," said he, " my name is Ralph,
   Of every bushel I'd take half,
   Of every bushel that I should grind,
   So that I might a good living find." Cho.

7. Says the old man, " You're a silly blade !
   You have not learned your old father's trade,
   And by such terms no man could live,
   So the mill unto thee I'll not give." Cho.

8. He called to him his youngest son,
   Saying, " My glass it is almost run,
   And if I would you the miller make
   Come tell to me what toll you'd take." Cho.

9. " Father," said he, " I'm your youngest son,
   Your darling and your bonny one,
   And before I would a good living lack
   I'd take the whole and false swear the sack." Cho.

10. Says the old man, " You're a crafty blade !
    You have well learned your old father's trade,
    So take the mill, a good living provide,"
    And the good old father closed his eyes and died. Cho.

No. 94. *The Miller.*

The miller has always been game for the village satirist, and this particular song is one of the most popular ever written upon that subject. J.A.F.L. gives a text like this Nova Scotia variant, described as a somewhat disordered version of the famous broadside ballad, *The Miller's Advice to His Three Sons on Taking Toll*, Roxburghe Collection, III, 681.

See also Bell, pp. 194–195 ; Dixon, pp. 204–206 ; Baring-Gould, No. 12 ; Cox, No. 155.

95.

Mush a Doody

Sung by Mrs. William McNab, Halifax, who picked it up at the little settlement of Tangier.

1. THERE was an old woman, she had na bairns,
   She took the punch jug in her airms,
   And she sang, " Mush-a-lula boo,
   Will you ne'er be empty till I be fu'."

   Chorus.
   Mush a doody ah,
   Mush a doody ah,
   Lul ah doodine.

2. " When I am in my grave
   No costly tombstones will I have,
   But I'll have a grave that is wide and deep
   And a jug of punch at my head and feet." Cho.

No. 95. *Mush a Doody.*

96.

Boston Burglar

Andante

I was born in Boston, a city you all know well Brought
up by honest parents, the truth to you I'll tell. Brought up by honest
parents, and reared most tender-ly Till I became a
sporting blade at the age of twenty-three.

Sung by Mr. Tom Henneberry, Halifax, and by Mr. Edward Hartley.

1. I was born in Boston, a city you all know well,
   Brought up by honest parents, the truth to you I'll tell,
   Brought up by honest parents, and reared most tenderly,
   Till I became a sporting blade at the age of twenty-three.

2. My character was taken, and I was sent to jail,
   My friends and my relations tried to get me out on bail,
   The jury found me guilty, the clerk he wrote it down,
   The Judge announced my sentence, twenty-one years in Charleston.

3. I saw my dear old father a-standing at the bar,
   I saw my dear old mother pulling out her old grey hair,
   A-pulling out of her old grey locks while tears do dim her eye,
   " My son, my son, what have you done that you're bound for Charleston ? "

206

4. They put me on an east-bound train one cold December day,
   And every station we passed by you would hear the people say,
   " There goes the Boston burglar, in custody he is bound,"
   While some cried louder than others, " He is bound for Charleston."

5. Come, all ye rambling sailors, a warning take by me,
   Give over all night walking, shun all bad company,
   For if you surely do, boys, you'll likewise be like me
   In serving all of twenty-one years in a penitentiary.

6. There is a girl in Boston, a girl I love so well,
   If ever I gain my liberty with her I'm going to dwell,
   If ever I gain my liberty that enemy I will shun,
   Street walking and bad company, and likewise drinking rum.

No. 96. *Prisoner's Song*; *or The Boston Burglar.*

See Pound, No. 23, and compare *The Sheffield Apprentice*, EFSSA, No. 97, from which presumably it has been adapted.

97.

The Three Gallant Huntsmen

Moderato.

It is of three gallant huntsmen, three jolly lads were they   Were

John and William Johnston, now mark those words I say   Their

daily hunt being over on Wicklow mountain high   When

"Hark oh hark," cries Johnston, "I hear a woman's cry."

Sung by Mr. Ben Henneberry, Devil's Island.

1. It is of three gallant huntsmen, three jolly lads were they,
    Were John and William Johnston, now mark those words I say,
    Their daily hunt being over on Wicklow mountain high,
    When, " Hark, oh hark," cried Johnston, " I hear a woman's cry."

2. " Oh, may you be an idle girl ?" bold Johnston he did say,
    " Or may you be a robber, our lives to take away ? "
    " No, no, I am no pirate, sir, for them I do deny,
    For they have robbed me here to-night and left me here to die.

3. " They have robbed me of my gay gold watch, likewise five hundred pounds,
    And they have left me here alone, my hair pinned to the ground.
    Oh, take me home, oh, take me home," this fair one she did say,
    " My father he is a wealthy man and your kindness he will repay."

4. Oh, Johnston being a kind young man, he placed her on behind,
   He wrapped his cloak around her form to shield her from the wind;
   They rode away without delay and came to Cumberland's hill,
   When she put a bugle to her mouth and blew it hard and shrill.

5. She being the leader of the gang they came at her command,
   And nine of those daring robbers brought those huntsmen to a stand.
   " Deliver up your gold to us without any more delay,
   Or on those lonely mountains your lives we'll take away."

6. Johnston being a smart young man he discharged his carabine
   And two of those daring robbers to death he did consign,
   Then William followed after with heavy balls of lead,
   And Gormon with his blunderbolt the rest of them shot dead.

7. The maid she mounted a milk-white steed to scale the mountains high,
   But Johnston followed in quick pursuit while she did him defy,
   But his rifle-ball proved her downfall, and her blood did stain the lea.
   " Hurrah, hurrah ! " cried Johnston, " we have gained a victory."

8. In the saddle-bags were found five hundred pounds in gold,
   Which they had robbed and plundered all on the mountain bold,
   Caused many the widow and orphan child in sorrow to complain,
   But now in death they're sleeping, and we're off to our hunt again.

No. 97. *The Three Gallant Huntsmen.*

The issue of *The Chapbook* edited by C. Lovat Fraser, Sept. 15, 1920, gives this song **under** the caption *The Three Merry Butchers and the Highwaymen*, date *circa* 1730. In this older **text** the huntsmen are butchers, and have the £500 with them, which makes them worth the robbing. Sharp has an interesting variant, EFSSA, No. 50.

98.

Alphabet Song

Sung by Mr. Ben Henneberry, Devil's Island.

1. A is the anchor that lays at our bow,
   And B is the bowsprit that sits in the bow,
   C is the capstan that always goes round,
   And D is the derrick that hoists in the rum.

   ### Chorus.
   So merry, so merry, so merry are we,
   No mortals on earth are like sailors at sea,
   To me edory, idory, odory dong,
   Give sailors some grog and there's nothing goes wrong.

210

2. E is the ensign the masthead do flew,
   And F is the forecastle where is the crew,
   G is the gewel-block hangs at the yardarm,
   And H is the hawser that never will stand.   Cho.

3. I is the island our sternsail boom shipper,
   And J is the jib so neatly doth set,
   And K is the keelson our ship's sunken hole,
   And L is the lanyard that holds the good hole.   Cho.

4. M is the mainmast wrought stout and strong,
   N is for needlepoint never goes wrong,
   And O is for oars of our jolly boat,
   And P is the pennant so neatly does float.   Cho.

5. Q is for quarterdeck built stout and strong,
   And R is the rudder guides us along,
   And S is the sailors as I've heard said,
   And T.U.V.W.X.Y.Z.

ALPHABET SONG

As sung by Mr. Hiram O. Hilshie, Dartmouth.

1. A is the anchor of our gallant ship,
   B is the bowsprit so neatly did fit,
   C is the capstan that always goes round
   And D is the derrick we hoist on our rum.

   ### Chorus.

   So merry, so merry, so merry are we,
   No mortals on earth are like sailors at sea,
   To me edory, idory odery dong,
   Give sailors some grog and there's nothing goes wrong.

2. E is the ensign that on our fore flew,
   F is the forecastle held all our crew,
   G is our grog which seldom goes round,
   H is the halliards that hoist in our rum.   Cho.

3. I is the .   .   .   .   .   .
    J is the jib .   .   .   .   .   .
    K is the keelson that lays in the hole,
    L is the lanyards .   .   .   . Cho.

4. M is the mainmast so stout and so strong,
    N is the needle that never went wrong,
    O is the oars of our gallant boat,
    P is the pennant was always afloat. Cho.

5. Q is the quarterdeck we all walk upon,
    R is the rudder hung on the stern,
    S is the sailors .   .   .   .   .
    And T.U.V.W.X.Y.Z.

ALPHABET SONG (Lumberman's)

Sung by Mr. Charlie Hartlan, South-East Passage.

1. Oh, A is the axes you very well know,
    B is for boys who can handle them so,
    C is the chopping as now we begin,
    And D is the danger we always stand in.

    Chorus.

    Hi derry, do derry, hi derry down,
    .   .   .   .
    Not a myrtle * on earth are as happy as we,
    Give the chanty boys grog and there's nothing goes wrong.

2. E is the echo the woods does ring,
    F is the foreman, the head of the gang,
    G is the grindstone, smooth and so round,
    And H is the handle that turns it around. Cho.

3. I is the iron that's marking the pine,
    J is the jolly boys falling behind,
    K is the keen edge our axes does keep,
    And L is the lice which over us creep. Cho.

* Probably mortal.

212

4. M is the moss we stow in our camp,
    N is the needle we mend up our pants,
    O is the owl that hoots us at night,
    And P is the pine which always falls right.   Cho.

5. Q is the quirls * that we won't allow,
    R is the river we drive our logs through,
    S is the sled so stout and so strong,
    T is the teams that hauls them along.   Cho.

6. U is the use as our teams they stand true,
    V is the valley our logs they go through,
    W   .   .   .   .

7. X.Y.Z. these last few letters I can't put in rhyme,
    So fare you young darling, I'll tell you in time,
    The train at the crossing the whistle does blow,
    So fare you young darling, to the woods I must go.   Cho.

* Probably quarrels or quarrelling.

No. 98. *Alphabet Song.*

For the sailorman's song see Eckstorm, pp. 233–234; and J.A.F.L., 38, 298, where it is given not as a song but as a sailor's toast from the Bahamas. The chorus in both is omitted.

For the lumberman's song or shanty-boy's alphabet see Gray, pp. 10–14; Rickaby, No. 6; J.A.F.L., 35, 413–414; Eckstorm, pp. 30–32.

It is interesting to see how the difficulty of rhyming the last letters of the alphabet is overcome in these variants. One ends abruptly thus:

W is for woods we leave in the spring
And so I have sung all I'm going to sing,

while another carries the rhyme on to the letter v. When the Nova Scotia variant A is sung, the climax is most effective.

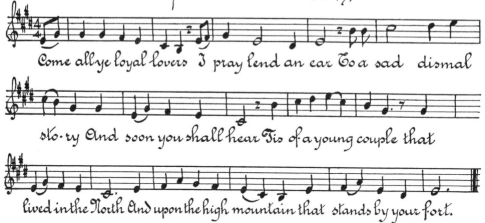

99

Come all ye loyal lovers I pray lend an ear To a sad dismal sto-ry And soon you shall hear 'Tis of a young couple that lived in the North And upon the high mountain that stands by your fort.

Sung by Mr. Gordon Young, Devil's Island.

1. COME, all ye loyal lovers, I pray lend an ear
   To a sad, dismal story, and soon you shall hear.
   'Tis of a young couple that lived in the North
   And upon the high mountain that stands by your fort.

2. The lady was the daughter of a rich gentleman
   By the name of McFarlan, and of the same clan.
   Young William was born in the Highlands Glen Isle
   And by blood relation his cousin did style.

3. But when that their parents their tidings did hear
   They acted a part that was cruel and severe.
   A letter they sent down to Inverness
   Which brought up a party young William to press.

4. And as for the pressing they gave no time we hear,
   He asked but one blessing was a word with his dear,
   Which caused that fair damsel to weep bitterly,
   May the heavens forgive you for your cruelty.

5. With vows then they parted, and with words not a few,
   A ring from her finger she instantly drew,
   Which he was not to part with come death or come life,
   Until the happy moment he would make her his wife.

6. He marched for America, his orders being so.
   He proved a loyal soldier, his valour did show,
   And for his good conduct no one could he blame
   Till at length from a corporal to a sergeant he came.

7. It was near Fort Niagara in the year 'sixty-nine,
   To frequent the wild woods which he oft did incline,
   To frequent the wild woods of some distant place,
   To breathe in his favour his name to servate.

8. But among the savage Indians at length there he fell,
   And how he was murdered we cannot well tell,
   But early next morning he was found lying dead,
   With five Indians lying by him for the want of their heads.

9. Was cut off by his broadsword as we understood,
   And the place all around him was nothing but blood,
   The finger from far off his hand it was cut,
   On which was the ring from his true love he got.

10. And at this very moment in Scotland we hear
    A most dreadful spectre to his love did appear,
    And like a wild aspect he gazed in her face,
    Saying, " Mary, dear Mary, do not me embrace.

11. " For I am but a spirit a-shining in blood,
    While my body lies murdered in American woods.

    .   .   .   .

    .   .   .   .

12. " There's five wounds in my body and three in my side,
    From hatchets and arrows, they are both deep and wide,
    And my long yellow lock for a premium was sold
    And also my finger with the pure ring of gold,

13. " Which you drew upon it as a token of love.
    Love is powerfuller than death, for it does me remove.
    Now my only desire is for you, my dear,
    And until you are with me I will still wander here."

215

14. Early next morning to her father she run,
    Saying, " Father, dear father, what have you done ?
    My true love young Willie appeared to me in blood,
    And his body lies murdered in American woods.

15. " He showed me his wounds and each bleeding sore,
    Therefore my joys on this earth are no more."
    This beautiful damsel in one week expired,
    I hope she enjoys all the love she desires.

No. 99. *American Woods.*

100.

AS NOW WE ARE SAILING

(Sung to the tune of *Captain Conrod*, No. 108.)

This song was sung by Charlie Hartlan, South-East Passage.

1. As now we are sailing out of Sheet Harbour Bay
   And soon will be sailing around Scaterie,

   .   .   .   .

   .   .   .   .

2. Here comes the McClune with ladies on board,
   The best-looking girls Newfoundland could afford.
   Come, all you young men, and take my advice,
   When the factory close up there is a chance for a wife.

3. And now we are leaving the coast Labrador,
   I pray to the Lord I'll come back here no more,

   .   .   .   .

   For to hear the dogs bark and the sea pigeons sing.

No. 100. *As Now We Are Sailing.*

This is only a fragment, all Mr. Hartlan could remember. He tells me it was written about a schooner that took men to Labrador to work in a lobster factory. These few lines may recall memories to sea-faring men who live on the coast of Nova Scotia.

101.

Back Bay Hill

One day in December I'll never for-get A charming young

creature I first met Her eyes shone like diamonds, she was

dressed up to kill. She was slipping and tripping down Back Bay

Chorus

Hill And sing fall de dol doodle dum fall de dol doodle dum

fall de dol doodle dum, lidy I die.

Sung by Mr. Frank Faulkner,
South-East Passage.

1. ONE day in December I'll never forget,
    A charming young creature I first met,
    Her eyes shone like diamonds, she was dressed up to kill,
    She was slipping and tripping down Back Bay Hill,

    Chorus.
    And sing fall de dol doodle dum,
    Fall de dol doodle dum,
    Fall de dol doodle dum,
    Lidy I die.

2. I says, " My fair creature, you will me excuse."
    To partake of my arm she did not refuse ;
    Her arm slipped in mine, I felt love's thrill,
    They made it all right on Back Bay Hill.   Cho.

217

3. The very next day to church we did go,
   Which made all the people talk, you must know.
   Said the priest, " Will you wed ? " Says I, " That we will,"
   And it's buckled we were on Back Bay Hill.   Cho.

4. Now we are married, children have three,
   Me and the missus can never agree.
   She called one Bridget, the other one Bill,
   Says I, " Call the other one Back Bay Hill."   Cho.

5. Come, all you young fellows, take warning by me
   If ever in need of a wife you may be,
   I'll tell you where you will get your fill,
   Slipping and tripping down Back Bay Hill.   Cho.

No. 101. *Back Bay Hill.*

My singer learned this song while sealing in 1902.   He says it was composed near Prospect, a fishing village in Halifax County, but it is quite probable it has been imported.   The name Back Bay may be changed to any hill in the place where the song is sung.

102.

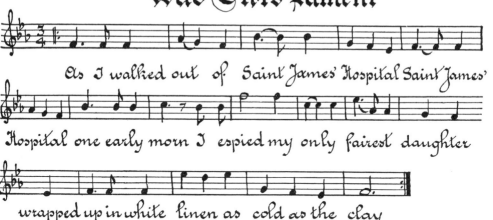

As I walked out of Saint James' Hospital Saint James'
Hospital one early morn I espied my only fairest daughter
wrapped up in white linen as cold as the clay

Repeat for Chorus.

Sung by Mr. Edward Hartley, Dartmouth.

1. As I walked out of St. James' Hospital,
    St. James' Hospital one early morn,
    I espied my only fairest daughter
    Wrapped up in white linen as cold as the clay.

    Chorus.

    So beat your drums and play your pipes merrily,
    And play the dead march as you carry me on,
    Take me to the churchyard and throw the ground over me,
    I'm a young maiden, and I know I've done wrong.

2. Once on the street I used to look handsome,
    Once on the street I used to dress gay ;
    First to the ale-house, then to the dance-hall,
    Then to the poor-house, and now to my grave.   Cho.

3. O come, dear mother, and sit down beside me,
    And sit down beside me and pity my case,
    For my head it is aching, my heart it is breaking,
    With sore lamentations I know I've done wrong.   Cho.

4. O send for the minister to pray o'er my body ;
    O send for the doctor to heal up my wounds ;
    O send for the young man that I first fell in love with
    That I may see him before I am gone.   Cho.

5. Let four pretty maidens with a bunch of red roses,
    Let four pretty maidens to sing me a song ;
    Let four pretty maidens with a bunch of red roses
    To place on my coffin to carry me on.   Cho.

No. 102. *Bad Girl's Lament.*

The words of this song, which have their origin in one known as *The Irish Rake,* current in Ireland as early as 1790, are interchangeable with the more familar song, *The Dying Cowboy.* As this was originally an old soldier's song it has a military chorus which is incongruous in its present setting.

For *The Bad Girl's Lament* see J.A.F.L., 25, 276–278 ; Mackenzie, No. 119.

For *The Dying Cowboy* see Pound, No. 77 ; J.A.F.L., 24, 341 ; 22, 258–259 ; 25, 153–154 and 276–278 ; Yeats, No. 4, Fifth Year ; Cox, No. 53, where in addition to the texts there are numerous references given.   Lomax, pp. 74–76.   The Nova Scotia variant is very similar to all the above.

103.

Banks of Newfoundland (1)

Come all you rakes and rambling boys I have you to beware It's when you sail those packet ships Blue dungaree jumpers wear But buy your monkey jackets boys Keep them at your command And beware of the cold norwester On the Banks of Newfoundland

Sung by Mr. Richard Hartlan, South-East Passage.

1. COME, all you rakes and rambling boys,
   I have you to beware,
   It's when you sail those packet ships
   Blue dungaree jumpers wear.
   But buy your monkey-jackets, boys,
   Keep them at your command,
   And beware of the cold nor'wester
   On the Banks of Newfoundland.

2. We had on board two Irish chaps,
   Pat Murphy and Joe Moore.
   The passage to the westward
   Those sailors suffered sore.
   They pawned their clothes in Liverpool
   And sold right out of hand,
   Not thinking of the cold nor'wester
   On the Banks of Newfoundland.

221

3. We had on board an Irish girl,
   Bridget Power was her name,
   On one she proved a marriage,
   On one she had a claim.
   She cut up all her underclothes
   To make mittens for his hands,
   Before she'd see her true love free *
   On the Banks of Newfoundland.

4. I had a dream the other night,
   I dreamed that I was home,
   I dreamed that me and my true love
   Was away down Marabone.
   I dreamed I was on Scotland Road
   With a jar of ale on hand,
   But when I woke my heart was broke
   On the Banks of Newfoundland.

5. We'll scrub her up, we'll scrub her down,
   With holy stone find sand,
   And bid adieu to the Virgin Rocks
   On the Banks of Newfoundland.

6. Oh, now we're off of Sandy Hook
   Where the Highlands are buried in snow,
   And the pilot boat ahead of us,
   Into New York we will go.
   We'll call for liquor merrily
   With a jar of ale in hand,
   And when we're here we can't be there
   On the Banks of Newfoundland.

* Probably freeze.

No. 103. *The Banks of Newfoundland* (1).

Many songs are written about the Banks of Newfoundland, for hardships endured there make an interesting theme for a story. See Colcord, pp. 92–93; Eckstorm, pp. 220–221, where v. 5 of this variant is given as chorus; Mackenzie, No. 161. Also paper-covered volume by James Murphy, Newfoundland, Sept. 1923, entitled *Songs Their Fathers Sung*.

104.

The Banks of Newfoundland (2)

Andante

On Saint Patrick's day the seventeenth from New York we set sail Kind fortune did favour us With a sweet and pleasant gale We bore away from Americay The wind being off the land With courage brave we ploughed the wave Bound down for Newfoundland.

Sung by Mr. Ben Henneberry, Devil's Island.

1. On St. Patrick's Day the seventeenth
    From New York we set sail,
   Kind fortune did favour us
    With a sweet and pleasant gale.
   We bore away from Americay
    The wind being off the land,
   With courage brave we ploughed the wave
    Bound down for Newfoundland.

2. Our captain's name was Nelson
    Just twenty years of age,
   As true, as brave a sailor lad
    As ever ploughed the wave.
   The *Eveline* our brig was called
    Belonging to McLean,
   With courage brave we ploughed the wave
    Bound down for Newfoundland.

3. When three days out, to our surprise
   Our captain he fell sick,
   And shortly was not able
   To show himself on deck.
   The fever raged, which made us fear
   That death was near at hand,
   We bore away from Halifax
   Bound down for Newfoundland.

4. We made the land, but knew it not,
   For strangers we were all,
   Our captain was not able
   To come on deck at all.
   Then we were obliged to haul
   Our brig from off the land,
   With laden hearts we put to sea
   Bound down to Newfoundland.

5. All that long night we ran our brig
   Till nine o'clock next day.
   Our captain at the point of death
   To our record did say,
   " We'll bear away for Cape Canso,
   Now, boys, come lend a hand
   And trim your topsail to the wind
   Bound down for Newfoundland."

6. At three o'clock we sighted a light
   Which we were glad to see,
   The smallpox it being raging,
   (That's what it proved to be),
   And at four o'clock in the afternoon
   As judge as God's command,
   We anchored her safe in Arichat
   Bound down for Newfoundland.

7. And for help and medicine
   Ashore then we did go,
   Our captain at the point of death
   Our sympathy to show.

At five o'clock in the afternoon
As judge as God's command,
In Arichat he breathed his last
Bound down for Newfoundland.

8. All that long night we did lament
For our departed friend,
And we were praying unto God
For what had been his end.
We'll pray the God will guide us
And keep us by his hand,
And give us fair wind while at sea
Bound down for Newfoundland.

No. 104. *The Banks of Newfoundland* (2).

The only variant found is Mackenzie, No. 87. The authorship of the song is credited to Captain Cale White of Maitland, Colchester County, N.S.

105

Barrack Street

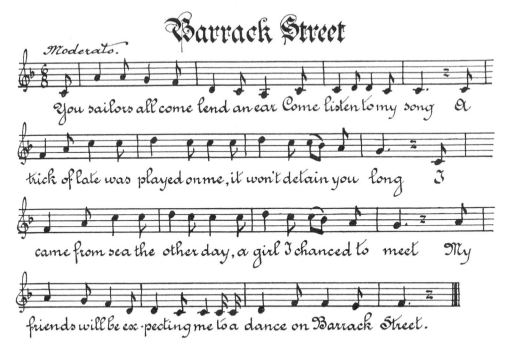

Moderato.

You sailors all come lend an ear Come listen to my song A
trick of late was played on me, it won't detain you long I
came from sea the other day, a girl I chanced to meet My
friends will be ex-pecting me to a dance on Barrack Street.

Sung by Mr. Ben Henneberry, Devil's Island.

1. YOU sailors all, come lend an ear, come listen to my song,
   A trick of late was played on me, it won't detain you long.
   I came from sea the other day, a girl I chanced to meet,
   " My friends will be expecting me to a dance on Barrack Street."

2. I said, " My pretty fair one, I cannot dance too well,
   Besides, I am to Windsor bound, where all my friends do dwell.
   I've been to sea these last two years, I've saved up £30,
   My friends will be expecting me this night in Windsor town."

3. " If you cannot dance, my love, you shall stand a treat,
   Have a glass or two of brandy, and something for to eat.
   At six o'clock this evening I'll meet you on the train,
   So don't forget to give a call when you come to town again."

4. She seemed to be so civil I took her on the car,

   The people on the other side I thought I heard them say,
   " I think, old chap, you'll need a cab before you get away."

5. At eight o'clock that evening the drinking did begin,
   And when all hands had got their fill the dancing did begin.
   Me and my love danced all around unto a merry tune,
   When she says, " Dear, we will retire to a chamber all alone."

6. The dancing being over, to bed we did repair,
   And there I fell fast asleep, the truth I will declare.
   My darling with my £30, gold watch and chain had fled,
   And left me here, poor Jack alone, left naked in the bed.

7. I looked all around me, nothing could I spy
   But a woman's shirt and apron upon the bed did lie.
   I wrung my hands and tore my hair, crying, " What shall I do ?
   Fare you well, sweet Windsor town, I'm sure I'll ne'er see you."

8. Everything being silent, and the hour but twelve o'clock,
   I put on my shirt and apron and steered for Cronon's wharf,
   And when I did get on board the sailors all did say,
   " I think, old chap, you've had a duck since you have been away.

9. " Is those the new spring fashions which have lately come on shore ?
   Where is the shop you bought them at, do you think there's any more ? "
   The captain, he says, " Jack, I thought you were to Windsor bound,
   You might have got a better suit than that for £30."

10. " I might have got a better suit if I'd a had the chance.
    I met a girl in Water Street ; she asked me to a dance.
    I danced my own destruction ; I'm stripped from head to feet,
    I'll take my oath I'll go no more to a dance on Barrack Street."

11. Come, all you young sailor lads, a warning take by me,
    Be sure and choose your company when you go on a spree ;
    Be sure keep out of Barrack Street, or else you'll rue the day,
    With a woman's shirt and apron they'll rig you out for sea.

No. 105. *Barrack Street.*

The scene of this song is now Market Street, Halifax, and the title is more familiarly known
as *Woman's Shirt and Apron.* An interesting comparison is the Bothy ballad, Ord, pp. 278–279,
where Jock Hawk's Adventures are very similar, even to the remarks of other people about the
ill-fortune the hero is to suffer. The editor describes it as a real Bothy song sung in all the
farm kitchens and at feeing markets some forty or fifty years ago, describing a Glasgow incident
of a time prior to the Forbes Mackenzie Act. It is curious that the two songs are so alike.

106

Brigantine Sinorca

Allegro.

Oh now we're off of Shelburne And there we lay aground The
caulkers they go round her And soon her leak was found They
caulk her up with oakum As tight as tight could be   And
squared away our yards And we put her out to sea Then it's
watch her, trig her See her how she goes Her stun s'ls and her
stay sails set The wind began to blow She's one of the fastest sailers that
ever sailed the sea She's the Brigantine Sinor-ca She belongs to Port Med-way.

Chorus

Sung by Mr. Richard Hartlan, South-East
Passage.

OH, now we're off of Shelburne
  And there we lay aground,
The caulkers they go round her
  And soon her leak was found.
They caulk her up with oakum
  As tight as tight could be,
And squared away our yards
  And we put her out to sea.

Chorus.

Then it's watch her, trig her,
  See her how she goes,
Her stuns'ls and her staysails set
  The wind began to blow.
She's one of the fastest sailers
  That ever sailed the sea,
She's the brigantine *Sinorca*,*
  She belongs to Port Medway.

* Spelled phonetically.

No. 106. *Brigantine "Sinorca."*

Shelburne and Port Medway are both Nova Scotia towns, prosperous in the happy and romantic days of the sailing-vessel.

107.

Canso Strait

In Canso Strait our vessel lay, We just arrived in from the Bay. Our vessel built both stout and strong And to Gloucester she does belong.

Sung by Chas. Hartlan and Frank Faulkner, South-East Passage.

1. In Canso Strait our vessel lay,
   We just arrived in from the Bay,
   Our vessel built both stout and strong,
   To Glou-ces-ter she does belong.

2. We were homeward bound and ready for sea
   When our drunken captain got on a spree.
   He came on board and to us did say,
   " Get your anchor, boys, and fill away."

3. We weighed our anchor at his command,
   And with all sails set we left the land,
   We left old Sand Point early
   And headed her out against a dead beat sea.

4. The night came on, dark clouds lower,
   The wind did howl and breakers roar,
   An angry squall and the angry sky
   It put her down at half-mast high.

5. Her jib sheets parted, which lighted her,
   She came head to the wind and rose again.
   Our jibs take in and new sheet bent,
   And straightway aft to our captain went.

6. We kindly asked him to shorten sail
   Or we'd be lost in a dreadful gale ;
   He cursed and swore if the wind would blow
   He'd show us how his boat could go.

7. When up spoke one of our gallant men,
   " There's twelve of us right here on hand,
   We'll reef her down, and to sea we'll go,
   If you refuse you'll be tied below."

8. We reefed her down on her own success,
   She's like a bird seeking for a rest.
   We are headed up Cape Shore now,
   She knocks the white foam from her bow.

9. Never again will I ever sail
   With a drunken captain and a heavy gale.

No. 107. *Canso Strait.*

108.

Captain Conrod

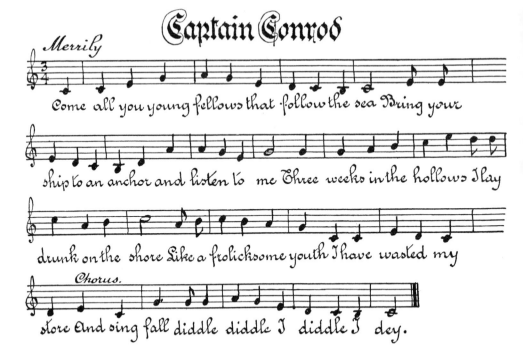

Merrily

Come all you young fellows that follow the sea Bring your
ship to an anchor and listen to me Three weeks in the hollows I lay
drunk on the shore Like a frolicksome youth I have wasted my

Chorus.

store And sing fall diddle diddle I diddle I dey.

Sung by Mr. Ben Henneberry, Devil's Island.

1. COME, all you young fellows that follow the sea,
   Bring your ship to an anchor and listen to me.
   Three weeks in the hollows I lay drunk on the shore,
   Like a frolicksome youth I have wasted my store.

   Chorus.

   And sing fall diddle diddle, I diddle I dey.

2. Some frolicksome game put an end to my fun,
   Oh, friends were damn scarce when my money was gone.
   I drawed my advance up for to finish the toll,
   And said drink with my friends like a good-hearted soul.   Cho.

3. I put my bag on my back and down I did wag
   With a bottle of brandy stowed snug in my bag.
   In a brig called the *Mary* belonging to Starr
   I went down roaring drunk like a jolly Jack Tar.   Cho.

4. 'Twas on Monday morning we gave her full sail,
   The wind from the nor'west did blow a sweet gale,
   My heart with the horrors did beat pitter pat,
   And the tears in my eyes like a ferry-house rat.   Cho.

5. When eight bells did strike I went aft for to steer,
   All sorts of strange voices ran into my ear.
   With whispering all by me I dare not look round,
   And there I stood trembling while the cold sweat run down.   Cho.

6. Says oh, I'll go down get a wee sup of grog,
   My head then was going nine knots by the log,
   But when I got there just as sure as you're born,
   There was not a drop in the bottle, not a blessed horn.   Cho.

7. The mate like myself being a damn drunken beast,
   While I was ashore on my brandy did feast,
   When I went there just as sure as you're born
   He never left a drop in the bottle, not one blessed horn.   Cho.

8. Oh, now we are ploughing all on the rough sea,
   The horrors is over, thank God I am free,
   And since I am here I've got nothing to do,
   I'll sing of our captain just one verse or two.   Cho.

9. Our captain an old Methodist preacher had been,
   One of the stingiest old beggars that ever was seen,
   Salt cod and religion he gave us to eat,
   And then once a week one small chunk of meat.   Cho.

10. When twelve o'clock come he goes down for to eat,
    Like a hard dying angel he'll stretch out his feet,
    He turned his eyes up to the blessing of God,
    With a plate of boiled rice and a junk of salt cod.   Cho.

11. When he is tired and * reading his book
    He'll go down forward and fight with the cook.
    He walks on the quarter-deck smoking his pipe,
    With his face griddled up like an old piece of tripe.   Cho.

* Probably " of."

233

12. Now our voyage is over, our voyage is up,
     At Halifax Harbour we'll coil up our ropes,
     We'll let go both anchors and moor stem and stern,
     With a plentiful table we'll spin then this yarn.   Cho.

13. All things shall be ready ; all things shall be right ;
     There'll be roast beef and mutton to eat day and night ;
     There'll be no short allowance or rusty salt cod,
     So to hell with Starr's *Mary* and Captain Conrod.

No. 108. *Captain Conrod.*

According to the singer, this was composed by Harry Rissal, a seaman with whom Mr. Henneberry's brother sailed. Starr was the name of a well-known Halifax firm, in sailing-ship days, and Captain Conrod a Halifax man.

109.

Charles G. Anderson

Sympathetically

Come all ye human countrymen, with pity lend an ear And hear my feeling sto-ry you can't but shed a tear I'm held in close con-fine-ment and bound in irons strong Sur-rounded by stony granite walls and sentenced to be hung.

Sung by Mr. Ben Henneberry, Devil's Island.

1. COME, all ye human countrymen, with pity lend an ear,
   And hear my feeling story—you can't but shed a tear.
   I'm held in close confinement and bound in irons strong,
   Surrounded by stony granite walls and sentenced to be hung.

2. Charles Gustavus Anderson is my right and proper name ;
   Since I have been in custody I ne'er denied the same.
   I came from decent parents although I die in scorn,
   And believe me now I much lament that ever I was born.

3. It was my sad misfortune that brought me to this place,
   To die an ignominious death, my parents to disgrace.
   With sorrow, when I parted them, their hearts were pierced thro',
   Their sorrows were not worn away before they will renew.

4. My father was a shipwright, I might have been the same,
   He taught me good examples, to him I leave no blame.
   Likewise my tender mother, who for me suffered sore,
   When she hears this sad announcement I'm sure she'll suffer more.

5. Oh, dear and loving mother, if I could but see your face,
   I'd kiss thy lips of tenderness, and take my last embrace.
   I'd bathe you in my tears of grief before my final hour,
   I'd then submit myself to God, to His holy will and power.

6. Brothers and sisters all, adieu, who are near and dear to me,
   So far beyond the ocean, whose faces I ne'er shall see.
   The happy days I spent with you on my native shore,
   Farewell, sweet Udavilla, I will never see you more.

7. Ah, if I could recall my days again, how happy I would be,
   To live at home amongst my friends, in love and unity.
   When I think of former innocence, and those I left behind,
   'Tis God and only Him that knows the horrors of my mind.

8. No books of consolation are here that I can read,
   I profess the Church of England, by nation I'm a Swede.
   Those words that are addressed to me, I can't well understand,
   I must die like a heathen, here in a foreign land.

9. It's near the town of Gottenburgh where I was bred and born,
   Here in the city of Halifax I end my life in scorn ;
   Pity my misfortunes and a warning take from me,
   Shun all evil company and beware of mutiny.

10. Since I left my tender parents, it's but a few years ago,
    Of the dreadful fate that awaits me, it's little I did know.
    I got into bad company who have seduced me,
    For to become a murderer and a pirate on the sea.

11. I shipped on board the *Saladin*, as you may understand,
    She was bound to Valparaiso, McKenzie had command.
    We arrived there in safety without the least dismay,
    When Fielding came on board of us, curse on that fatal day.

12. 'Twas him that seduced us to do that horrid crime ;
    Though we might have prevented it if we had thought in time.
    We shed the blood of innocence, the same we don't deny,
    And stained our hands in human blood, for which we have to die.

13. Oh, God, I fear your vengeance, and judgment much I dread,
    To stand before Your judgment-seat with my hands imbued in blood.
    I deserve Your indignation, but Your pardon still I crave.
    Oh, Lord, have mercy on my soul beyond the gloomy grave.

14. The sheriff and his officers all came to him in gaol;
    He knew their awful message well but never seemed to fail.
    They placed the fatal halter on, to end all shame and strife;
    With his own hands he greased the cord that cut the thread of life.

15. He was led to the gallows and placed on that awful stand.
    He viewed the briny ocean and then the pleasant land.
    The rope adjusted through the ring, which quickly stopped his breath.
    So ended his career in the violent jaws of death.

No. 109. *Charles Gustavus Anderson.*

See note accompanying *George Jones* in this volume. Also Mackenzie, No. 113. The phrase " I ne'er denied the same," is very common in murder songs. See *Charles Guiteau*, Pound, No. 65, A, v. 2, and *The Death of Bendall*, No. 65, B, v. 2.

110.

George Jones

Good people all, come listen to my melancholy tale My dying declaration Which I have penn'd in jail My present situ- ation May to
all a warning be And a caution to all seamen to beware of mutin-y.

Sung by Mr. Ben Henneberry, Devil's Island.

1. Good people all, come listen to my melancholy tale,
   My dying declaration which I have penn'd in jail.
   My present situation may to all a warning be,
   And a caution to all seamen to beware of mutiny.

2. George Jones is my name, I am from the county Clare,
   I quit my aged parents and left them living there.
   I being inclined for roving, at home I would not stay,
   And much against my parents' will I shipped and went to sea.

3. My last ship was the *Saladin*, I shudder at her name,
   I joined her in Valparaiso on the Spanish Main.
   I shipped as cabin steward which proved a fatal day,
   A demon came aboard of her which led us four astray.

4. I agreed to work my passage, the ship being homeward bound,
   With copper ore and silver and over thousand pounds ;
   Likewise two cabin passengers on board of her did come,
   The one was Captain Fielding, the other was his son.

238

5. He did upbraid our captain before we were long at sea,
   And one by one seduced us into a mutiny ;
   The tempting prize did tempt his eyes, he kept it well in view,
   And by his consummate art he's destroyed us all but two.

6. On the fourteenth night of April I am sorry to relate,
   We began his desperate enterprise—at first we killed the mate ;
   Next we killed the carpenter, and overboard him threw,
   Our captain next was put to death with three more of the crew.

7. The watch were in their hammocks when the work of death begun,
   The watch we called, as they came up we killed them one by one ;
   These poor unhappy victims lay in their beds asleep,
   We called them up and murdered them, and hove them in the deep.

8. There were two more remaining still below and unprepared,
   The hand of God protected them that both their lives were spared ;
   By them we're brought to justice and both of them are free.
   They had no hand in Fielding's plan, nor his conspiracy.

9. An oath was next administered to the remainder of the crew,
   And like a band of brothers we were sworn to be true.
   This was on Sunday morning when the bloody deed was done,
   When Fielding brought the Bible and swore us every one.

10. The firearms and weapons all we threw into the sea,
    He said he'd steer for Newfoundland, to which we did agree,
    And secret all our treasure there in some secluded place ;
    If it was not for his treachery that might have been the case.

11. We found with Captain Fielding (for which he lost his life)
    A brace of loaded pistols, likewise a carving-knife ;
    We suspected him for treachery which did enrage the crew ;
    He was seized by Carr and Galloway and overboard was threw.

12. His son exclaimed for mercy, as being left alone,
    But his entreaties were soon cut off, no mercy there shown.
    We served him like his father was who met a watery grave,
    So we buried son and father beneath the briny wave.

13. Next it was agreed upon before the wind to keep,
    We had the world before us then, and on the trackless deep ;
    We mostly kept before the wind as we could do no more,
    And on the twenty-eighth of May we were shipwrecked on the shore.

14. We were all apprehended, and into prison cast,
    Tried and found guilty, and sentence on us passed,
    Four of us being condemned and sentenced for to die,
    And the day of execution was the thirtieth of July.

15. Come, all you pious Christians, who God is pleased to spare,
    I hope you will remember us in your pious prayer ;
    Make appeals to God for us, for our departing souls.
    I hope you will remember us when we depart and mould.

16. Likewise the pious clergymen, who for our souls did pray,
    Who watched and prayed along with us, whilst we in prison lay ;
    May God reward them for their pains, they really did their best,
    They offered holy sacrifice to God to grant us rest.

17. And may the God of mercy, who shed His blood so free,
    Who died upon the holy cross all sinners to set free.
    We humbly ask His pardon for the gross offence we gave,
    May He have mercy on our souls when we descend the grave.

18. We were conveyed from prison, unto the gallows high,
    Ascended on the scaffold, whereon we were to die.
    Farewell, my loving countrymen, I bid this world adieu,
    I hope this will a warning be to one and all of you.

19. They were placed upon the fatal drop, their coffins beneath their feet,
    And their Clergy were preparing them, their Maker for to meet ;
    They prayed sincere for mercy, whilst they humbly smote their breast,
    They were launched into eternity, and may God grant them rest.

No. 110. *George Jones.*

No. 2 in the group of songs of the *Saladin* mutiny, which are the last dying thoughts of three of the four men hanged for murder in Halifax. In an issue of the *Acadian Recorder* of 1924 " Occasional " tells that they were composed by a fisherman, and suggested by the confession of the men. " Mr. Forhan saw the four men hanged. He was six years old at the time. His father and mother and he stood on the spot where the Victoria General Hospital now stands, and saw the two wagons come from the penitentiary. They were surrounded by a squad of soldiers with fixed bayonets. They came up Tower Road, and when they arrived the wagons turned in west and when 200 yards from the spot where the gallows were erected, the troops formed a circle around it. This was the exact spot, and after they dropped we started for home, and on top of the citadel, looking back, saw the heads of the four men still hanging on the gallows."

For an excellent prose account of the mutiny see MacMechan, *Old Province Tales*, pp. 209–238. For the song, *Adventure Magazine*, Oct. 20, 1925; Mackenzie, No. 112.

111.

Saladin's Crew

Andante

Come all ye good people who wish to live long And pray lend an ear to a criminal song Take warning by me while now I lie in jail Her halter is ready my fate to be-wail.

Sung by Mr. Ben Henneberry, Devil's Island.

1. COME, all ye good people who wish to live long,
   And pray lend an ear to a criminal song.
   Take warning by me while now I lie in jail,
   Her halter is ready my fate to bewail.

2. I was reared by the hand of the kindest affection,
   My parents oft taught me to be a perfection.
   Pride filled their bosoms while their hearts beat with joy
   When they thought on the hopes of their well-cherished boy.

3. But the *Saladin's* crew on this distant shore
   Have proved their misfortune since I left their door.
   Being wearied I left them of their kind control,
   But my fate known to all men, alas my poor soul.

4. I wish now that none of you my right name to know,
   For it would prove their ruin, and pleasure overthrow;
   Some day you call me your Rich Hazelton,
   But they never will know of the fate of their son.

241

5. I ask now for mercy, but I'm afraid there's no hope,
    There's a true and just God, in His mercy wide scope ;
    It extends to the vilest, He can pardon us all,
    Even Fielding, curse Fielding, that proved my downfall.

6. Oh, now for one view of the sweet scenes of youth,
    If I could but live home surrounded by truth ;
    If I could but see them, those hills and those dales,
    And could hear the sweet songsters of my own native land.

7. If I could but meet her, or see her once more,
    The girl of my bosom, the lass I adore,
    Who taught me to love in a far distant land
    When I grasped with affection her lily-white hand.

No. 111. "*Saladin's*" *Crew.*

Third of the *Saladin* trio and hitherto unpublished as far as I can learn. See note accompanying *George Jones.*

112.

Coloured Girl from the South

Moderato

The master had a coloured girl He fetched her from the south Her

hair in curl so mighty much She could not shut her mouth Come

ha ha ha ha ha ha ha A girl from the South Her hair in curl so

mighty much She could not shut her mouth

Sung by Mr. Richard Hartlan, South-East Passage.

1. THE master had a coloured girl,
     He fetched her from the south,
   Her hair in curl so mighty much
     She could not shut her mouth.

Chorus.

To me ha ! ha ! ha ! ha ! Ha ! ha ! ha !
     A girl from the south,
   Her hair in curl so mighty much
     She could not shut her mouth.

2. Oh, her eyes they were very small,
     They both run into one,
   And if a fly got into one
     By golly you would see fun.   Cho.

243

3. Oh, master had no hook at all
   For to hang up his coat and hat,
   For on the darky's nose of his
   He hung his coat and hat.   Cho.

4. He sent her to the tailor's shop
   To buy him a suit of clothes.
   She took one fearful long breath
   She swallowed him, tailor and all.   Cho.

No. 112. *Coloured Girl from the South.*

This song of slavery times is widely current in the southern States. See Scarborough, *On the Trail of the Negro Folk-Songs*, pp. 66–68 ; White, *American Negro Folk-Songs*, pp. 152–156 and p. 450, where a chorus is given like the Nova Scotia text.

113.

Cumberland's Crew

Sung by Mr. Ben Henneberry, Devil's Island.

1. COME, shipmates, and gather and join in my ditty,
   It's of a terrible battle which happened of late ;
   Let each good Union tar shed a sad tear of pity
   When he thinks of the once gallant *Cumberland*'s fate.

2. On the eighth day of March told a terrible story,
   Many a brave tar through this world bid adieu ;
   Our flag it was wrapped in the mantle of glory
   By the heroic deeds of the *Cumberland's* crew.

3. On that ill-fated day about ten in the morning
   The sky it was clear, and bright shone the sun,
   The drums of the *Cumberland* sounded a warning
   And told every seaman to stand by his gun.

4. Then up spoke our captain with stern resolution,
   " My boys, of this monster, now don't be dismayed.
   We're sworn to maintain our beloved constitution
   And die for our country.   We are not afraid."

5. " To fight for the Union our cause it was glorious,
   For the Stars and the Stripes we will stand ever true,
   We will sink in our quarters or conquer victorious,"
   Was the answer with cheers from the *Cumberland's* crew.

6. Now our gallant ship fired, her guns dreadfully thundered,
   Her broadside like hail on the rebel did pour ;
   The people gazed on struck with terror and wonder,
   The shots struck her sides and glanced harmlessly o'er.

7. But the pride of our navy could never be daunted,
   The dead and the wounded her decks we did strew,
   And the Star Spangled banner above them is flying,
   Was nailed to the mast by the *Cumberland's* crew.

8. We fought her three hours with stern resolution,
   Those rebel found cannons could never avoid,
   The blood of cessation * had no part to guile † them,
   The blood from her scuppers lay crimson the tide.

9. She struck us amidships, our planks she did sever,
   Her sharp iron prong pierced our noble ship through,
   And still as we sank on that dark rolling river,
   " We will die at our guns," cried the *Cumberland's* crew.

* " Secession " in Gray's variant.   † " Quail " in Gray's variant.

10. Columbia my birthplace with freedom communion,*
Our flag it ne'er floated so proudly before,
But the honour of those who fought for the Union
Above its broad folds exultingly soar.

11. But when our dear sailors in battle assembled,
God bless the dear banner, the red, white and blue,
Above its bright stripes will cause tyrants to tremble
And sink at our guns like the *Cumberland's* crew.

   * Gray—" Columbia is the gem of the brightest communion."

No. 113. *"Cumberland's" Crew.*

See Rickaby, No. 39; Dean, pp. 36–37; for further references Gray, pp. 162–165. The
United States frigate *Cumberland* was commanded by Lieutenant George Morris and was sunk
by the *Merrimac* off Newport News, Virginia, in March 1862. See *Maggie Mac* in this volume.

114.

Dutchman's Song

Amongst the pines and hemlocks Way down at the mid white shore There lies the prettiest cook house Named by P.H. Moore We went into the bunk room Where the Dutchmens always sleep It wasn't swept for a month or more (The Dutchmen always creep.)

Sung by Charlie Hartlan, South-East Passage.

1. AMONGST the pines and hemlocks
     Way down at the mid white shore,
   There lies the prettiest cookhouse
     Named by P. H. Moore.
   We went into the bunk room
     Where the Dutchmens always sleep,
   It wasn't swept for a month or more
     (The Dutchmen always creep).

2. We gathered round the table
     To have a little fun,
   First she begin to . . .
     Was the poker just begun.

No. 114. *Dutchman's Song.*

Fragment of a lumberman's song.

115

The Flemmings of Torbay

Andante

The thrilling news we heard last week Is in our memories yet Two fishermen from Newfoundland Saved from the jaws of death Two fine young men born in Torbay Who went adrift at sea On the eighteenth day of April From the schooner Jubilee.

Sung by Patrick Williams, Devil's Island, Nova Scotia.

1. THE thrilling news we heard last week
   Is in our memories yet,
   Two fishermen from Newfoundland
   Saved from the jaws of death.
   Two fine young men born in Torbay
   Who went adrift at sea,
   On the 18th day of April
   From the schooner *Jubilee*.

2. They left to persevere their voyage
   Near the Grand Banks stormy shore,

Where many a hardy fisherman
    Was never heard of more.
For twelve long days and stormy nights
    These hardy fishermen stood,
Fagged, heart-sore and hungry,
    No water nor no food.

3. Lost on the seas all these long days
    While bitter was each night,
No one to speak a friendly word,
    No sail to heave in sight.
Exhausted, cold and hungry
    These two poor brothers lay
To gaze on sky and water
    Throughout each weary day.

4. The horrors of this story,
    The Flemmings of Torbay,
Two fishermen of Newfoundland
    While in their dories lay.
At last a vessel hove in sight
    And saw that floating speck,
The *Jessie Maurice* was her name,
    Coal laden for Quebec.

5. The wheelsman being a well-trained yachtsman
    Discerned her through the misty haze,
These two exhausted fishermen
    Now adrift so many a day.
The captain being a kind-hearted man
    Who just came up on deck,
And his order he gave to hard a port
    And shape her for the wreck.

6. Two hours or more while wind did roar
    The *Jessie* sailed around
To see if any tidings
    Of the dory could be found.
The crew was stationed in the bow
    All anxious her to hail,
When the captain eyed her in the fog
    Just aft the weather rail.

7.   Our brave commander right away
      Gave orders for to launch
   The jolly boat that hung astern
      Of good old oak so staunch.
   Two tough old seamen standing there
      All at the word to go,
   And the captain standing in the stern
      Soon took the boat in tow.

8   The captain grasped the painter
      And hauled her to the barque,
   For those on board were still as death
      Their features cold and dark.
   A sling was then prepared below
      Where these two men were placed,
   While tender-hearted mariners
      Their work did nobly face.

9.   No signs of life were in these men
      As they were placed to bed,
   But still our captain held out hopes
      The vital spark not fled.
   He watched for days and sleepless nights
      To bring those men around,
   And on the second day he discerned
      But just a feeble sound.

10.   The first to speak was Peter,
      The eldest of the two,
   He told the captain who he was,
      A part of the *Jubilee's* crew.
   And when in April on the Banks
      By chance did go astray,
   And was left exposed in an open boat
      Throughout cold, weary days.

11.   Our captain then the stuns'l set,
      And he shaped her for Quebec.
   He took on board the dory
      And all left of the wreck.

He watched these men with a mother's care
      And in their berth they lay,
And he saved the lives of those two men
      Once more to see Torbay.

12.   So let us pray for those away
          Saved from the dory's wreck,
      To heal their wounds as sore they lay
          In hospital in Quebec,
      And guide them in their homes of peace
          So keep a cheerful smile,
      These men safe from the jaws of death
          That on the seas must toil.

13.   Long live the *Jessie's* gallant crew
          All as her captain bold.
      Their names should be recorded
          In letters of bright gold.
      And send them peace and happiness
          In every port they lay,
      Those plucky boys that saved the lives
          Of the Flemmings of Torbay.

No. 115. *The Flemmings of Torbay.*

Songs Their Fathers Sung, James Murphy, Newfoundland, Sept. 1923, gives the only printed copy of this song I have seen. To the Archives of Halifax I am indebted for a note from the *Evening Mercury* of May 31, 1888, under a Quebec date-line of May 18, 1888, which gives an interesting account of the story. When the *Jessie Maurice* picked up the Newfoundland dory they noticed a piece of net partly across the stern and partly in the water. In the centre of the boat was a water-keg, fog-horn, oars and an oilskin coat. Huddled in the bow and curled under the seat was the body of a man; his brother was discovered later. How they survived is a mystery, for William states, " I must have been unconscious for five days." Both men were taken to Quebec, where their legs were amputated.

My singer completes the story in most romantic manner by assuring me that Queen Victoria sent a pair of artificial limbs to the elder brother. I have been unable to substantiate this as the Flemmings both died some time ago and the author of the song, Johnny Burke of St. John's, remembers little now concerning the event.

116.

I ar-rived in Fox River Febru-ary the tenth 'twas a week in the
city with pleasure I spent While a looking in the paper the
notice to find Wanted fifty old bums for the Fox River Line

Sung by Dr. Perry Cochrane, Wolfville.

1. I ARRIVED in Fox River February the tenth.
   'Twas a week in the city with pleasure I spent.
   While a-looking in the paper the notice to find
   Wanted fifty old bums for the Fox River line.

2. There were Dutchmen, Italians, Irishmen, Jews,
   All walking up Wall Street to hear the great news,
   With a pair of old larrigans and a broad axe to grind
   Was fifty old bums for the Fox River line.

3. I went up to Star Soley the very next day,
   " You are too late," Star Soley did say,
   " For the teams they left here at a quarter of nine
   With fifty old bums for the Fox River line.

4. " To please your desire I'll do what I can,
   By the cut of your jib you're a fine working man.
   Go back to headquarters and there you will find
   George Allan's camp on the Fox River line."

5.   I am working for Allan the very next day,
      Twenty dollars per month I heard was my pay,
      After working six weeks I summed up my time
      And I was eight cents in debt to the Fox River line.

6.   I left Allan's, the camp my abode,
      I picked up my turkey and walked down the road.
      I was working for Rector and smiling divine,
      He's a light number two on the Fox River line.

7th verse unknown.

8.   The girls of Fox River are charming and fair,
      They wear their pink wrappers to shade their red hair.
      There's a time in each year when we all do combine
      To raise a shindig on the Fox River line.

No. 116. *Fox River Line.*

Dr. Cochrane first heard this as a boy at Fox River, N.S. In Joggins it is known as *The Scantaling Line.* It is sung all over the province where the words are changed to suit the locality. The theme of v. 5, where the hero is in debt at the end of his service, is common in this type of song. "Turkey" is the lumberman's term for the sack holding his belongings.

117

The Ghostly Sailors

You may all smile if you want to But perhaps you'll lend an
ear For it's men and boys together Well on for fifty
years I've sailed upon the ocean In summer's pleasant
days And through the stormy winter When the
howling winds did rage

Sung by Mr. Gordon Young, Devil's Island.

1. YOU may all smile if you want to
       But perhaps you'll lend an ear.
    For men and boys together
       Well on for fifty years,
    I've sailed upon the ocean
       In summer's pleasant days,
    And through the stormy winter
       When the howling winds did rage.

2. I've been tossed about on Georgia Shoals,
       Been fishing in the Bay,
    Down south in early seasons,
       Most anywhere would pay.

I've been in different vessels
   On the western Banks and Grand,
I've been in herring vessels
   That went to Newfoundland.

3. There I saw storms I tell you,
   And things looked rather blue,
But somehow I was always
   Quite lucky and got through.
I will not brag, however,
   I won't say much, but then
I am not much easier frightened
   Than most of other men.

4. Last night as we were sailing
   We were off shore a ways,
I never will forget it
   In all my mortal days.
It was in the grand dog watches
   I felt a thrilling dread
Came over me as if I heard
   One calling from the dead.

5. Right over our rail there clambered
   All silent one by one,
A dozen dripping sailors,
   Just wait till I am done.
Their faces were pale and sea wan,
   Shone through the ghostly night,
Each fellow took his station
   As if he had a right.

6. They moved about before us
   Till land was most in sight,
Or rather I should say so
   The lighthouse shone its light.
And then those ghostly sailors
   Moved to the rail again,
And vanished in an instant
   Before the sons of men.

7. We sailed right in the harbour,
    And every mother's son
Will tell you the same story
    The same as I have done.
The trip before the other
    We were on Georgia then,
We ran down another vessel
    And sank her and her men.

8. These were the same poor fellows,
    I hope God rest their souls,
That on our old craft ran over
    And sank on Georgia Shoals.
So now you have my story,
    It is just as I say.
I do believe in spirits
    Until this very day.

No. 117. *The Ghostly Sailors.*

Sailors have always been and will probably always be superstitious men. The tale this song relates speaks for itself. Mr. Young says it is the experience of a Gloucester fisherman going to Newfoundland for its spring and summer bait.

118.

Granite Mill

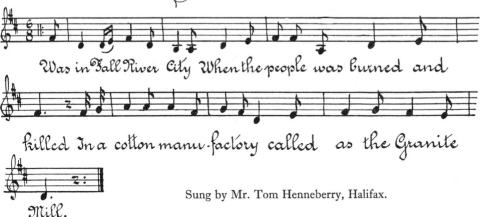

Was in Fall River City When the people was burned and killed In a cotton manu-factory called as the Granite Mill.

Sung by Mr. Tom Henneberry, Halifax.

1. Was in Fall River City
     When the people was burned and killed,
   In a cotton manufactory
     Called as the Granite Mill.
   At seven o'clock the firebells rang
     But oh, it was too late,
   The flames they were fast spreading
     And at a rapid rate.

2. They were men and women there
     And children too, I'm told,
   Who might have been saved from out of the flames
     If the truth was only known.
   But oh, the villains that locked the doors
     And told them to keep still,
   It was the bosses and overseers
     That burning Granite Mill.

3. The first scene was a touching one
     From a maid so young in years,
   She was standing by a window and
     Her eyes were filled with tears.

She cried, " Oh, save me !   Save me ! "
    She called her mother's name,
But her mother could not save her
    And she fell back in the flame.

4. The next scene was a horrible one
    Just as it caught my eye.
They were leaping from a window
    From up so very high,
And the only means of their escape
    Was sliding down a rope,
And just as they were half way down
    The burning strands they broke.

5. Christ, Christ, what a horrible mess,
    They were mangled, burned and killed,
Six stories high, and falling from
    The burning Granite Mill.
But I hope their spirits has fled
    To a better place far still,
Up high, up high, up in the sky
    Above the Granite Mill.

No. 118. *Granite Mill.*

Mr. Tom Henneberry, who learned this song about sixty years ago, says it describes an incendiary fire in Fall River, New York, of about that time.

119.

Guysboro Song

Moderato

Come all ye landsmen and young sailors too While I relate the hardships that I have gone through I have suffered some hardships and pain in my time Oh I put them together and composed the rhyme

Sung by Mr. Ben Henneberry, Devil's Island.

1. Come, all ye landsmen, and young sailors too,
   While I relate the hardships that I have gone through.
   I have suffered some hardships and pain in my time,
   Oh, I put them together and composed the rhyme.

2. In the county of Guysborough my first breath I drew,
   'Twas the poorest county that ever I knew,
   The people were poor, and I think they were proud;
   It is no harm to think if you don't think too loud.

3. When a boy very young both my parents did die,
   They left me alone my heart's fortune to try.
   My father's own brother turned me out of doors,
   But he paid for it since for he died very poor.

4. Then I sailed with my uncle to the Labrador,
   With him and his son for three seasons or more,
   But I had to work hard both by night and by day,
   And to make it still worse I had very small pay.

5. I determined one winter to remain on shore,
   I went to New York to make a short voyage more.
   It seems as misfortune was always on me,
   I slipped on the ice and I broke my knee.

6. When I was laid up for more than a year
   I was well attended by my sister dear,
   But, poor girl, she sickened, and shortly did die.
   She was the only one I had in this world wide.

7. I found it impossible for to live there,
   I tried every means that was handsome and fair.
   I had a dressing-case given me by a friend,
   Even that I pawned my boots for to mend.

8. I shipped then as captain, from captain to mate,
   A trip down to Canso I drank all my freight ;
   I drank all my freight, and I drowned two boys,
   And for my term's actions I lost my employ.

9. One fall very late I went to Ingonish,
   To bring up a crew that had been there to fish,
   But we were cast away off the middle Cape,
   And out of thirteen only four did escape.

10. Then for the eastern Indies I longed for a chance,
    I did go as master to the isle of France,
    Where I had the misfortune to break my good knee,
    So lame in both legs, boys, for life I'll be.

11. So now I'm a cripple, I will be all my days,
    I think it high time for to order my ways,
    Now I'm intended to lead a new life,
    I'll go no more roving, but try and get a wife.

No. 119. *Guysboro Song.*

120.

Hanstead Boys

The Hanstead Boys they have no sleds They slide down the hills On the herring heads One

Sung by Dr. Perry Cochrane, Wolfville.

THE Hanstead boys they have no sleds,
They slide down the hills on the herring heads ;
The Hanstead boys they have no combs,
They comb their heads with the herring bones.

No. 120. *Hanstead Boys.*

This would have been given as a song of Port Greville, N.S., if I had not happened to find it in Botsford, *Folk-Songs of Many Peoples*, vol. 2, where the words Hanstead Boys are given as Cape Cod Girls, and the song known as a Cape Cod Chanty. The one stanza of the Nova Scotia text is given as two, and a chorus added.

Indian Song (1)

Oh here's to the old Ind-ian who sits in his canoe And paddles the

waters so noble and blue And thinks of the time when the

land was his own A-mongst those pale faces there never was known.

Sung by Charlie Hartlan, South-East Passage.

OH, here's to the old Indian who sits in his canoe
And paddles the waters so noble and blue,
And thinks on the time when the land was his own
Amongst those pale faces there never was known.

No. 121. *Indian Song* (1).

It would be interesting to know the origin of this song, which is obviously not a folk-song. I have found no reference to it, but Professor Robins remembers it as sung by his father.

Indian Song (2)

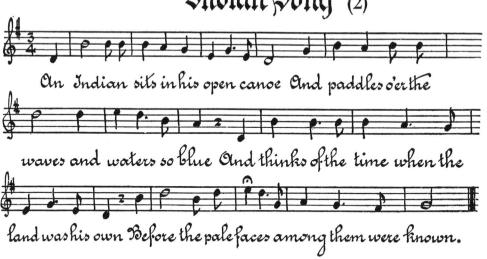

An Indian sits in his open canoe And paddles o'er the
waves and waters so blue And thinks of the time when the
land was his own Before the pale faces among them were known.

Sung by Mr. Ben Henneberry, Devil's Island.

1. An Indian sits in his open canoe
   And paddles o'er the waves and waters so blue,
   And thinks of the time when the land was his own
   Before the pale faces among them were known.

2. When first the red men was lord of the soil
   They lived at their ease, free from sorrow and toil,
   They hunted the otter, the beaver and deer,
   And roamed through the wild wood with nothing to fear.

3. When first the pale faces they came to our land
   We met them like brothers and gave them our hand.
   We knew they were weary and needed repose,
   But ne'er did we dream that the white men were foes.

4. Oh, while we lived happy with our white folks around
   We gave them the best of our own hunting-ground.
   They paid us in trinkets which pleased us awhile,
   And caused us like children, upon them to smile.

5. But soon they began to encroach on our rights,
    Their numbers increased and they put us to flight,
    They drove us away from our own native shores
    And the smoke of our camp fires shall rise there no more.

6. They built their large cities all over the land
    And on our rich meadow their farm houses stand.
    They cleared all the country from Texas to Maine,
    And the Indian may seek for his wigwam again.

7. The pride of our forest before them did go ;
    The white pine and cedar their hatchets laid low ;
    The otter and beaver their hunters have slain ;
    They have driven the red deer away from the plain.

8. The graves of our forefathers, where are they now ?
    They've been rudely run over and turned by the plough.
    Our rich, rolling meadow which once was our own
    The buffalo and Indian will never more roam.

9. Oh, now we'll go westward, far back in the wood
    Where the white man is unknown and the hunting is good.
    No more shall the white man intrude on our home
    Or cause the poor Indian in sorrow to roam.

10. Here's adieu to our children, our forefathers brave,
    Now we'll go westward and find there a grave,
    Till the Great Spirit calls us away from the plain
    And there we will meet and be happy again.

No. 121. *Indian Song* (2).

122.

In the Month of October

In the month of October eighteen eighty-two Billy Williams from Bangor he scared up a crew And forty brave fellows of us he did take And he landed us over and across head Moose Lake Singing

Chorus

Fall the diddle derro right toodle I dey.

Sung by Mr. Allan Hartlan,
South-East Passage.

1. In the month of October eighteen-eighty-two,
    Billy Williams from Bangor he scared up a crew,
    And forty brave fellows of us he did take,
    And he landed us over and across head Moose Lake.

    Chorus.

    Singing fall the diddle derro, right toodle I dey.

2. Oh, we have a chopper, from Bangor came he,
    The best he can do is to lodge every tree.   Cho.

            .   .   .   .   .   .

            .   .   .   .   .   .

3. Oh, we have a cook, from Bangor came he,
    The dirtiest old beggar you ever did see.
    Cold beans and raw dough he gave us to eat,
    About twice a week a big feed of salt meat.   Cho.

265

4. At five in the morning our boss he would shout,
   " Come, bullies ; come, bullies ; come, bullies, roll out."
   When you roll out was all you could see
   Was a darn dirty cook and that lousy cookee.   Cho.

No. 122. *In the Month of October.*

For a more complete version of this lumberman's song see Gray, pp. 60–62.

123.

Irish Labourer

Andante

I am an Irish labourer Both hearty stout and strong For idleness I never love, to my race it don't be-long I've still the strength and will to toil for the want of a life so dear But told where'er I ask for work There's no Irish wanted here

Repeat for Chorus

Sung by Patrick Williams, Devil's Island.

1. I AM an Irish labourer, both hearty, stout and strong,
   For idleness I never love, to my race it don't belong.
   I've still the strength and will to toil for the want of a life so dear,
   But told where'er I ask for work, " There's no Irish wanted here. "

Chorus.

Then you may think it a misfortune to be christened Pat or Dan,
To me it is an honour to be called an Irishman,
And you may live to see the day, it will come, oh, never fear,
When ignorance gives way to sense, " You are welcome Irish here."

2.   When your country was in danger but a few short years ago
You were not so particular about who should fight the foe.
When the men were needed for the ranks to reserve our rights so dear
Among the bravest of the brave it was, " Irish wanted here ! " Cho.

3.   For generous hearts and charity you could search this wide world round,
For Paddy's hospitality 'twas likes was never found,
He'd give the clothes from off his back, his blood for friends so dear,
But for justice and for envy's vile there's no Irish wanted here. Cho.

4.   Then turn your hearts to kindness, take poor Paddy from the wall,
For God in heaven made this world and lots of room for all,
So stretch your arms across the sea to that little isle so dear
And give the Irish girls and boys glad welcome over here. Cho.

No. 123. *Irish Labourer.*

See also Dean, p. 65.

124.

Joe Livermore

Moderato

Come sit down beside me Come listen awhile I'll sing you a song that will cause you to smile About this old villain he's very well known And he sails the Columbia from Eastport town Singing down down derry

Chorus

down

Sung by Mr. Hiram O. Hilshie, Dartmouth.

1. COME sit down beside me, come listen awhile,
   I'll sing you a song that will cause you to smile
   About this old villain, he's very well known,
   And he sails the *Columbia* from Eastport town.

   Chorus.

   Singing down, down derry down.

2. As we sailed from Eastport when we first left the land
   With watery eye as we sailed from the strand,
   This old villain would holler and bawl,
   " Then lay aft, ye damn lubbers, and give us a haul."   Cho.

3. When we got to Eastport it was on the lucky day,
   Each man took his chest and no longer would stay,
   If we can't do no better, boys, we'll stay on the shore
   And we'll never go to sea with old Joe Livermore.   Cho.

4. Now he says, if you want to hear any more of this rogue,
   Look under his coat and you'll see the old foge'.
   He has a snuff-coloured coat and he's known very well,
   He has a thing on his nose what they call the hotel.   Cho.

No. 124. *Joe Livermore.*

125.

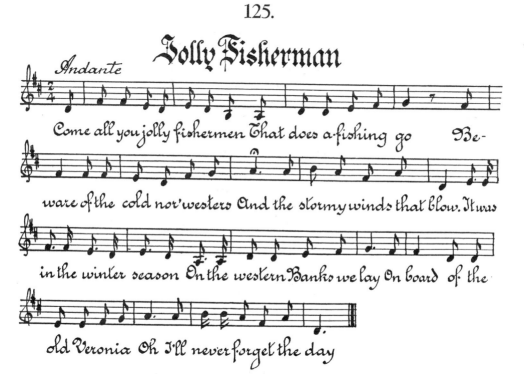

Sung by Mr. Richard Hartlan, South-East Passage.

    1. COME, all you jolly fishermen,
        That does a-fishing go,
      Beware of the cold nor'westers
        And the stormy winds that blow.
      It was in the winter season
        On the western Banks we lay
      On board of the old *Veronia*,
        Oh, I'll never forget the day.

2. It was stormy in the morning
     Just as the dawn of light,
   When we went out to haul our trawls
     We returned again all right.
   " Bait up again, my jolly boys,"
     I heard our captain say,
   " It's halibut here it's to be had,
     We must haul again to-day."

3. " Oh, three can go in a dory," said he,
     " If it comes the worst do blow,
   We'll pay down buoy line astern,
     Adrift you never can go."
   Oh, three of us went in a dory
     And away us boys did go,
   The wind south-east a breezing up
     And every sign of snow.

4. Oh, we got our trawls all right,
     And might have reached her too,
   But when we got our lights in sight
     We broke our oars in two.
   I overboard an anchor,
     Thinking to ride it out,
   But our buoy line soon parted,
     For I tell you it was not stout.

5. My dory mate he kept her straight
     While the other one kept her free,
   For if we'd a got a broadside to it
     Capsized we would be.
   My dory mate he kept her straight
     While the other one kept her free,
   While I rigged a drug of halibut
     And cast it in the sea.*

* This was to cover the water with oil to make it quiet beside the boat.

6. Oh, early the next morning
     We took our turn about,
   And pulling away to leeward
     And keeping a sharp look out.
   " Sail oh !   Sail oh ! my jolly boys,
     The joyful bells do ring,"
   There lay the old *Veronia*
     And to Williams we convened.

7. " Oh, wasn't you afraid ? "
     Oh, I guess so.
   We're all right at last,
     By baling with our sou'westers
   We saved our little craft."

No. 125. *Jolly Fisherman.*

Mr. Hartlan says the incident related took place off the western Banks. He knew the schooner when a boy, and distinctly remembers a time when she was in Halifax for two winters. The song was probably composed by members of the crew.

126.

Liverpool Girls

From Car-diff down to Cali-for-ni-a I went to
live in that country it was my in-tent But drinking bad
whiskey like every darn fool Soon got me ex-ported back
Chorus
to Liverpool. To me roll roll Julia roll The Liverpool
girls will take us in tow.

Sung by Mr. Ben Henneberry,
Devil's Island.

1. FROM Cardiff down to California
   I went to live in that country it was my intent,
   But drinking bad whiskey like every darn fool
   Soon got me exported back to Liverpool.

   Chorus.

   To me roll, roll, *Julia*, roll,
   The Liverpool girls will take us in tow.

2. The *Alaska* lies out in the Bay,
   She's waiting for fair winds to get under way.
   The sailors on board are so sick and so sore,
   Their whiskey all gone and they can't get no more.   Cho.

272

3. Our mate he comes forward with his jacket so blue,
   He's a-hunting up jobs for the sailors to do.
   " Your jib topsail has it," he loudly did bawl,
   Said, " Shin aloft, Paddy, and them overhaul."   Cho.

4. Our captain he's damning because there's no wine,
   And to leave those pretty fair maids so far behind.
   " Your fore and main topsail now set, Mr. Brown,
   We'll beat the flush packet, the tacker *McGown*."   Cho.

5. One night off Cape Horn I shall never forget,
   And when I remember I think on it yet.
   She was driving bows under, the sailors all wet,
   A-scudding twelve knots with her skysails all set.   Cho.

6. Now back to those northern docks I will go
   To see those pretty fair maids that had us in tow.
   We'll go up to Jack Casey's and have a gay time,
   Drink ale, wine and brandy till we are stone blind.   Cho.

7. Oh, here's to our captain, wherever he be,
   He's a friend to the sailor on land or on sea,
   But here's to our mate, he's a dirty old brute,
   I hope when he dies to hell he will skoot.

Chorus.

To me roll, roll, *Julia*, roll,
The Liverpool girls have got us in tow.

No. 126. *Liverpool Girls.*

273

127.

Loakie's Boat

Moderato

Old Loakie's boat is painted green A ha Old Loakie's boat is

Chorus

painted green She's the finest boat you ever seen A

ha doodle I dey.

Sung by Mr. and Mrs. Edward Hartley, Dartmouth.

1. OLD Loakie's boat is painted green—A-ha,
   Old Loakie's boat is painted green,
   She's the finest boat you ever seen,

   Chorus.

   A-ha, doodle I dey.

2. Old Loakie he sailed down the shore—A-ha,
   Old Loakie he sailed down the shore
   To catch some fish from Labrador.   Cho.

3. Old Loakie he looked all around—A-ha,
   Old Loakie he looked all around,
   " My wife is dead, the blinds are down."   Cho.

4. " Oh," says Loakie, " I don't care "—-A-ha,
   " Oh," says Loakie, " I don't care
   For I'll get another in the fall of the year."   Cho.

No. 127. *Loakie's Boat.*

My singers tell me this was composed about a man of the name who came from Lunenburg.

128.

Ye landsmen all on ye I call And jolly sea-men too While I relate the hardships great I've late-ly gone through For Ha-vana bound in the Philosophy And from St. John set sail It was on the fourth of No-vember In a sweet and a pleasant gale.

Sung by Mr. Ben Henneberry, Devil's Island.

1. YE landsmen all, on ye I call,
   And jolly seamen too,
   While I relate the hardships great
   I've lately gone through.
   For Havana bound in the *Philosophy*,
   And from St. John set sail,
   It was on the fourth of November
   In a sweet and a pleasant gale.

2. Full seven hands we had on board,
   Likewise our captain too.
   The first few days we sailed the sea
   Right fair the wind did blow.
   But to our grief we soon found out
   Our vessel she was weak,
   We had to pump both night and day
   Most dismally did she leak.

3. All our headgear had been gone,
     And bowsprit carried away,
   Yet we arrived at Havana
     As plainly you may see,
   Where we discharged our cargo
     And got repaired again.
   Once moored her anchor, our sweet lives
     Had crossed the raging main.

4. We had not long been out of port
     Before we were run down,
   We had to put right back again
     Unto Havana town.
   Our headgear being gone,
     And topmast carried away,
   We had to lay there for repairs
     Till the twenty-third day.

5. The first few days we sailed the sea
     Right fair the wind did blow,
   Our vessel, she being very light,
     Across the ocean flew.
   Our chronometer being out
     In reckoning got astray,
   And on the seventh of January
     We were cast away.

6. It's early the next morning
     To view our forlorn state,
   Our cook and captain, they being gone,
     And likewise our chief mate.
   There was five of us did reach the shore
     But only three alive,
   The other two of our ship's crew
     The cold could not survive.

7. Oh, when we were safe landed
     We knew not where to run,
   But a-wandering through frost and snow
     At length we heard a gun.
   It was providence for us poor souls
     For to protect our lives,
   In port once more we're safe on shore
     With our sweethearts and our wives.

8. Now to conclude and finish
       Of this my doleful song,
    I wish well to those kind friends
       That in Pope's Harbour do belong.
    For all your kindness shown to us,
       Both the living and the dead,
    May the God above who we all love
       Shower blessings on your heads.

No. 128. *Loss of the " Philosophy."*

Mr. Henneberry says : " This is a true story. Pope's Harbour is in Halifax County. The cook was frozen between decks, and in the morning was as large as a puncheon from water being frozen around him. The story was told me from my father, who learned it from the old people when he was quite small. The song was composed by one of the survivors of the wreck."

129.

Louisiana Lowlands

Merrily

Way down Louisiana, boys, not many years ago There lived a coloured gentleman whose name was Pompey Snow This Pompey Snow he started to have a little fun. And first he thought he'd *Chorus* refresh himself with a good stiff glass of rum. So they buried him in the Lowlands, Low-lands In the Louisiana Lowlands low In the Louisiana Lowlands Low-lands In the Louisiana Lowlands low

Words and music contributed by Prof. A. McMechan, Halifax.

(As sung by Robert Haddow in Knox College, Toronto, *circa* 1883).

1. WAY down Louisiana, boys, not many years ago,
    There lived a coloured gentleman whose name was Pompey Snow.
    This Pompey Snow he started to have a little fun,
    And first he thought he'd refresh himself with a good stiff glass of rum.

Chorus.

So they buried him in the Lowlands, Lowlands,
In the Louisiana Lowlands, low.
In the Louisiana Lowlands, Lowlands,
In the Louisiana Lowlands, low.

2. The fire-bells are ringing, boys, there is a fire in town ;
    The hook-and-ladder company is first upon the ground ;
    The Phœnix she is ready, the volunteers are here,
    The steamer she is left behind, and without her engineer.   Cho.

3. This little boy had an augu-er that bored two holes at once,
    This little boy had an augu-er that bored two holes at once,
    And some were shuffling cards, and some were rattling dice—
    This little boy turned his head around and he blew out all the lights.   Cho.

No. 129. *Louisiana Lowlands.*

See *Sweet Trinity: or The Golden Vanity* (*Vallady*) in this volume, of which the third stanza of this song is evidently a parody.   The first stanza is from an old minstrel song.

130.

Lumbering Boy

You leave your kind old mother your father and sisters three For there is something tells me Your face I never shall see Early the next morning Harry started on his way He met with a lumbering quay Which caused him for to stay.

Sung by Charlie Hartlan, South-East Passage.

1. COME, all you wild Canadian boys,
   That leave your native home,

   .   .   .   .   .   .

   .   .   .   .   .   .

2. And everything was needed
   To work upon the farm,
   You leave your kind old mother,
   Your father and sisters three,
   For there is something tells me
   Your face I never shall see.

3. Oh, early the next morning
   Harry started on his way,
   He met with a lumbering quay
   Which caused him for to stay.
   He worked along for three long months,
   And oft times he'd write home,
   Saying, " The winter months will soon be done
   And I'll be coming home."

4. Oh, early the next morning
   As he drew from his bunk,
   Not a smile upon his brow
   Which called his chum from outside the door
   Whose name was Charlie Boyle.
   It's " Charlie dear, I had a dream
   Which fills my heart with woe.
   There must be something matter home
   And it's there I'd better go."

5. His comrades only laughed at him
   Which cheered him for a while,
   " It's time to go, Harry,
   It's time to fall the pines."
   He worked along till three o'clock
   All on that fatal day,
   When a hanging limb fell down upon him
   And scruched him through the clay.

6. " Oh, pick me up ; oh, pick me up,
   And send my body home,"

   .   .   .   .   .   .

   God knows her heart was broken
   When she saw her only son.

No. 130. *Lumbering Boy.*

See Rickaby, *The Hanging Limb*, No. 26 (from Ontario) ; also J.A.F.L., 31, 75–76.

131

Maggie Mac

Was on a Monday morning just at the break of day I

spied a lofty steamship to an anchor in the bay When a man from our

masthead our topmast so high There's something up to windward like a

housetop I es-py And we'll hoist up our flag and long may it wave

Over the Union so noble and so brave. We'll hoist up our flag And

long may it wave Over the station as she slumbers in the grave

Sung by Mr. Ben Henneberry, Devil's Island.

1. Was on a Monday morning just at the break of day,
    I spied a lofty steamship to an anchor in the bay,
    When a man from our masthead, our topmast so high,
    " There's something up to windward like a housetop I espy."

    Chorus.

    And we'll hoist up our flag and long may it wave
    Over the Union so noble and so brave,
    We'll hoist up our flag and long may it wave
    Over the station as she slumbers in the grave.

2. Our captain took up his telescope, he spied all o'er the blue,
   " Come, all you jolly comrades, and I will tell you true,
   That object you see yonder just like a turtle's back,
   It is the rebel monster, they call it *Maggie Mac.*"   Cho.

3. Our decks were cleared for action, our guns were pointed true,
   But yet the rebel monster came steaming o'er the blue ;
   On she kept coming, when fifty yards apart
   She sent a ball whistling which was the beat of many's the heart.
   Cho.

4. We gave her to her broadside and to her ribs a steel,
   No damage did we do to her and no danger did she feel,
   And then the noble captain in a thundering voice he spoke,
   " Haul down your flying colours or I'll sink your Yankee boat."
   Cho.

5. Our captain on the quarter-deck his face grew pale with rage,
   And turning to the rebel in a thundering voice he said,
   " My men is true and loyal, and under me will stand,
   Before I pull my colours down you can sink me and be hanged."
   Cho.

No. 131. "*Maggie Mac.*"

Properly called the *Merrimac*, this ship was a southern commerce raider which destroyed much shipping in the north, but was finally sunk in a notable encounter with the *Monitor*. Professor Clawson of the University of Toronto recalls the song as being current in New Brunswick 30 years ago, beginning :

'Twas on a Sunday morning the Yankee frigate lay,

while he recalls the word " monster " in my variant as " Monitor." The last line of v. 2 he sings :

It is the rebel *Monitor*, the iron *Merrimac.*

132.

The Mary L. MacKay

With a swing

Oh come all you hearty haddockers Who winterfishing go And brave the seas upon the Banks In stormy winds and snow And ye who love hard driving Come listen to my lay Of the run we made from Portland On the Mary L. MacKay

Sung by Edmund Henneberry,
Devil's Island.

1. Oh come, all you hearty haddockers,
      Who winter fishing go,
    And brave the seas upon the Banks
      In stormy winds and snow,
    And ye who love hard driving
      Come listen to my lay
    Of the run we made from Portland
      On the *Mary L. MacKay.*

2. We hung the muslin on her,
      The wind began to hum,
    Twenty hardy Nova Scotia men
      Most full of Portland rum.
    Mainsail, foresail, jib and jumbo
      On that wild December day,
    As we passed out Cape Elizabeth
      And slugged for Fundy Bay.

284

3. We slammed her by Monhegan
   As the gale began to scream,
Our vessel took to dancing
   In a way that was no dream.
A howler o'er the toprail
   We steered sou'west away,
Oh, she was a hound for running
   Was the *Mary L. MacKay*.

4. " Storm along and drive along,
   Punch her through the ribs,
Don't mind your boarding combers
   As the solid green she dips.
Just mind your eye and watch the wheel,"
   Our skipper, he did say,
" Clear decks we'll sport to-morrow
   On the *Mary L. MacKay*."

5. Oh, the seas were looking ugly
   And the crests were heaving high,
Our vessel simply scooped her
   Till our decks were never dry.
The cook he mouthed his pots and pans
   And unto us did say,
" You'll get nothing else but mugups
   On the *Mary L. MacKay*."

6. We laced a hawser to the wreck
   And caulked the cable box.
We tested all our shackles
   And our fore and mainsail blocks.
We double gripped our dories
   While the gang began to pray
For a breeze to tear the bits from out
   The *Mary L. MacKay*.

7. We slammed her to Matinicus,
   The skipper hauled the log,
" Sixteen knots ! Lord Harry,
   Ain't she just the gal to jog ? "
The half-canned wheelsman shouted
   As he swung her on her way,
" Just watch me tear the mainsail off
   The *Mary L. MacKay*."

8. The rum was passing merrily
     And the gang was feeling grand,
   Long necks dancing in her wake
     From where we left the land.
   Our skipper he kept sober
     For he knew how things would lay,
   And made us furl the mainsail on
     The *Mary L. MacKay*.

9. Under foresail and her jumbo
     We tore wildly through the night,
   The foaming, surging whitecaps
     In the moonshine made a sight,
   Would fill your hearts with terror, boys,
     And wish you were away
   At home in bed, and not aboard
     The *Mary L. MacKay*.

10. Over on the Lurcher Shoals
      The seas were running strong,
    The roaring, angry breakers
      From three to four miles long,
    And this wild inferno, boys,
      We soon had hell to pay,
    We didn't care a hoot aboard
      The *Mary L. MacKay*.

11. We laced our wheelsman to the box
      As he steered her through the gloom,
    A big sea hove his dory mate
      Right over the main boom.
    It tore the oil pants off his legs
      And you could hear him say,
    " There's a power of water flying o'er
      The *Mary L. MacKay*."

12. Our skipper didn't care to make
      His wife a widow yet,
    He swung her off to Yarmouth Cape
      With just her foresail set,
    And passed Forchu next morning
      And shut in at break of day,
    And soon in sheltered harbour lay
      The *Mary L. MacKay*.

13. From Portland, Maine, to Yarmouth Sound
    Two twenty miles we ran,
    In eighteen hours, my bully boys,
    Now beat that if you can.
    The gang said 'twas seamanship,
    The skipper he kept dumb,
    But the force that drove our vessel was
    The power of Portland rum.

No. 132. *The "Mary L. MacKay."*

I am grateful to Mr. Murray Gibbon of the Canadian Pacific Railways at Montreal for the name of the author of this excellent song, which my singers had attributed to a resident of the little village of Chezzetcook, N.S. It was written as a poem by Mr. Frederick William Wallace and published in the *Canadian Fisherman* in 1914. Somewhere Mr. Henneberry must have heard the poem and set it to the interesting melody with which it is now known along the coast as a song.

Mr. Wallace has kindly given me permission to use this text, which is the story of an experience of his on the fishing schooner, the *Effie Morrissey*. "This vessel, under Captain Bartlett, has become famous in numerous expeditions to the Arctic," writes Mr. Wallace. "Books have been written about her trips, particularly the Palmer Putman expedition." The trip described in the song was made in December 1913.

133.

McCarthy's Song

Long shall I remember one day last December My fob lined with silver my heart full of glee Being out on a frolic determined to travel Intending great Halifax city to see.

Sung by Mr. Ben Henneberry, Devil's Island.

1. LONG shall I remember one day last December,
   My fob lined with silver, my heart full of glee,
   Being out on a frolic, determined to travel,
   Intending great Halifax city to see.

2. I crossed Taylor's Bay Harbour in very good order,
   From back to Pope's Harbour both up hill and down ;
   I took into my noddle to get a full bottle,
   Oh, at the Brian's tavern, that hole of renown.

3. At the hotel I arrived ; I was kindly invited,
   Led into the barroom as you may suppose,
   With Brian's ale and water, and wine in the corner
   They bid me sweet kindly with a how-do-you-do.

4. I called for a flagon, all hands I then treated,
   All hands I then treated and paid the cash down.
   Says this Brian, " My dear fellow, come let us be mellow,
   You have plenty of money, I pray you sit down."

5. Being easily persuaded myself then I seated,
   All hands again treated with full bumpers round.
   Being fond of the cratur my head got elated,
   On the floor they soon made me a bed of shakedown.

6. It's there I lay groaning and horrors bemoaning,
   Not one to control, not a heed to my call;
   They battered and bruised me and sorely abused me,
   I'm sure that they broke both my liver and all.

7. My room then I ordered in very poor quarters,
   A chamber more fierce than the frozen north pole.
   No friend to come near me, and no one to cheer me
   But a bucket of cold water to nourish my soul.

8. Oh, early next morning the landlord gave warning
   To pay for my quarters and what I did call.
   I paid to each farthing each treat that was called on,
   He swore black and blue I paid nothing at all.

9. Then my good guardian angel cries, " Flee from the danger,"
   He told my heart it was time to begone.
   Like Lot leaving Sodom and wicked Gomorrah
   For home then I started quite feeble alone.

10. Each step as I walked I staggered and halted,
    My heart's blood been gushing through his mouth and nose,
    When Hilshy and Glawson like big kind Samaritans
    Conducted me safely to old Mrs. Haws.

11. Next day I was greeted and most kindly treated,
    On my wounds that was bleeding she poured oil and wine;
    With motherly feeling she nursed and relieved me,
    Her words full of sweetness, they seemed divine.

12. My health being regained I offered her payment,
    She freely forgave me her labour and time.
    May the great God reward her both here and hereafter
    Then in glory eternal I hope she may shine.

13. Now my frolic is over, no more I'll be rover,
    Good-bye to Pope's Harbour and Halifax town.
    Here I'll die easy with Henry and Sarah,
    A bonnie Scotch laddie that cares not a frown ;

14. And Brian's ale and water I'll ne'er taste hereafter,
    But home keep a bottle my sorrows to drown.
    My Irish blood would scorn at the name of the informer,
    Excise men I'll call on to pull this house down.

No. 133. *McCarthy's Song.*

Island singers tell me that this was composed by Michael McCarthy, school teacher at Taylor's Bay Harbour, N.S. Later, in 1865, he taught on Devil's Island. Mr. McCarthy was evidently a man of talent, for his prowess as a musician was known far and wide. Besides playing the violin, he composed music, but he never played in public. As a teacher he was also famous, for his children thronged to him both in school and out. From daylight to dark he taught them, and when lessons were over he played and they simply had to dance before he would let them go home. He had no relations in Nova Scotia, and when drink became his master he was forced to go to the poorhouse, where he died. He is remembered by the people as an exceptionally good teacher and musician.

134.

McNab's Island

It's Sergeant John McCafferty And Corporal God knows
Who They'll make you march to the roll of the drums And
company army too Then it's forty hours a day me boys (And
Chorus
be-ing in the reg-u-lar ar-my too) A tor ror lol a lido A tor ror a lol a ley

Sung by Mr. Richard Hartlan, South-East Passage.

1. It's Sergeant John McCafferty
   And Corporal God Knows Who,
   They'll make you march to the roll of the drums
   And company army too.
   Then it's forty hours a day me boys
   (And being in the regular army too.)

   Chorus.
   A tor ror lol a lido,
   A tor ror a lol a ley.

2. I went down to McNab's Island, boys,
   To box the Indian's ear,
   And sure we got bald-headed
   And never lost a hair.   Cho.

291

3. I got blisters on me heels
   And bunions on me toes,
   And shouldering the gun in the red hot sun
   Got blisters on me nose.   Cho.

No. 134. *McNab's Island.*

McNab's Island includes part of the fortification of Halifax Harbour. Mr. Hartlan says the song has another stanza which he cannot remember.

135.

Meagher's Children

Sung by Mr. Ben Henneberry, Devil's Island.

1. GOOD people, read these verses
   Which I have written here,
   And when you have perused them
   You can but shed a tear.
   In eighteen hundred and forty-four,
   April the eleventh day,
   Two little girls on Preston Road
   Into the woods did stray.

2. Their father and their mother
     Both sick in bed did lay,
   When their two little children
     About the door did play.
   It was hand in hand together
     They were seen to leave the door.
   The eldest was but six years old,
     And the youngest only four.

3. Oh, Jane Elizabeth, Margaret Meagher,
     Was their right and proper name,
   Yet two as fair a creature
     As nature ever framed.
   They walked along together,
     Most cheerfully did play,
   But mark what followed after,
     How soon they lost their way.

4. It's in the lonely wilderness
     They spent a dismal day,
   When night came on they thought of home
     Their screaming cries gave way.
   The frosty gale blew very hard,
     Not a star to yield them light,
   The beasts of prey they heard all day
     And a screaming owl by night.

5. They might have been discovered
     Only for that simple way,
   You Preston Negroes wash your hands
     And wipe off your disgrace.
   You cruel Browns who heard them cry
     And would not take them in,
   May God reward and punish you
     According to your sin.

6. Oh, when the shocking news at last
     Did reach the Preston ground,
   Every manly heart with pity beswelled
     And oft with grief atoned,
   Crying, " Where, Meaghers, your babies are lost,
     And you are left alone,
   It is true they say as Burns remarked
     And man was made to mourn."

7. Oh, early the next morning
　　Went out one hundred men,
When they saw poor Meagher's anguish
　　Searching the lonely glen.
First cast their eyes to heaven
　　And then down on the grove,
With screams and groans and dying cries
　　Distracted as they go.

8. Oh, all that day they searched
　　But alas it was in vain,
For in the lonely wilderness
　　Those infants did remain.
At times they strolled * to listen
　　But could not hear a sound,
Until twelve o'clock on Tuesday
　　A bloody leg was found.

9. Oh, gentle readers, what a sight
　　If we could but them behold,
A-dying in the wilderness
　　Through hunger, grief and cold.
Not a mother by to close an eye
　　Nor a friend to shed a tear,
A pirate's heart would surely melt
　　Their dying cries to hear.

10. On the fourteenth day of April
　　Went out a valiant crew
To search the hills and very woods
　　As huntsmen used to do.
From Halifax and Dartmouth,
　　Preston and Porter's Lake,
Twelve hundred men assembled
　　A final search to make.

11. Was Peter Curry found them
　　About twelve o'clock that day,
On a melancholy mountain
　　Among lumps of breathless clay.
Their hair was dragged out of their heads,
　　Their clothes in pieces torn,
Their tender flesh from hand to feet
　　With prickling thorns were gored.

* stopped (?)

12. The frost that fell upon their hearts
      Their blood began to chill,
   Their feebleness could not obey
      With all its heart and will.
   Headlong filled their souls
      Unwilling took its way,
   And left their dismal bodies
      On a dismal rock to lay.

13. No longer did they leave them
      For the beasts and birds to tear,
   On these small biers they laid them
      And greeted them with a tear.
   To their father's house they carried them
      Their mother to behold.
   She kissed them a thousand times over
      Though they were dead and cold.

14. Their father quite distracted
      And overcome with grief,
   Their neighbours tried to comfort them
      But could bring no relief.
   The cries of dear, dear mother
      Was dreadful for to hear,
   To think death had deprived her
      Of those loved most dear.

15. The rain was fast down falling
      And dismal was the day,
   While gazing on Elizabeth
      We thought we heard her say,
   " Return, you loving neighbours,
      Return, dry up your tears,
   For here we lay in this cold, cold clay
      Till Christ himself appears."

16. As early the next morning
      As in one coffin lay,
   Between Allan's vale and Allan's farm
      Their little graves were made.
   One thousand there assembled
      Their last farewell to take,
   Was rich and poor lamented sore
      For these poor children's sake.

17. Five pounds reward was offered
       For the man that did them find,
     But Curry he refused it
       Like a Christian true and kind.
     May the Lord for ever bless him
       And grant him length of day,
     The humble blessed D.G.B.
       May he ever sing his praise.

18. Ye tender folks of Halifax
       Who did turn now so kind,
     I hope in heaven hereafter
       Your true reward you'll find.
     And likewise those of Dartmouth
       Who turned out, rich and poor,
     And also those of Preston
       All along the eastern shore.

19. Now to conclude and finish
       This my doleful song,
     I beg you to excuse me
       For writing it so long.
     I hope another theme like this
       I may never have to pen,
     It is my first, I hope the last,
       God grant it so.   Amen.

No. 135. *Meagher's Children.*

The scene of the tragedy recorded in this tale lies about three miles from Dartmouth, N.S., and many hearts have been touched by the sad misfortune of the children. It is rather a coincidence that this song begins and goes on somewhat after the pattern of that very old ballad *The Children in the Wood*, although there is no actual relation between them. The last two lines of v. 15 are similar to *Peter Rambelay*, v. 13. The facts recorded in the ballad are historically correct, and may be found in Mrs. Lawrence's *History of the Township of Preston*.

136.

Ocean Queen

Moderato

Was in the winter season All in the frost and snow We leave our noble harbour And down to Georges go Where winds do loudly whistle, blow heavy on our sail As we go off a spouting just like a frightened whale.

Sung by Mr. Ben Henneberry,
Devil's Island.

1. Was in the winter season, all in the frost and snow,
   We leave our noble harbour and down to Georges go,
   Where winds do loudly whistle, blow heavy on our sail,
   As we go off a-spouting just like a frightened whale.

2. Our sails are always good and strong, made of the best of duck,
   Our rigging is manilla and rove through patent block,
   Our vessel built of white oak and finished with great taste
   To ride the heavy norther gale and stand the winter's test.

3. And on the banks of Georges no tongue can e'er describe
   The roughness of the weather, the swiftness of the tide.
   Where ice congeals like mountains and heavy winds do blow,
   And we poor sons of Neptune great hardships must go through.

4. Hail, rain and thunder, and breakers on each side,
    But yet our noble vessel majestically do ride,
    But hark one moment, listen, for what I say is true,
    The *Ocean Queen* is missing, and have drowned all her crew.

5. Nine there were in number, all in the prime of life,
    Commanded by a captain who leaves a tender wife.
    One fortnight they were married ; from her he did depart,
    And now she's left a widow with a sad and broken heart.

6. It's true she's not the only one who's left alone to weep,
    There's fathers, sons and brothers that drowned in the deep,
    But I hope God will reward her for we know the grief she feeled,
    There is a balm of Gilead that every wound can heal.

No. 136. "*Ocean Queen.*"

The singer's story is that this boat was so exceptionally fine that nine captains sailed in her as crew, going from Gloucester to the Banks of Georges off Cape Sable, from which they were never heard of again.

137

On the Lakes of Ponchartrain

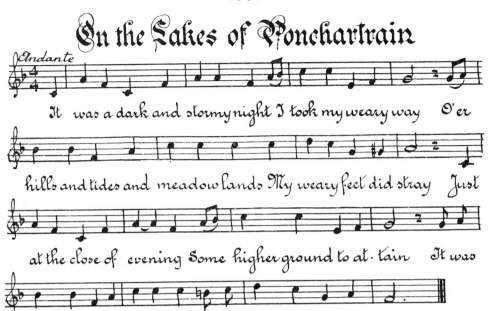

It was a dark and stormy night I took my weary way O'er hills and tides and meadow lands My weary feet did stray Just at the close of evening Some higher ground to at-tain It was there I met a Creole girl on the lakes of Ponchar-train.

Sung by Mrs. Thomas Osborne, Eastern Passage.

1. It was a dark and stormy night
    I took my weary way,
    O'er hills and tides and meadow lands
    My weary feet did stray.
    Just at the close of evening
    Some higher ground to attain,
    It was there I met a Creole girl
    On the lakes of Ponchartrain.

2. " Good evening, my pretty fair maid,
    My money does me no good;
    If it were not for the alligators
    I would sleep out in the wood."
    " You are welcome, welcome, stranger,
    To my cottage, though 'tis plain,
    For we never turn a sailor out
    On the lakes of Ponchartrain."

3. She took me to her mother's cottage
    And treated me quite well,
    Her hair rung down in ringlets
    And about her shoulder fell.
    I tried to paint her beauty
    But my efforts were in vain,
    For handsome was that Creole girl
    On the lakes of Ponchartrain.

4. I asked her if she'd marry me.
    She said that never could be,
    For she had had a true lover
    And he had gone to sea.
    For she had had a true lover
    And true to him she'd remain
    Until he came back to his Creole girl
    On the lakes of Ponchartrain.

5. " Adieu, adieu, my pretty fair maid,
    I shall never see you more,
    Though I'll never forget your kindness
    In that cottage by the shore."
    Long may this social gathering last
    O'er this wide and spreading main,
    We will all drink a toast to that Creole girl
    On the lakes of Ponchartrain.

No. 137. *On the Lakes of Ponchartrain.*

Pontchartrain is the name of a lake in Louisiana. See Pound, No. 55; J.A.F.L., 35, pp. 387–388. The more common name of the song, and that given by Mr. Enos Hartlan, is *The Creole Girl.*

138.

Peter Rambelay

Andante

My name is Peter Rambelay As you may understand I was born in Prince Edward Island Close by the ocean strand In eighteen hundred and eighty-one When the flowers were brilliant to view I left my native counteree My fortune to pursue.

Sung by Richard Hartlan, South-East Passage.

1. My name is Peter Rambelay
    As you may understand.
    I was born in Prince Edward Island
    Close by the ocean strand.

2. In eighteen hundred and eighty-one
    When the flowers were brilliant to view,
    I left my native counteree
    My fortune to pursue.

3. I landed in New Brunswick,
    That lumbering counteree.
    I hired in the lumbering woods
    Which proved my destiny.

4. I hired in the lumbering woods
       For to cut the tall spruce down.
    While loading sleds all from the yard
       I received my deathly wound.

5. There's adieu unto my dearest friends,
       Unto my mother dear.
    She reared a boy that fell as soon
       As he left her tender care.

6. But little did she ever thought
       When she sang to me lullabies,
    What country I would travel in
       Or what death I would die.

7. Here's adieu unto my father,
       It was him who sent me here ;
    It was him who sent me here to die
       And treatment too severe.

8. It is not right to press a boy
       For him to try to keep me down,
    For it will make him leave his home
       When he is far too young.

9. It's adieu to Prince Edward Island
       And the Island girls so true.
    May they long live to roam the island
       Where my first breath I drew.

10. I will never see those lofty ships
       As they go sailing by
    With a flag a-flying in the air
       Above the canvas high.

11. There's one thing that I ask him,
       And that I humbly crave,
    To have a holy father
       To bless my peaceful grave.

12. All in the city of $\begin{Bmatrix} \text{Boling} \\ \text{Alton} \end{Bmatrix}$ town
Where my crushed remains do lay
To await the Saviour's coming
On the resurrection day.

13. To wait for some holy father
For to bless my humble grave,
And here I will lay in that cold, cold clay
Until Christ himself appears.

No. 138. *Peter Rambelay.*

This is one of the most interesting of the native songs in this collection, for the composer evidently knew the ballad, *Mary Hamilton.* Compare v. 6 with Child, 173, A. 15 :

Oh little did my mother think,
The day she cradled me,
What lands I was to travel through,
What death I was to dee.

Also B. 17 :

Little did my mother think,
First time she cradled me,
What land I was to travel on,
Or what death I would die.

This song is widely known in Nova Scotia. Other collectors give the name as *Ambelay*, but my singers insist upon *Rambelay*. Eckstorm, pp. 98–103, gives the scene of the song as the Miramichi River about 1880, and suggests that the hero wrote it himself when dying from being crushed by falling logs. Barry, p. 264, says that two persons independently have given the author as Lawrence Gorman, the woods poet. See also Gray, pp. 63–69; Mackenzie, No. 116.

139.

Prentice Boy

Moderato

To a New York trader I do belong To sail the sea around and round I
had not sailed a league but one When I fell in love with a young woman

Chorus

Whack fal lal I dey   Whack fal lal I dey

Sung by Mr. Ben Henneberry, Devil's Island.

1. To a New York trader I do belong
    To sail the sea around and round.
    I had not sailed a league but one
    When I fell in love with a young woman.

            Chorus.

        Whack fal lal I dey,
        Whack fal lal I dey.

2. And to my captain I then did go
    And told to him my sad grief and woe.
    " I love a girl as I love my life,
    What would I give if she was my wife." Cho.

3. " Begone, you foolish and simple boy,
    To love a girl you can ne'er enjoy,
    For she has sweethearts on land and sea,
    And she'll be married before you're free." Cho.

4. " Oh, never mind, I'll go and try,
   Perhaps she might but fancy I,
   Perhaps she might but fancy I,
   Although I am but a prentice boy."   Cho.

5. Me and my shipmates we did agree
   To go ashore and have a spree,
   And to dance with me she was no way shy,
   And toss off a glass with her prentice boy.   Cho.

6. I bought her ribbons, I bought her gloves,
   And safe conveyed them unto my love,
   And in taking them she was no way shy,
   Although they came from a prentice boy.   Cho.

7. Now come all young prentices, where'er you be,
   Never flirt your love in low degree,
   But love that girl as you love your life
   And when you're leaving make her your wife.   Cho.

No. 139. *Prentice Boy.* (*To a New York trader.*)

140.

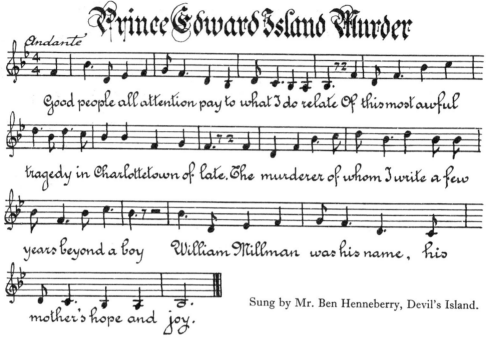

Prince Edward Island Murder

Good people all attention pay to what I do relate Of this most awful tragedy in Charlottetown of late. The murderer of whom I write a few years beyond a boy William Millman was his name, his mother's hope and joy.

Sung by Mr. Ben Henneberry, Devil's Island.

1. GOOD people, all attention pay to what I do relate,
   Of this most awful tragedy in Charlottetown of late.
   The murderer of whom I write a few years beyond a boy,
   William Millman was his name, his mother's hope and joy.

2. She reared him up so tenderly, and did a mother's part,
   Ne'er dreamed the time was so near at hand that he would break her heart;
   Yes, break both parents' hearts, I can't describe the sorrow they will feel,
   No matter where on earth they go their grief is with them still.

3. The memory of that much-loved son the parents eyes behold
   With murder of the deepest dye on his immortal soul.
   To look upon the fine young man no one would ever thought
   Such a horrible crime as that could enter his young heart,

4. Against the girl that he had vowed he never would deceive,
   Poor innocent she could do naught but his false vows believe.
   Shame on that base deceiver who led that girl astray,
   And baser still, to hide his sin, he took her life away.

5. It is of her we now must speak, her cruel death recall,
   Her broken-hearted parents, the saddest thought of all.
   Their hearts were filled with grief ; they were mourning for their son,
   And while their tears were falling fast this cruel deed was done.

6. Was Mary Tuplin young and fair, her household duties o'er,
   Went forth to meet her lover as she oft had done before,
   And as she walked along the path one look at home she cast,
   Though in her heart she never dreamed that it would be her last.

7. They met.   Poor girl, what horrid sight, what anguish did she bear !
   Could her poor rigid corpse but speak, alas ! what would we hear ;
   What agonizing cries and prayers to him her life to spare,
   As he raised a weapon in his hand she sees a pistol there.

8. Her fair young life he took, and when the last faint hope was gone,
   He to the river dragged her, then tied to her a heavy stone,
   And as he threw her body in he slyly looked around,
   " No one shall ever think of this.   She never will be found."

9. But O the eye of God was on his every movement there,
   And soon before the neighbours all traces did lay bare.
   Her body was discovered soon beneath the flowing wave,
   At the bottom of the river he had planned to be her grave.

10. Her parents laid her in the tomb close by her brother's side,
    Their happiness for ever gone ; their peace of mind denied.
    Shame on that base deceiver who led that girl astray
    And crueller still to hide his sin he took her life away.

11. Now, all young girls, a warning take before it is too late,
    Be cautious in your conduct, lest you meet the same sad fate.
    When in company with men be prudent and take care,
    Place no temptation in their way ; of flatterers beware.

12. They may seem kind and gentle words they whisper in your ear,
    But seek advice from those who know and prove they're sincere ;
    And mothers that have children dear at every day and hour
    Pray to the God who rules above to keep them by his father.*

* power (?)

307

13. From Millman's eyes the streaming tears in bitter anguish fell,
     While to his friends and all he knew he bid a last farewell.
     " Cover up my eyes," he says, " that I may never see
     The gallows, or the awful rope that now awaited me."
     So Millman paid the penalty, he lies beneath the sod,
     We leave him to the tender mercy of a most loving God.

No. 140. *Prince Edward Island Murder.*

There are many murder songs current in Nova Scotia. Only a year or two ago a man named Bevis was hanged in Halifax, and ballads are sung now which tell the story. Mr. Henneberry gives the composer of this song as Mrs. C. A. Barren, Halifax. The murder, he says, took place about forty-five years ago. Apparently the murderer meant to place the body in a deep hole, but by a mistake it was found on a shoal with the incriminating rock which he had put on as a weight.

141.

Prisoner's Song

Oh it's hard to be locked up in prison Kept a-way from your

own heart's delight With cold iron bars all a-round you.

Chorus

And a stone for your pillow by night Lonely and sad

Sadly a-lone Sitting in my cell all a-lone I've been thinking of the

days that's gone by me The days when I know I have done wrong.

Sung by Mr. Edward Hartley, Dartmouth.

Oh, it's hard to be locked up in prison,
Kept away from your own heart's delight,
With cold iron bars all around you,
And a stone for your pillow by night.

Chorus.

Lonely and sad ; sadly alone,
Sitting in my cell all alone,
I've been thinking of the days that's gone by me,
The days when I know I have done wrong.

No. 141. *Prisoner's Song.* (*It's hard to be.*)

See Mackenzie, No. 121.

142.

Sable Island Song

On the stormy western ocean Just eighty miles from land Lies a barren little island Composed of grass and sand.

Sung by Mr. Albert Whare, Eastern Passage.

1. On the stormy western ocean,
    Just eighty miles from land,
  Lies a barren little island
    Composed of grass and sand.

2. I signed the government articles
    To stay down there a year
  To take care of government property,
    The government clothes to wear.

3. They say that it's wear government clothes,
    But it's always wear your own,
  Wear government clothes on Sunday,
    Or it's pack your bag for home.

4. You're chasing crazy horses
    From daylight until dark,
  Or you're hunting up wild cattle
    Down by famous Gordeau * Park.

* Named for the Deputy Minister of Marine of 1903 or 1904, who had 88,000 trees planted there. These trees were brought from all parts of the world as an experiment. One grew to the top of a six-foot fence, but the sandy soil refused to supply nourishment and within a year or two all had died.

5. Ye go out picking cranberries
    For the government guys to chew,
  For to help to buy some more salt horse
    For to feed the lifeboat crew.

6. There's a Nova Scotia gentleman
    Came down here for cook,
  He's always washing up old clothes
    While the crew they live on look.*

7. Doughnuts as big as ringbolts
    That go around your head,
  A plate of rusty porridge,
    And a junk of deep-sea lead.

8. Salt horse that died of hunger,
    Cranberries † stewed in glue,
  And a duff made out of armour
    That a tiger couldn't chew.

9. Now my story's ended,
    And I can't sing any more.
  Get off Sable Island
    Or you'll be crazy in a year.

* View.

† Cranberries grew on the island in profusion, and for many years were sent up to Halifax to be sold.

No. 142. *Sable Island Song* (1).

The author of this song is said to be one of the sons of the well-to-do in Halifax who was sent to Sable Island shortly after Gordeau Park was attempted to be cured of his fondness for the cup. This was the custom in the old days, and is even done occasionally to-day.

The " crazy horses " mentioned are wild ponies which used to be sent up to Halifax every year to be sold.

143.

Sable Island Song

Moderato.

There's a little trail a winding To a little pile of sand To a place called the Main Station Where the forty steeves are banned We eats salt pork three times a day And potatoes we have none We thought to steal from other boys And only call that fun.

Sung by Mr. Allan Hartlan, South-East Passage.

1. THERE'S a little trail a winding
    To a little pile of sand,
   To a place called the Main Station
    Where the forty steeves are banned.
   We eats salt pork three times a day
    And potatoes we have none,
   We thought to steal from other boys
    And only call that fun.

2. Some people lived in the castle
    On top of the sandy hill,
   For minding other's business
    Their tongues were never still.
   The forty steeves all gathered round,
    Included * it was tough.
   They all made up their minds
    To go down and call their bluff.
      * Probably "concluded."

3. One of the forty steeves
   Nailed a postal on the door.
   King and queen of the castle
   Came out looking awful sore.
   King and queen of the castle
   They rang the governor right away.
   The governor asked whɛt the matter was,
   Those words the king did say :

4. " Some of your forty steeves come down
   And nailed a postal on the door,
   We want it taken out this very night
   Or we'll be out for war."
   The governor was dumbfounded
   And to the king replied,
   " I believe you blame the forty steeves
   For stealing your supplies."

5. The governor he came over
   And told us to take it off,
   But the forty steeves they were tough
   And at him only guffed.

No. 143. *Sable Island Song* (2).

This was composed on Sable Island, where Mr. Allan Hartlan was employed at the Main Station. In 1926 the wireless men lost some potatoes and accused the Main Station men of taking them. A fortnight later the potatoes were found in the cellar behind a barrel. This exonerated the Main Station staff, but they decided to make up a song about it, composing verse and verse about to see who could do the best. The first verse is my singer's composition. The music is also original. The " king " and " queen " are the wireless operator and his wife. The " governor " is the superintendent. The song has no intrinsic value, but illustrates that the song-making instinct is not dormant.

144.

The Seizure of the E. J. Horton

Moderato

Ye sons of Uncle Samuel Come listen for a while I'll
tell you of a capture that was done in Yankee style Of the schooner E. J.
Horton and her gallant band Commanded by brave Knowlton, a true
son of Yankee land.

Sung by Mr. Ben Henneberry, Devil's Island.

1. YE sons of Uncle Samuel, come listen for awhile,
   I'll tell you of a capture that was done in Yankee style,
   Of the schooner *E. J. Horton* and her gallant band,
   Commanded by brave Knowlton, a true son of Yankee land.

2. The schooner *E. J. Horton* in a British harbour lie,
   She was taken by the sweepstakes while cruising in disguise ;
   Our treaty they rejected, our government they defy,
   They have captured our fishermen, now Johnny mind your eye.

3. On the seventeenth of April, eighteen seventy-one,
   Those bold, undaunted heroes their daring work began.
   While Johnny's son was sleeping with grave on * their brain
   Those sons of Uncle Samuel took the *Horton* back again.

* red ruin (Eckstorm).

3¹4

4. It's early the next morning they began to look about,
    They found a gold prospector, and the *Horton* had slipped out.
    While the news of her reception was circulating round
    Those sons of Uncle Samuel for their native home was bound.

5. Oh, Johnny, there'll be a bully time in Gloucester to-night,
    There'll be heavy guns a-firing, and torches burning bright,
    The drums will play Yankee doodle and make the hedges * ring,
    Young America is shouting, " The *Horton* has got in."

6. Now you new Dominion government, I warn you now, beware.
    Why don't you sign the treaty, and settle this affair ?
    Why don't you do to others as you wish others do to you ?
    And don't abuse your neighbours as old Johnny used to do.

* welkin (Eckstorm).

No. 144. *Seizure of the " E. J. Horton."*

The event which provoked the writing of this song was one which evidently caused intense excitement in Gloucester upon the return of the vessel. Strangely the Halifax files reveal nothing. Mr. Henneberry's account, however, agrees with that of Eckstorm, for he tells of the *Horton's* capture by the cutter *Kingfisher* belonging to the Dominion government, as she had been fishing inside the limits. She was stripped of her sails and a watch put on her while the rest of the crew went ashore and " got drunk." Eckstorm continues with a thrilling tale of the vanquished captain posing as a gold prospector and with great ingenuity recovering the stored sails and capturing his own vessel back again, in which he returned to his home port triumphant. Captain and crew were given a bonus of $1000 each. For further notes see Eckstorm, pp. 303-315.

315

145.

Song of the Tangier Gold Mines

Moderato

Oh in eighteen hundred and sixty-one All in the month of May When

Nova Scotia was very poor As I oft times heard them say But

since I've got the secret A story I'll unfold Back of Tangier and Pope's

Harbour Where they're digging out the gold.

Words and music composed by Mrs. Catherine Hart of Tangier, A.D. 1861. Sung by her nephew, Mr. Hiram O. Hilshie, Dartmouth.

1. OH, in eighteen hundred and sixty-one,
    All in the month of May,
    When Nova Scotia was very poor,
        As I ofttimes heard them say ;
    But since I've got the secret,
        A story I'll unfold,
    Back of Tangier and Pope's Harbour
        Where they're digging out the gold.

2. It's all through the country,
        Those golden veins do run ;
    And those who have not much to do
        They only think of fun,
    With their pick upon their shoulder,
        And their shovel in their hand,
    Seeking out the golden veins
        Among the rocky land.

3.　There are farmers and fishermen,
　　　　Likewise sailors too ;
　　Blacksmiths and shoe-makers
　　　　Among the jovial crew.
　　Carpenters and shop-keepers,
　　　　As I've been lately told,
　　All leave their wives and sweethearts
　　　　For the sake of " Tangier gold."

4.　Just go up on the diggings,
　　　　If you'll not believe me ;
　　And walk up through Gold Street,
　　　　It's there you soon shall see——
　　The houses they are building,
　　　　And the trees they have cut down ;
　　And in the course of eighteen months,
　　　　I guess they'll have a town.

5.　They have crushing pans and horses too,
　　　　For them who take the lead ;
　　Their houses shall all be furnished well
　　　　With everything they need.
　　They shall all live in splendour,
　　　　Those hearts that are so bold ;
　　For their precious lives they venture
　　　　For the sake of Tangier gold.

6.　If the gold does turn out plenty,
　　　　How rich the folks will be ;
　　Their houses won't be empty,
　　　　Of molasses, flour or tea,
　　Rum, sugar and tobacco,
　　　　And all other things in store.
　　Success attend the miners,
　　　　It's a blessing to the shore.

317

7. If you happen to get rich,
     Now of it make good use.
  Don't lie, steal or murder,
     Your neighbours don't abuse.
  Don't spend your gold in drunkenness,
     You'll find it is a sin ;
  But try and build a larger church,
     Let all the folk get in.

8. If you meet a poor widow,
     Let her be young or old,
  See you don't molest her,
     But bestow on her some gold.
  And if you give it freely
     You'll have good luck, you know,
  For relieving the poor widow,
     Who was in the midst of woe.

9. A verse about the ladies now,
     I'm sure there ought to be ;
  They go upon the diggings,
     The miners for to see.
  Some they are acquainted with,
     And others they don't know ;
  There's one young lady fell in love
     With California Joe.

10. Now, here's to the miners !
     To them I do suppose
  Digging gold, it is hard work,
     That all of them well know.
  And should you wish to marry,
     Don't lead a single life,
  And do no longer tarry,
     But present yourself a wife.

11. Now if my song displeases you,
       I'm sure I'm not to blame ;
     It was not made to tease you,
       For I speak no person's name.
     I only have composed it
       To make your work go light.
     And those who can peruse it
       May pass away the night.

12. And now my song is ended,
       I have no more to sing ;
     And to the one who made it,
       Give gold to make a ring.
     And to a child who sings it,
       Of sweeties—give it some ;
     But of a man, of your own clan,
       He deserves a drink of rum.

13. And now my jolly miners,
       I wish you all success ;
     And the one who has composed this song,
       'Twill puzzle them to guess.

No. 145. *Song of the Tangier Gold Mines.*

Note from Archives at Halifax : " The Tangier Gold Mines opened in 1860. The district covers 30 square miles and has 12 lodes of auriferous quartz. The ground is honeycombed with pits and shafts for miles. Gold was not found in quantities, but lucrative shore-workings were engaged in for some time. . . ." Unfortunately it has never been as lucrative as the dreams of the composer of this song. California Joe, mentioned in v. 9, is the hero of a song by that name, Lomax, p. 139.

146.

Sweet Fair Ella

Down by some drooping willow Where the violets gently bloom There lies a sweet fair Ella So silent in her tomb.

Sung by Mr. Edward Hartley, Dartmouth.

1. Down by some drooping willow
    Where the violets gently bloom
   There lies a sweet, fair Ella
    So silent in her tomb.

2. She died not broken-hearted
    Nor in sickness her befell,
   But in one moment parted
    From the one she loved so well.

3. " Come, love," said he, " let's wander
    Down by yon meadow so gay,
   And understood we'll ponder
    Upon our wedding day."

4. " Those woods are dark and dreary
    And I am afraid to stray,
   Of wandering I am weary
    And I would retrace my way."

5. " Retrace your way ? No, never.
    Never more in those woods you shall roam,

    .   .   .   .
    .   .   .   .

6. Down on her knees before him
    She begged him to spare her her life.
   Deep down into her bosom
    He plunged that fatal knife.

7. " Oh, Willie, I'll forgive you
    With my last dying breath,"
   And her heart it ceased her * beating,
   And her eyes were closed in death.

* its (?)

No. 146. *Sweet Fair Ella.*

This song was written following the murder of Pearl Bryan in 1896. See Pound, No. 43;
Richardson, pp. 30–31; Cox, No. 38; J.A.F.L., 20, pp. 264–265; 22, 370–372; 28, 168–169;
30, 344; 39, 116–118; 42, 301–303.

147.

Tacking of a Full Rigged Ship Off Shore

Sung by Mr. Ben Henneberry, Devil's Island.

1. THE weather leach our topsails shiver,
    Bowline strain and our lea shroud slack,
   Our braces taut and the least boom quivers,
   The waves was a-coming storm cloud black.

321

2. Open one point on the weather bow,
   The lighthouse tall on Fire Island Head,
   There's a shade of doubt on the captain's brow
   As the pilot he watches the heathing * lead.

3. I stand at the wheel with an eagle eye
   To see in the sky as ashore I gaze,
   When the muttered order, a " full and by,"
   Is suddenly changed to a " full for stays."

4. Now a ship bends lower before the breeze
   As a broadside fair till a blast she lays,
   And she swifter springs to the rising sea
   As the pilot calls, " Stand by for stays."

5. Then silence all ; it's each in his place
   With his gathered coils in his hardened hand,
   By tack and bowline, sheet and brace
   There the watchman patient stands.

6. As the light on Fire Island she draws near
   Her trumpet wings the pilot shout,
   From his post at the bowsprit, " Heel ! " I hear,
   The welcome cry of, " Ready about ! "

7. There's no time to spare.   It's touch and go
   As our captain growled, " Down helm !   Hard down ! "
   My weight on the whirling spoke I throw
   As heaven grown black with the storm clouds frown.

8. High o'er the night heads flies the spray
   As she met the shock of a plunging sea,
   And my shoulder stiff to the wheel I lay
   As I answer, " Aye, aye, sir, hard a lee."

9. The swivelling lip of a startled steed,
   Our ship lies fast to the eye of the wind,
   A dangerous shoal on the lee we seed,
   The headland white we will leave behind.

* Probably "heaving."

10. Our topsails shiver ; our jib collapsed,
    They belly and tug to the growling sleet,
    The mainsail flaps and the spanker slacks
    And thunders the order, " Tacks and sheet."

11. Amid the rattle of blocks and the tramp of the crew
    Hisses the rain of the rushing squall.
    Our sails are backed from clew to clew
    And now is the moment to mainsail haul.

12. Our heavy yards like baby's toys
    By fifty strong arms are swiftly swung.
    She held her way, and I looked with joy
    For the first white spray o'er the bulwarks flung.

13. " Let go and haul," is the last command,
    Our headsails filled to the blast once more,
    Astern to leeward lies the land
    With its breakers white on a shingly shore.

14. No matter for the reef, the rain or the squall,
    I can steady the helm to the open sea,
    The first mate clambers, " Delay there all,"
    And the captain's breath once more come free.

15. So now off shore let the good ship fly,
    It's little care I how hard it blows,
    In my forecastle bunk in my jacket dry
    Eight bells is struck and my watch is below.

No. 147. *Tacking of a Full-Rigged Ship Off Shore.*

Although not a folk-song, this is included for its interest in the way songs are made. Mr. Henneberry read this poem of Walter F. Mitchell, a native of Nantucket Island, and finding it brimful of nautical phrases he adapted a tune and has made it into a song. Eckstorm, pp. 216–219, has also found it sung by fishermen of the Atlantic coast, adopted almost 70 years after it was printed. He reports that it has been made famous by William Palmer, an old deep-water sailor " who could put it over in real deep-water fashion."

148

'Twas in the Town of Parsboro

Sung by Dr. Perry Cochrane, Wolfville, N.S. McLellan belonged to Spencer's Island, Dunkerson to Advocate.

1. 'Twas in the town of Parsboro one dark and stormy night
    When the gallant slugger Dunkerson got ready for a fight.
    He was full of rotten whiskey and was feeling very spry
    And he said he'd lick McLellan or he'd know the reason why.

2. He ran across McLellan about nine o'clock that night,
    He was feeling very ugly, and also very tight.
    He threw his coat upon the floor and bared his mighty arms
    And he challenged Baxter there to fight in Bill Mahoney's barn.

3. Said Baxter to old Dunkerson, " You are a mighty man,
    You're six feet tall and over but I'll lick you if I can.
    You're a drunkard and a coward, and you've been telling lies,"
    And with that he hit old Dunkerson a wallop between the eyes.

4. Old Dunkerson he staggered but he kept his balance well
   For nearly half a minute, then to the floor he fell.
   The gallant Baxter mounted him and handled him so rough
   That inside of fifteen seconds he yelled he'd had enough.

5. Then up from off the stable floor old Dunkerson arose.
   He went straight up to Mrs. Hiltz to wash his bloody nose.
   That mother used him kindly though he had no wealth ;
   She put him in a nice warm bed and nursed him back to health.

6. And now he quickly home did go, down o'er the hills and brooks,
   Down through the town of Port Greville until he came to Cook's ;
   His pockets they were empty and a tear was in his eye,
   He wanted some provisions or he would surely die.

7. Now when the Portland House was reached, and feeling dry and hot,
   For along the road and in the place he could not get a drop,
   Old Katy and old Sandy, it is secret though, of course,
   Leander and he did go into the house when the Scott Act was in force.

8. And now my friends come look at him after his drunken rabble,
   His eyes all blacked, his nose all skinned, his face looked like the devil,
   And now in peace we leave him just as quickly as we can,
   For he was so badly licked by a sober and perhaps a wiser man.

No. 148. *'Twas in the Town of Parsboro.*

The Scott Act was one of the first attempts at temperance in this country. Parsboro is a
town in Nova Scotia.

149.

Unicorn

When I was young and in my prime To the seas I had to go My

parents died when I was young The truth to you I'll show But of

all the times that ever I had Since the hour I was born Was

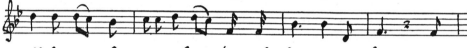

going home to the old country On board of the Uni-corn.

Sung by Mr. Ben Henneberry, Devil's Island.

1. WHEN I was young and in my prime
   To the seas I had to go.
   My parents died when I was young,
   The truth to you I'll show.
   But of all the times that ever I had
   Since the hour I was born,
   Was going home to the old country
   On board of the *Unicorn*.

2. I shipped on board of a steamer,
   Was bound for Liverpool,
   And many's the time I cursed the day
   That I was such a fool;
   It was watch and watch both night and day
   From our warm bunks we were torn,
   To go aloft and send down yards
   On board of the *Unicorn*.

3. A few days after we set sail
     A storm it did arise,
   The winds did blow from the east
     And dismal were the skies ;
   We furled our sails, sent down our yards
     And storm staysail bent on,
   And a dismal drilling we did get
     On board of the *Unicorn*.

4. As soon as daylight does appear
     All hands must then turn to,
   For well you know our mates and men
     Can show us what to do
   With a scrubbing brush and a holy stone
     As soon as the day did dawn,
   And that is the music they gave us
     On board of the *Unicorn*.

5. Now for to give the devil his due
     All things went very well,
   We had plenty provisions, fresh and salt,
     The truth to you I'll tell ;
   We had plenty provisions, fresh and salt,
     But the bread was hard as horn.
   It would do darn well for holy stone
     On board of the *Unicorn*.

6. So after her twelve days rain and fog
     To the land we did draw near,
   And when the fog it did hold up
     There we espied Cape Clare.
   Those twelve days it seemed longer to me
     Than voyage around Cape Horn,
   So you well may judge what music we had
     On board of the *Unicorn*.

7. At length we arrived at Liverpool
      And we laid there all the day,
    Until we got orders for Glasgow
      And straight did sail away ;
    The Glasgow girls they were very kind
      And did not treat me with scorn,
    So I packed up my duds and I bid farewell
      To the darned old *Unicorn*.

No. 149. " *Unicorn*."

150.

Sung by Mr. Ben Henneberry, Devil's Island, and Miss Aletha Edwards, Eastern Passage.

1. YOUNG CHARLOTTE lived on the mountain side
      On a very lonely spot,
    No dwelling was there for five miles round
      Except her father's cot.

328

2. On many's the cold and frosty night
      Young swains would gather there.
   Her father kept a social abode,
      And she was very fair.

3. He longed to see his daughter dressed
      As gay as a city belle.
   She was the only child he had
      And he dearly loved her well.

4. One New Year's Eve as the sun went down
      She looked with wistful eye
   Along the crowded window forth
      As the merry sleighs passed by.

5. Restless was her watchful eye
      Till his well-known voice she heard,
   Came bounding up by the cottage door
      Young Charles in a sleigh appeared.

6. " About fifteen miles from here there is
      A merry ball to-night,
   Although the air is piercing cold
      Our hearts are warm and light."

7. " O Charlotte dear," her mother cried,
      " Those blankets round you fold,
   For it is a bitter cold night without
      And you'd get your death of cold."

8. " O no, O no, mama," she cried,
      She laughed like a gypsy queen.
   " To drive in blankets muffled up
      I never could be seen.

9. " My silken cloak is warm enough,
      It's lined throughout you know,
   And besides I have a silken scarf
      To shield my face from the cold."

329

10. Her gloves and bonnet they being on
      She jumped into the sleigh,
And away they dashed by the mountain side,
      Far over the hills away.

11. " There's music in those merry bells
      As over the hills we go.
What a creaking noise the runners make
      As they glide the frozen snow !

12. " Such a night as this I ne'er did see,
      My reins I scarce can hold ! "
Young Charlotte spoke with a feeble voice,
      " I am exceeding cold."

13. He cracked the whip, he urged his steed
      Much faster than before,
Until another five miles round
      In silence they passed o'er.

14. " How fast, how fast the frozen snow
      Is gathering on my brow ! "
Young Charlotte spoke in a feeble voice,
      " I'm growing warmer now."

15. Over the hills and through the vales
      And out to the starlight,
Until the village inn was reached
      And the ballroom came in sight.

16. When the inn was reached young Charles jumped out
      And offered her his hand,
And there she stood * like a monument
      And had no power to stand.

17. He called her once, he called her twice,
      But she answered not a word.
He offered her his hand again
      But still she never stirred.

* sat (?)

18. And when he took her by the hand
It was as hard as stone.
He tore the mantle from off her face
And the bright light upon it shone.

19. And quickly to the light he held,
Her frozen corpse he bore.
Young Charlotte was a stiff, cold corpse
And word spoke never more.

20. And when he found that she was dead
Tears from his eyes did flow,
He said, " My young intended bride,
You never me more will go."

21. He took her to the sleigh again,
And with her he rode home ;
When he arrived at her father's door,
O how her parents moan !

22. They mourn for the loss of their daughter dear,
Young Charles wept o'er in gloom,
Until at length it broke his heart
And they * slumbered in her tomb.

* he (?)

No. 150. *Young Charlotte.*

The author of this song is given in various sources as William Lorenzo Carter, a blind poet of Benson or Bensontown, Vermont.   It is widely current in the United States and Canada.,

See also Gray, pp. 94–97 ; Pound, No. 44 ; Sandburg, pp. 58–59 ; Lomax, pp. 239–242 ; J.A.F.L., 22, pp. 367–370 ; J.A.F.L., 25, pp. 156–168, gives a complete story of author and song with 22 verses in text ; 39, 119–121 ; Dean, pp. 57–58 ; Cox, No. 80 ; Mackenzie, No. 60.

The writing of this song is supposed to have taken place before 1833.

INDEX OF TITLES

The references are to pages

A CATALOG OF SELECTED
DOVER BOOKS
IN ALL FIELDS OF INTEREST

A CATALOG OF SELECTED DOVER
BOOKS IN ALL FIELDS OF INTEREST

DRAWINGS OF REMBRANDT, edited by Seymour Slive. Updated Lippmann, Hofstede de Groot edition, with definitive scholarly apparatus. All portraits, biblical sketches, landscapes, nudes. Oriental figures, classical studies, together with selection of work by followers. 550 illustrations. Total of 630pp. 9⅛ × 12¼.
21485-0, 21486-9 Pa., Two-vol. set $29.90

GHOST AND HORROR STORIES OF AMBROSE BIERCE, Ambrose Bierce. 24 tales vividly imagined, strangely prophetic, and decades ahead of their time in technical skill: "The Damned Thing," "An Inhabitant of Carcosa," "The Eyes of the Panther," "Moxon's Master," and 20 more. 199pp. 5⅜ × 8½. 20767-6 Pa. $4.95

ETHICAL WRITINGS OF MAIMONIDES, Maimonides. Most significant ethical works of great medieval sage, newly translated for utmost precision, readability. Laws Concerning Character Traits, Eight Chapters, more. 192pp. 5⅜ × 8½.
24522-5 Pa. $4.50

THE EXPLORATION OF THE COLORADO RIVER AND ITS CANYONS, J. W. Powell. Full text of Powell's 1,000-mile expedition down the fabled Colorado in 1869. Superb account of terrain, geology, vegetation, Indians, famine, mutiny, treacherous rapids, mighty canyons, during exploration of last unknown part of continental U.S. 400pp. 5⅜ × 8½. 20094-9 Pa. $7.95

HISTORY OF PHILOSOPHY, Julián Marías. Clearest one-volume history on the market. Every major philosopher and dozens of others, to Existentialism and later. 505pp. 5⅜ × 8½.
21739-6 Pa. $9.95

ALL ABOUT LIGHTNING, Martin A. Uman. Highly readable non-technical survey of nature and causes of lightning, thunderstorms, ball lightning, St. Elmo's Fire, much more. Illustrated. 192pp. 5⅜ × 8½. 25237-X Pa. $5.95

SAILING ALONE AROUND THE WORLD, Captain Joshua Slocum. First man to sail around the world, alone, in small boat. One of great feats of seamanship told in delightful manner. 67 illustrations. 294pp. 5⅜ × 8½. 20326-3 Pa. $4.95

LETTERS AND NOTES ON THE MANNERS, CUSTOMS AND CONDITIONS OF THE NORTH AMERICAN INDIANS, George Catlin. Classic account of life among Plains Indians: ceremonies, hunt, warfare, etc. 312 plates. 572pp. of text. 6⅛ × 9¼. 22118-0, 22119-9, Pa. Two-vol. set $17.90

ALASKA: The Harriman Expedition, 1899, John Burroughs, John Muir, et al. Informative, engrossing accounts of two-month, 9,000-mile expedition. Native peoples, wildlife, forests, geography, salmon industry, glaciers, more. Profusely illustrated. 240 black-and-white line drawings. 124 black-and-white photographs. 3 maps. Index. 576pp. 5⅜ × 8½. 25109-8 Pa. $11.95

THE BOOK OF BEASTS: Being a Translation from a Latin Bestiary of the Twelfth Century, T. H. White. Wonderful catalog real and fanciful beasts: manticore, griffin, phoenix, amphivius, jaculus, many more. White's witty erudite commentary on scientific, historical aspects. Fascinating glimpse of medieval mind. Illustrated. 296pp. 5⅜ × 8¼. (Available in U.S. only) 24609-4 Pa. $6.95

FRANK LLOYD WRIGHT: ARCHITECTURE AND NATURE With 160 Illustrations, Donald Hoffmann. Profusely illustrated study of influence of nature—especially prairie—on Wright's designs for Fallingwater, Robie House, Guggenheim Museum, other masterpieces. 96pp. 9¼ × 10¾. 25098-9 Pa. $8.95

FRANK LLOYD WRIGHT'S FALLINGWATER, Donald Hoffmann. Wright's famous waterfall house: planning and construction of organic idea. History of site, owners, Wright's personal involvement. Photographs of various stages of building. Preface by Edgar Kaufmann, Jr. 100 illustrations. 112pp. 9¼ × 10.
23671-4 Pa. $8.95

YEARS WITH FRANK LLOYD WRIGHT: Apprentice to Genius, Edgar Tafel. Insightful memoir by a former apprentice presents a revealing portrait of Wright the man, the inspired teacher, the greatest American architect. 372 black-and-white illustrations. Preface. Index. vi + 228pp. 8¼ × 11. 24801-1 Pa. $10.95

THE STORY OF KING ARTHUR AND HIS KNIGHTS, Howard Pyle. Enchanting version of King Arthur fable has delighted generations with imaginative narratives of exciting adventures and unforgettable illustrations by the author. 41 illustrations. xviii + 313pp. 6⅛ × 9¼. 21445-1 Pa. $6.95

THE GODS OF THE EGYPTIANS, E. A. Wallis Budge. Thorough coverage of numerous gods of ancient Egypt by foremost Egyptologist. Information on evolution of cults, rites and gods; the cult of Osiris; the Book of the Dead and its rites; the sacred animals and birds; Heaven and Hell; and more. 956pp. 6⅛ × 9¼.
22055-9, 22056-7 Pa., Two-vol. set $21.90

A THEOLOGICO-POLITICAL TREATISE, Benedict Spinoza. Also contains unfinished *Political Treatise*. Great classic on religious liberty, theory of government on common consent. R. Elwes translation. Total of 421pp. 5⅜ × 8½.
20249-6 Pa. $7.95

INCIDENTS OF TRAVEL IN CENTRAL AMERICA, CHIAPAS, AND YUCATAN, John L. Stephens. Almost single-handed discovery of Maya culture; exploration of ruined cities, monuments, temples; customs of Indians. 115 drawings. 892pp. 5⅜ × 8½. 22404-X, 22405-8 Pa., Two-vol. set $15.90

LOS CAPRICHOS, Francisco Goya. 80 plates of wild, grotesque monsters and caricatures. Prado manuscript included. 183pp. 6⅜ × 9⅜. 22384-1 Pa. $5.95

AUTOBIOGRAPHY: The Story of My Experiments with Truth, Mohandas K. Gandhi. Not hagiography, but Gandhi in his own words. Boyhood, legal studies, purification, the growth of the Satyagraha (nonviolent protest) movement. Critical, inspiring work of the man who freed India. 480pp. 5⅜ × 8½. (Available in U.S. only)
24593-4 Pa. $6.95

ILLUSTRATED DICTIONARY OF HISTORIC ARCHITECTURE, edited by Cyril M. Harris. Extraordinary compendium of clear, concise definitions for over 5,000 important architectural terms complemented by over 2,000 line drawings. Covers full spectrum of architecture from ancient ruins to 20th-century Modernism. Preface. 592pp. 7½ × 9⅝. 24444-X Pa. $15.95

THE NIGHT BEFORE CHRISTMAS, Clement Moore. Full text, and woodcuts from original 1848 book. Also critical, historical material. 19 illustrations. 40pp. 4⅝ × 6. 22797-9 Pa. $2.50

THE LESSON OF JAPANESE ARCHITECTURE: 165 Photographs, Jiro Harada. Memorable gallery of 165 photographs taken in the 1930's of exquisite Japanese homes of the well-to-do and historic buildings. 13 line diagrams. 192pp. 8⅜ × 11¼. 24778-3 Pa. $10.95

THE AUTOBIOGRAPHY OF CHARLES DARWIN AND SELECTED LETTERS, edited by Francis Darwin. The fascinating life of eccentric genius composed of an intimate memoir by Darwin (intended for his children); commentary by his son, Francis; hundreds of fragments from notebooks, journals, papers; and letters to and from Lyell, Hooker, Huxley, Wallace and Henslow. xi + 365pp. 5⅜ × 8. 20479-0 Pa. $6.95

WONDERS OF THE SKY: Observing Rainbows, Comets, Eclipses, the Stars and Other Phenomena, Fred Schaaf. Charming, easy-to-read poetic guide to all manner of celestial events visible to the naked eye. Mock suns, glories, Belt of Venus, more. Illustrated. 299pp. 5¼ × 8¼. 24402-4 Pa. $7.95

BURNHAM'S CELESTIAL HANDBOOK, Robert Burnham, Jr. Thorough guide to the stars beyond our solar system. Exhaustive treatment. Alphabetical by constellation: Andromeda to Cetus in Vol. 1; Chamaeleon to Orion in Vol. 2; and Pavo to Vulpecula in Vol. 3. Hundreds of illustrations. Index in Vol. 3. 2,000pp. 6⅛ × 9¼. 23567-X, 23568-8, 23673-0 Pa., Three-vol. set $41.85

STAR NAMES: Their Lore and Meaning, Richard Hinckley Allen. Fascinating history of names various cultures have given to constellations and literary and folkloristic uses that have been made of stars. Indexes to subjects. Arabic and Greek names. Biblical references. Bibliography. 563pp. 5⅜ × 8½. 21079-0 Pa. $8.95

THIRTY YEARS THAT SHOOK PHYSICS: The Story of Quantum Theory, George Gamow. Lucid, accessible introduction to influential theory of energy and matter. Careful explanations of Dirac's anti-particles, Bohr's model of the atom, much more. 12 plates. Numerous drawings. 240pp. 5⅜ × 8½. 24895-X Pa. $5.95

CHINESE DOMESTIC FURNITURE IN PHOTOGRAPHS AND MEASURED DRAWINGS, Gustav Ecke. A rare volume, now affordably priced for antique collectors, furniture buffs and art historians. Detailed review of styles ranging from early Shang to late Ming. Unabridged republication. 161 black-and-white drawings, photos. Total of 224pp. 8⅜ × 11¼. (Available in U.S. only) 25171-3 Pa. $13.95

VINCENT VAN GOGH: A Biography, Julius Meier-Graefe. Dynamic, penetrating study of artist's life, relationship with brother, Theo, painting techniques, travels, more. Readable, engrossing. 160pp. 5⅜ × 8½. (Available in U.S. only) 25253-1 Pa. $4.95

HOW TO WRITE, Gertrude Stein. Gertrude Stein claimed anyone could understand her unconventional writing—here are clues to help. Fascinating improvisations, language experiments, explanations illuminate Stein's craft and the art of writing. Total of 414pp. 4⅜ × 6⅜. 23144-5 Pa. $6.95

ADVENTURES AT SEA IN THE GREAT AGE OF SAIL: Five Firsthand Narratives, edited by Elliot Snow. Rare true accounts of exploration, whaling, shipwreck, fierce natives, trade, shipboard life, more. 33 illustrations. Introduction. 353pp. 5⅜ × 8½. 25177-2 Pa. $8.95

THE HERBAL OR GENERAL HISTORY OF PLANTS, John Gerard. Classic descriptions of about 2,850 plants—with over 2,700 illustrations—includes Latin and English names, physical descriptions, varieties, time and place of growth, more. 2,706 illustrations. xlv + 1,678pp. 8½ × 12¼. 23147-X Cloth. $75.00

DOROTHY AND THE WIZARD IN OZ, L. Frank Baum. Dorothy and the Wizard visit the center of the Earth, where people are vegetables, glass houses grow and Oz characters reappear. Classic sequel to *Wizard of Oz*. 256pp. 5⅜ × 8.
24714-7 Pa. $5.95

SONGS OF EXPERIENCE: Facsimile Reproduction with 26 Plates in Full Color, William Blake. This facsimile of Blake's original "Illuminated Book" reproduces 26 full-color plates from a rare 1826 edition. Includes "The Tyger," "London," "Holy Thursday," and other immortal poems. 26 color plates. Printed text of poems. 48pp. 5¼ × 7. 24636-1 Pa. $3.95

SONGS OF INNOCENCE, William Blake. The first and most popular of Blake's famous "Illuminated Books," in a facsimile edition reproducing all 31 brightly colored plates. Additional printed text of each poem. 64pp. 5¼ × 7.
22764-2 Pa. $3.95

PRECIOUS STONES, Max Bauer. Classic, thorough study of diamonds, rubies, emeralds, garnets, etc.: physical character, occurrence, properties, use, similar topics. 20 plates, 8 in color. 94 figures. 659pp. 6⅛ × 9¼.
21910-0, 21911-9 Pa., Two-vol. set $15.90

ENCYCLOPEDIA OF VICTORIAN NEEDLEWORK, S. F. A. Caulfeild and Blanche Saward. Full, precise descriptions of stitches, techniques for dozens of needlecrafts—most exhaustive reference of its kind. Over 800 figures. Total of 679pp. 8⅛ × 11. Two volumes. Vol. 1 22800-2 Pa. $11.95
Vol. 2 22801-0 Pa. $11.95

THE MARVELOUS LAND OF OZ, L. Frank Baum. Second Oz book, the Scarecrow and Tin Woodman are back with hero named Tip, Oz magic. 136 illustrations. 287pp. 5⅜ × 8½. 20692-0 Pa. $5.95

WILD FOWL DECOYS, Joel Barber. Basic book on the subject, by foremost authority and collector. Reveals history of decoy making and rigging, place in American culture, different kinds of decoys, how to make them, and how to use them. 140 plates. 156pp. 7⅞ × 10¾. 20011-6 Pa. $8.95

HISTORY OF LACE, Mrs. Bury Palliser. Definitive, profusely illustrated chronicle of lace from earliest times to late 19th century. Laces of Italy, Greece, England, France, Belgium, etc. Landmark of needlework scholarship. 266 illustrations. 672pp. 6⅛ × 9¼. 24742-2 Pa. $14.95

ILLUSTRATED GUIDE TO SHAKER FURNITURE, Robert Meader. All furniture and appurtenances, with much on unknown local styles. 235 photos. 146pp. 9 × 12. 22819-3 Pa. $8.95

WHALE SHIPS AND WHALING: A Pictorial Survey, George Francis Dow. Over 200 vintage engravings, drawings, photographs of barks, brigs, cutters, other vessels. Also harpoons, lances, whaling guns, many other artifacts. Comprehensive text by foremost authority. 207 black-and-white illustrations. 288pp. 6 × 9. 24808-9 Pa. $9.95

THE BERTRAMS, Anthony Trollope. Powerful portrayal of blind self-will and thwarted ambition includes one of Trollope's most heartrending love stories. 497pp. 5⅜ × 8½. 25119-5 Pa. $9.95

ADVENTURES WITH A HAND LENS, Richard Headstrom. Clearly written guide to observing and studying flowers and grasses, fish scales, moth and insect wings, egg cases, buds, feathers, seeds, leaf scars, moss, molds, ferns, common crystals, etc.—all with an ordinary, inexpensive magnifying glass. 209 exact line drawings aid in your discoveries. 220pp. 5⅜ × 8½. 23330-8 Pa. $4.95

RODIN ON ART AND ARTISTS, Auguste Rodin. Great sculptor's candid, wide-ranging comments on meaning of art; great artists; relation of sculpture to poetry, painting, music; philosophy of life, more. 76 superb black-and-white illustrations of Rodin's sculpture, drawings and prints. 119pp. 8⅜ × 11¼. 24487-3 Pa. $7.95

FIFTY CLASSIC FRENCH FILMS, 1912–1982: A Pictorial Record, Anthony Slide. Memorable stills from Grand Illusion, Beauty and the Beast, Hiroshima, Mon Amour, many more. Credits, plot synopses, reviews, etc. 160pp. 8¼ × 11. 25256-6 Pa. $11.95

THE PRINCIPLES OF PSYCHOLOGY, William James. Famous long course complete, unabridged. Stream of thought, time perception, memory, experimental methods; great work decades ahead of its time. 94 figures. 1,391pp. 5⅜ × 8½. 20381-6, 20382-4 Pa., Two-vol. set $23.90

BODIES IN A BOOKSHOP, R. T. Campbell. Challenging mystery of blackmail and murder with ingenious plot and superbly drawn characters. In the best tradition of British suspense fiction. 192pp. 5⅜ × 8½. 24720-1 Pa. $4.95

CALLAS: PORTRAIT OF A PRIMA DONNA, George Jellinek. Renowned commentator on the musical scene chronicles incredible career and life of the most controversial, fascinating, influential operatic personality of our time. 64 black-and-white photographs. 416pp. 5⅜ × 8¼. 25047-4 Pa. $8.95

GEOMETRY, RELATIVITY AND THE FOURTH DIMENSION, Rudolph Rucker. Exposition of fourth dimension, concepts of relativity as Flatland characters continue adventures. Popular, easily followed yet accurate, profound. 141 illustrations. 133pp. 5⅜ × 8½. 23400-2 Pa. $4.95

HOUSEHOLD STORIES BY THE BROTHERS GRIMM, with pictures by Walter Crane. 53 classic stories—Rumpelstiltskin, Rapunzel, Hansel and Gretel, the Fisherman and his Wife, Snow White, Tom Thumb, Sleeping Beauty, Cinderella, and so much more—lavishly illustrated with original 19th century drawings. 114 illustrations. x + 269pp. 5⅜ × 8½. 21080-4 Pa. $4.95

SUNDIALS, Albert Waugh. Far and away the best, most thorough coverage of ideas, mathematics concerned, types, construction, adjusting anywhere. Over 100 illustrations. 230pp. 5⅜ × 8½. 22947-5 Pa. $5.95

PICTURE HISTORY OF THE NORMANDIE: With 190 Illustrations, Frank O. Braynard. Full story of legendary French ocean liner: Art Deco interiors, design innovations, furnishings, celebrities, maiden voyage, tragic fire, much more. Extensive text. 144pp. 8⅞ × 11¾. 25257-4 Pa. $10.95

THE FIRST AMERICAN COOKBOOK: A Facsimile of "American Cookery," 1796, Amelia Simmons. Facsimile of the first American-written cookbook published in the United States contains authentic recipes for colonial favorites—pumpkin pudding, winter squash pudding, spruce beer, Indian slapjacks, and more. Introductory Essay and Glossary of colonial cooking terms. 80pp. 5⅜ × 8½. 24710-4 Pa. $3.50

101 PUZZLES IN THOUGHT AND LOGIC, C. R. Wylie, Jr. Solve murders and robberies, find out which fishermen are liars, how a blind man could possibly identify a color—purely by your own reasoning! 107pp. 5⅜ × 8½. 20367-0 Pa. $2.50

ANCIENT EGYPTIAN MYTHS AND LEGENDS, Lewis Spence. Examines animism, totemism, fetishism, creation myths, deities, alchemy, art and magic, other topics. Over 50 illustrations. 432pp. 5⅜ × 8½. 26525-0 Pa. $8.95

ANTHROPOLOGY AND MODERN LIFE, Franz Boas. Great anthropologist's classic treatise on race and culture. Introduction by Ruth Bunzel. Only inexpensive paperback edition. 255pp. 5⅜ × 8½. 25245-0 Pa. $6.95

THE TALE OF PETER RABBIT, Beatrix Potter. The inimitable Peter's terrifying adventure in Mr. McGregor's garden, with all 27 wonderful, full-color Potter illustrations. 55pp. 4¼ × 5½. (Available in U.S. only) 22827-4 Pa. $1.75

THREE PROPHETIC SCIENCE FICTION NOVELS, H. G. Wells. *When the Sleeper Wakes, A Story of the Days to Come* and *The Time Machine* (full version). 335pp. 5⅜ × 8½. (Available in U.S. only) 20605-X Pa. $6.95

APICIUS COOKERY AND DINING IN IMPERIAL ROME, edited and translated by Joseph Dommers Vehling. Oldest known cookbook in existence offers readers a clear picture of what foods Romans ate, how they prepared them, etc. 49 illustrations. 301pp. 6⅛ × 9¼. 23563-7 Pa. $7.95

SHAKESPEARE LEXICON AND QUOTATION DICTIONARY, Alexander Schmidt. Full definitions, locations, shades of meaning of every word in plays and poems. More than 50,000 exact quotations. 1,485pp. 6½ × 9¼. 22726-X, 22727-8 Pa., Two-vol. set $31.90

THE WORLD'S GREAT SPEECHES, edited by Lewis Copeland and Lawrence W. Lamm. Vast collection of 278 speeches from Greeks to 1970. Powerful and effective models; unique look at history. 842pp. 5⅜ × 8½. 20468-5 Pa. $12.95

THE BLUE FAIRY BOOK, Andrew Lang. The first, most famous collection, with many familiar tales: Little Red Riding Hood, Aladdin and the Wonderful Lamp, Puss in Boots, Sleeping Beauty, Hansel and Gretel, Rumpelstiltskin; 37 in all. 138 illustrations. 390pp. 5⅜ × 8½. 21437-0 Pa. $6.95

THE STORY OF THE CHAMPIONS OF THE ROUND TABLE, Howard Pyle. Sir Launcelot, Sir Tristram and Sir Percival in spirited adventures of love and triumph retold in Pyle's inimitable style. 50 drawings, 31 full-page. xviii + 329pp. 6½ × 9¼. 21883-X Pa. $7.95

THE MYTHS OF THE NORTH AMERICAN INDIANS, Lewis Spence. Myths and legends of the Algonquins, Iroquois, Pawnees and Sioux with comprehensive historical and ethnological commentary. 36 illustrations. 5⅜ × 8½.
25967-6 Pa. $8.95

GREAT DINOSAUR HUNTERS AND THEIR DISCOVERIES, Edwin H. Colbert. Fascinating, lavishly illustrated chronicle of dinosaur research, 1820's to 1960. Achievements of Cope, Marsh, Brown, Buckland, Mantell, Huxley, many others. 384pp. 5¼ × 8¼. 24701-5 Pa. $7.95

THE TASTEMAKERS, Russell Lynes. Informal, illustrated social history of American taste 1850's–1950's. First popularized categories Highbrow, Lowbrow, Middlebrow. 129 illustrations. New (1979) afterword. 384pp. 6 × 9.
23993-4 Pa. $8.95

DOUBLE CROSS PURPOSES, Ronald A. Knox. A treasure hunt in the Scottish Highlands, an old map, unidentified corpse, surprise discoveries keep reader guessing in this cleverly intricate tale of financial skullduggery. 2 black-and-white maps. 320pp. 5⅜ × 8½. (Available in U.S. only) 25032-6 Pa. $6.95

AUTHENTIC VICTORIAN DECORATION AND ORNAMENTATION IN FULL COLOR: 46 Plates from "Studies in Design," Christopher Dresser. Superb full-color lithographs reproduced from rare original portfolio of a major Victorian designer. 48pp. 9¼ × 12¼. 25083-0 Pa. $7.95

PRIMITIVE ART, Franz Boas. Remains the best text ever prepared on subject, thoroughly discussing Indian, African, Asian, Australian, and, especially, Northern American primitive art. Over 950 illustrations show ceramics, masks, totem poles, weapons, textiles, paintings, much more. 376pp. 5⅜ × 8. 20025-6 Pa. $7.95

SIDELIGHTS ON RELATIVITY, Albert Einstein. Unabridged republication of two lectures delivered by the great physicist in 1920–21. *Ether and Relativity* and *Geometry and Experience*. Elegant ideas in non-mathematical form, accessible to intelligent layman. vi + 56pp. 5⅜ × 8½. 24511-X Pa. $2.95

THE WIT AND HUMOR OF OSCAR WILDE, edited by Alvin Redman. More than 1,000 ripostes, paradoxes, wisecracks: Work is the curse of the drinking classes, I can resist everything except temptation, etc. 258pp. 5⅜ × 8½. 20602-5 Pa. $4.95

ADVENTURES WITH A MICROSCOPE, Richard Headstrom. 59 adventures with clothing fibers, protozoa, ferns and lichens, roots and leaves, much more. 142 illustrations. 232pp. 5⅜ × 8½. 23471-1 Pa. $3.95

PLANTS OF THE BIBLE, Harold N. Moldenke and Alma L. Moldenke. Standard reference to all 230 plants mentioned in Scriptures. Latin name, biblical reference, uses, modern identity, much more. Unsurpassed encyclopedic resource for scholars, botanists, nature lovers, students of Bible. Bibliography. Indexes. 123 black-and-white illustrations. 384pp. 6 × 9. 25069-5 Pa. $8.95

FAMOUS AMERICAN WOMEN: A Biographical Dictionary from Colonial Times to the Present, Robert McHenry, ed. From Pocahontas to Rosa Parks, 1,035 distinguished American women documented in separate biographical entries. Accurate, up-to-date data, numerous categories, spans 400 years. Indices. 493pp. 6½ × 9¼. 24523-3 Pa. $10.95

THE FABULOUS INTERIORS OF THE GREAT OCEAN LINERS IN HISTORIC PHOTOGRAPHS, William H. Miller, Jr. Some 200 superb photographs capture exquisite interiors of world's great "floating palaces"—1890's to 1980's: *Titanic, Ile de France, Queen Elizabeth, United States, Europa,* more. Approx. 200 black-and-white photographs. Captions. Text. Introduction. 160pp. 8⅞ × 11¾. 24756-2 Pa. $9.95

THE GREAT LUXURY LINERS, 1927–1954: A Photographic Record, William H. Miller, Jr. Nostalgic tribute to heyday of ocean liners. 186 photos of Ile de France, Normandie, Leviathan, Queen Elizabeth, United States, many others. Interior and exterior views. Introduction. Captions. 160pp. 9 × 12. 24056-8 Pa. $10.95

A NATURAL HISTORY OF THE DUCKS, John Charles Phillips. Great landmark of ornithology offers complete detailed coverage of nearly 200 species and subspecies of ducks: gadwall, sheldrake, merganser, pintail, many more. 74 full-color plates, 102 black-and-white. Bibliography. Total of 1,920pp. 8⅝ × 11¼. 25141-1, 25142-X Cloth. Two-vol. set $100.00

THE SEAWEED HANDBOOK: An Illustrated Guide to Seaweeds from North Carolina to Canada, Thomas F. Lee. Concise reference covers 78 species. Scientific and common names, habitat, distribution, more. Finding keys for easy identification. 224pp. 5⅜ × 8½. 25215-9 Pa. $6.95

THE TEN BOOKS OF ARCHITECTURE: The 1755 Leoni Edition, Leon Battista Alberti. Rare classic helped introduce the glories of ancient architecture to the Renaissance. 68 black-and-white plates. 336pp. 8⅜ × 11¼. 25239-6 Pa. $14.95

MISS MACKENZIE, Anthony Trollope. Minor masterpieces by Victorian master unmasks many truths about life in 19th-century England. First inexpensive edition in years. 392pp. 5⅜ × 8½. 25201-9 Pa. $8.95

THE RIME OF THE ANCIENT MARINER, Gustave Doré, Samuel Taylor Coleridge. Dramatic engravings considered by many to be his greatest work. The terrifying space of the open sea, the storms and whirlpools of an unknown ocean, the ice of Antarctica, more—all rendered in a powerful, chilling manner. Full text. 38 plates. 77pp. 9¼ × 12. 22305-1 Pa. $4.95

THE EXPEDITIONS OF ZEBULON MONTGOMERY PIKE, Zebulon Montgomery Pike. Fascinating first-hand accounts (1805–6) of exploration of Mississippi River, Indian wars, capture by Spanish dragoons, much more. 1,088pp. 5⅜ × 8½. 25254-X, 25255-8 Pa. Two-vol. set $25.90

A CONCISE HISTORY OF PHOTOGRAPHY: Third Revised Edition, Helmut Gernsheim. Best one-volume history—camera obscura, photochemistry, daguerreotypes, evolution of cameras, film, more. Also artistic aspects—landscape, portraits, fine art, etc. 281 black-and-white photographs. 26 in color. 176pp. 8⅜ × 11¼. 25128-4 Pa. $13.95

THE DORÉ BIBLE ILLUSTRATIONS, Gustave Doré. 241 detailed plates from the Bible: the Creation scenes, Adam and Eve, Flood, Babylon, battle sequences, life of Jesus, etc. Each plate is accompanied by the verses from the King James version of the Bible. 241pp. 9 × 12. 23004-X Pa. $9.95

WANDERINGS IN WEST AFRICA, Richard F. Burton. Great Victorian scholar/adventurer's invaluable descriptions of African tribal rituals, fetishism, culture, art, much more. Fascinating 19th-century account. 624pp. 5⅜ × 8½. 26890-X Pa. $12.95

FLATLAND, E. A. Abbott. Intriguing and enormously popular science-fiction classic explores the complexities of trying to survive as a two-dimensional being in a three-dimensional world. Amusingly illustrated by the author. 16 illustrations. 103pp. 5⅜ × 8½. 20001-9 Pa. $2.50

THE HISTORY OF THE LEWIS AND CLARK EXPEDITION, Meriwether Lewis and William Clark, edited by Elliott Coues. Classic edition of Lewis and Clark's day-by-day journals that later became the basis for U.S. claims to Oregon and the West. Accurate and invaluable geographical, botanical, biological, meteorological and anthropological material. Total of 1,508pp. 5⅜ × 8½.
21268-8, 21269-6, 21270-X Pa. Three-vol. set $26.85

LANGUAGE, TRUTH AND LOGIC, Alfred J. Ayer. Famous, clear introduction to Vienna, Cambridge schools of Logical Positivism. Role of philosophy, elimination of metaphysics, nature of analysis, etc. 160pp. 5⅜ × 8½. (Available in U.S. and Canada only) 20010-8 Pa. $3.95

MATHEMATICS FOR THE NONMATHEMATICIAN, Morris Kline. Detailed, college-level treatment of mathematics in cultural and historical context, with numerous exercises. For liberal arts students. Preface. Recommended Reading Lists. Tables. Index. Numerous black-and-white figures. xvi + 641pp. 5⅜ × 8½.
24823-2 Pa. $11.95

HANDBOOK OF PICTORIAL SYMBOLS, Rudolph Modley. 3,250 signs and symbols, many systems in full; official or heavy commercial use. Arranged by subject. Most in Pictorial Archive series. 143pp. 8⅛ × 11. 23357-X Pa. $6.95

INCIDENTS OF TRAVEL IN YUCATAN, John L. Stephens. Classic (1843) exploration of jungles of Yucatan, looking for evidences of Maya civilization. Travel adventures, Mexican and Indian culture, etc. Total of 669pp. 5⅜ × 8½.
20926-1, 20927-X Pa., Two-vol. set $11.90

DEGAS: An Intimate Portrait, Ambroise Vollard. Charming, anecdotal memoir by famous art dealer of one of the greatest 19th-century French painters. 14 black-and-white illustrations. Introduction by Harold L. Van Doren. 96pp. 5⅜ × 8½.
25131-4 Pa. $4.95

PERSONAL NARRATIVE OF A PILGRIMAGE TO ALMANDINAH AND MECCAH, Richard Burton. Great travel classic by remarkably colorful personality. Burton, disguised as a Moroccan, visited sacred shrines of Islam, narrowly escaping death. 47 illustrations. 959pp. 5⅜ × 8½.   21217-3, 21218-1 Pa., Two-vol. set $19.90

PHRASE AND WORD ORIGINS, A. H. Holt. Entertaining, reliable, modern study of more than 1,200 colorful words, phrases, origins and histories. Much unexpected information. 254pp. 5⅜ × 8½.   20758-7 Pa. $5.95

THE RED THUMB MARK, R. Austin Freeman. In this first Dr. Thorndyke case, the great scientific detective draws fascinating conclusions from the nature of a single fingerprint. Exciting story, authentic science. 320pp. 5⅜ × 8½. (Available in U.S. only)   25210-8 Pa. $6.95

AN EGYPTIAN HIEROGLYPHIC DICTIONARY, E. A. Wallis Budge. Monumental work containing about 25,000 words or terms that occur in texts ranging from 3000 B.C. to 600 A.D. Each entry consists of a transliteration of the word, the word in hieroglyphs, and the meaning in English. 1,314pp. 6⅜ × 10.
23615-3, 23616-1 Pa., Two-vol. set $35.90

THE COMPLEAT STRATEGYST: Being a Primer on the Theory of Games of Strategy, J. D. Williams. Highly entertaining classic describes, with many illustrated examples, how to select best strategies in conflict situations. Prefaces. Appendices. xvi + 268pp. 5⅜ × 8½.   25101-2 Pa. $6.95

THE ROAD TO OZ, L. Frank Baum. Dorothy meets the Shaggy Man, little Button-Bright and the Rainbow's beautiful daughter in this delightful trip to the magical Land of Oz. 272pp. 5⅜ × 8.   25208-6 Pa. $5.95

POINT AND LINE TO PLANE, Wassily Kandinsky. Seminal exposition of role of point, line, other elements in non-objective painting. Essential to understanding 20th-century art. 127 illustrations. 192pp. 6½ × 9¼.   23808-3 Pa. $5.95

LADY ANNA, Anthony Trollope. Moving chronicle of Countess Lovel's bitter struggle to win for herself and daughter Anna their rightful rank and fortune—perhaps at cost of sanity itself. 384pp. 5⅜ × 8½.   24669-8 Pa. $8.95

EGYPTIAN MAGIC, E. A. Wallis Budge. Sums up all that is known about magic in Ancient Egypt: the role of magic in controlling the gods, powerful amulets that warded off evil spirits, scarabs of immortality, use of wax images, formulas and spells, the secret name, much more. 253pp. 5⅜ × 8½.   22681-6 Pa. $4.50

THE DANCE OF SIVA, Ananda Coomaraswamy. Preeminent authority unfolds the vast metaphysic of India: the revelation of her art, conception of the universe, social organization, etc. 27 reproductions of art masterpieces. 192pp. 5⅜ × 8½.
24817-8 Pa. $5.95

CHRISTMAS CUSTOMS AND TRADITIONS, Clement A. Miles. Origin, evolution, significance of religious, secular practices. Caroling, gifts, yule logs, much more. Full, scholarly yet fascinating; non-sectarian. 400pp. 5⅜ × 8½.
23354-5 Pa. $6.95

THE HUMAN FIGURE IN MOTION, Eadweard Muybridge. More than 4,500 stopped-action photos, in action series, showing undraped men, women, children jumping, lying down, throwing, sitting, wrestling, carrying, etc. 390pp. 7⅞ × 10⅝.
20204-6 Cloth. $24.95

THE MAN WHO WAS THURSDAY, Gilbert Keith Chesterton. Witty, fast-paced novel about a club of anarchists in turn-of-the-century London. Brilliant social, religious, philosophical speculations. 128pp. 5⅜ × 8½. 25121-7 Pa. $3.95

A CEZANNE SKETCHBOOK: Figures, Portraits, Landscapes and Still Lifes, Paul Cezanne. Great artist experiments with tonal effects, light, mass, other qualities in over 100 drawings. A revealing view of developing master painter, precursor of Cubism. 102 black-and-white illustrations. 144pp. 8¾ × 6⅜. 24790-2 Pa. $6.95

AN ENCYCLOPEDIA OF BATTLES: Accounts of Over 1,560 Battles from 1479 B.C. to the Present, David Eggenberger. Presents essential details of every major battle in recorded history, from the first battle of Megiddo in 1479 B.C. to Grenada in 1984. List of Battle Maps. New Appendix covering the years 1967–1984. Index. 99 illustrations. 544pp. 6½ × 9¼. 24913-1 Pa. $14.95

AN ETYMOLOGICAL DICTIONARY OF MODERN ENGLISH, Ernest Weekley. Richest, fullest work, by foremost British lexicographer. Detailed word histories. Inexhaustible. Total of 856pp. 6½ × 9¼.
21873-2, 21874-0 Pa., Two-vol. set $19.90

WEBSTER'S AMERICAN MILITARY BIOGRAPHIES, edited by Robert McHenry. Over 1,000 figures who shaped 3 centuries of American military history. Detailed biographies of Nathan Hale, Douglas MacArthur, Mary Hallaren, others. Chronologies of engagements, more. Introduction. Addenda. 1,033 entries in alphabetical order. xi + 548pp. 6½ × 9¼. (Available in U.S. only)
24758-9 Pa. $13.95

LIFE IN ANCIENT EGYPT, Adolf Erman. Detailed older account, with much not in more recent books: domestic life, religion, magic, medicine, commerce, and whatever else needed for complete picture. Many illustrations. 597pp. 5⅜ × 8½.
22632-8 Pa. $8.95

HISTORIC COSTUME IN PICTURES, Braun & Schneider. Over 1,450 costumed figures shown, covering a wide variety of peoples: kings, emperors, nobles, priests, servants, soldiers, scholars, townsfolk, peasants, merchants, courtiers, cavaliers, and more. 256pp. 8⅜ × 11¼. 23150-X Pa. $9.95

THE NOTEBOOKS OF LEONARDO DA VINCI, edited by J. P. Richter. Extracts from manuscripts reveal great genius; on painting, sculpture, anatomy, sciences, geography, etc. Both Italian and English. 186 ms. pages reproduced, plus 500 additional drawings, including studies for *Last Supper, Sforza* monument, etc. 860pp. 7⅞ × 10¾. (Available in U.S. only) 22572-0, 22573-9 Pa., Two-vol. set $31.90

THE ART NOUVEAU STYLE BOOK OF ALPHONSE MUCHA: All 72 Plates from "Documents Decoratifs" in Original Color, Alphonse Mucha. Rare copyright-free design portfolio by high priest of Art Nouveau. Jewelry, wallpaper, stained glass, furniture, figure studies, plant and animal motifs, etc. Only complete one-volume edition. 80pp. 9⅜ × 12¼. 24044-4 Pa. $9.95

ANIMALS: 1,419 COPYRIGHT-FREE ILLUSTRATIONS OF MAMMALS, BIRDS, FISH, INSECTS, ETC., edited by Jim Harter. Clear wood engravings present, in extremely lifelike poses, over 1,000 species of animals. One of the most extensive pictorial sourcebooks of its kind. Captions. Index. 284pp. 9 × 12. 23766-4 Pa. $9.95

OBELISTS FLY HIGH, C. Daly King. Masterpiece of American detective fiction, long out of print, involves murder on a 1935 transcontinental flight—"a very thrilling story"—NY Times. Unabridged and unaltered republication of the edition published by William Collins Sons & Co. Ltd., London, 1935. 288pp. 5⅜ × 8½. (Available in U.S. only) 25036-9 Pa. $5.95

VICTORIAN AND EDWARDIAN FASHION: A Photographic Survey, Alison Gernsheim. First fashion history completely illustrated by contemporary photographs. Full text plus 235 photos, 1840–1914, in which many celebrities appear. 240pp. 6½ × 9¼. 24205-6 Pa. $8.95

THE ART OF THE FRENCH ILLUSTRATED BOOK, 1700–1914, Gordon N. Ray. Over 630 superb book illustrations by Fragonard, Delacroix, Daumier, Doré, Grandville, Manet, Mucha, Steinlen, Toulouse-Lautrec and many others. Preface. Introduction. 633 halftones. Indices of artists, authors & titles, binders and provenances. Appendices. Bibliography. 608pp. 8⅜ × 11¼. 25086-5 Pa. $24.95

THE WONDERFUL WIZARD OF OZ, L. Frank Baum. Facsimile in full color of America's finest children's classic. 143 illustrations by W. W. Denslow. 267pp. 5⅜ × 8½. 20691-2 Pa. $7.95

FOLLOWING THE EQUATOR: A Journey Around the World, Mark Twain. Great writer's 1897 account of circumnavigating the globe by steamship. Ironic humor, keen observations, vivid and fascinating descriptions of exotic places. 197 illustrations. 720pp. 5⅜ × 8½. 26113-1 Pa. $15.95

THE FRIENDLY STARS, Martha Evans Martin & Donald Howard Menzel. Classic text marshalls the stars together in an engaging, non-technical survey, presenting them as sources of beauty in night sky. 23 illustrations. Foreword. 2 star charts. Index. 147pp. 5⅜ × 8½. 21099-5 Pa. $3.95

FADS AND FALLACIES IN THE NAME OF SCIENCE, Martin Gardner. Fair, witty appraisal of cranks, quacks, and quackeries of science and pseudoscience: hollow earth, Velikovsky, orgone energy, Dianetics, flying saucers, Bridey Murphy, food and medical fads, etc. Revised, expanded In the Name of Science. "A very able and even-tempered presentation."—The New Yorker. 363pp. 5⅜ × 8. 20394-8 Pa. $6.95

ANCIENT EGYPT: ITS CULTURE AND HISTORY, J. E Manchip White. From pre-dynastics through Ptolemies: society, history, political structure, religion, daily life, literature, cultural heritage. 48 plates. 217pp. 5⅜ × 8½. 22548-8 Pa. $5.95

SIR HARRY HOTSPUR OF HUMBLETHWAITE, Anthony Trollope. Incisive, unconventional psychological study of a conflict between a wealthy baronet, his idealistic daughter, and their scapegrace cousin. The 1870 novel in its first inexpensive edition in years. 250pp. 5⅜ × 8½.   24953-0 Pa. $6.95

LASERS AND HOLOGRAPHY, Winston E. Kock. Sound introduction to burgeoning field, expanded (1981) for second edition. Wave patterns, coherence, lasers, diffraction, zone plates, properties of holograms, recent advances. 84 illustrations. 160pp. 5⅜ × 8¼. (Except in United Kingdom)   24041-X Pa. $3.95

INTRODUCTION TO ARTIFICIAL INTELLIGENCE: SECOND, EN-LARGED EDITION, Philip C. Jackson, Jr. Comprehensive survey of artificial intelligence—the study of how machines (computers) can be made to act intelligently. Includes introductory and advanced material. Extensive notes updating the main text. 132 black-and-white illustrations. 512pp. 5⅜ × 8½.   24864-X Pa. $8.95

HISTORY OF INDIAN AND INDONESIAN ART, Ananda K. Coomaraswamy. Over 400 illustrations illuminate classic study of Indian art from earliest Harappa finds to early 20th century. Provides philosophical, religious and social insights. 304pp. 6⅛ × 9⅜.   25005-9 Pa. $11.95

THE GOLEM, Gustav Meyrink. Most famous supernatural novel in modern European literature, set in Ghetto of Old Prague around 1890. Compelling story of mystical experiences, strange transformations, profound terror. 13 black-and-white illustrations. 224pp. 5⅜ × 8½. (Available in U.S. only)   25025-3 Pa. $6.95

PICTORIAL ENCYCLOPEDIA OF HISTORIC ARCHITECTURAL PLANS, DETAILS AND ELEMENTS: With 1,880 Line Drawings of Arches, Domes, Doorways, Facades, Gables, Windows, etc., John Theodore Haneman. Sourcebook of inspiration for architects, designers, others. Bibliography. Captions. 141pp. 9 × 12.   24605-1 Pa. $7.95

BENCHLEY LOST AND FOUND, Robert Benchley. Finest humor from early 30's, about pet peeves, child psychologists, post office and others. Mostly unavailable elsewhere. 73 illustrations by Peter Arno and others. 183pp. 5⅜ × 8½.
                                         22410-4 Pa. $4.95

ERTÉ GRAPHICS, Erté. Collection of striking color graphics: Seasons, Alphabet, Numerals, Aces and Precious Stones. 50 plates, including 4 on covers. 48pp. 9⅜ × 12¼.   23580-7 Pa. $7.95

THE JOURNAL OF HENRY D. THOREAU, edited by Bradford Torrey, F. H. Allen. Complete reprinting of 14 volumes, 1837–61, over two million words; the sourcebooks for Walden, etc. Definitive. All original sketches, plus 75 photographs. 1,804pp. 8½ × 12¼.   20312-3, 20313-1 Cloth., Two-vol. set $125.00

CASTLES: THEIR CONSTRUCTION AND HISTORY, Sidney Toy. Traces castle development from ancient roots. Nearly 200 photographs and drawings illustrate moats, keeps, baileys, many other features. Caernarvon, Dover Castles, Hadrian's Wall, Tower of London, dozens more. 256pp. 5⅜ × 8¼.
                                         24898-4 Pa. $6.95

AMERICAN CLIPPER SHIPS: 1833–1858, Octavius T. Howe & Frederick C. Matthews. Fully-illustrated, encyclopedic review of 352 clipper ships from the period of America's greatest maritime supremacy. Introduction. 109 halftones. 5 black-and-white line illustrations. Index. Total of 928pp. 5⅜ × 8½.
25115-2, 25116-0 Pa., Two-vol. set $17.90

TOWARDS A NEW ARCHITECTURE, Le Corbusier. Pioneering manifesto by great architect, near legendary founder of "International School." Technical and aesthetic theories, views on industry, economics, relation of form to function, "mass-production spirit," much more. Profusely illustrated. Unabridged translation of 13th French edition. Introduction by Frederick Etchells. 320pp. 6⅛ × 9¼. (Available in U.S. only)
25023-7 Pa. $8.95

THE BOOK OF KELLS, edited by Blanche Cirker. Inexpensive collection of 32 full-color, full-page plates from the greatest illuminated manuscript of the Middle Ages, painstakingly reproduced from rare facsimile edition. Publisher's Note. Captions. 32pp. 9⅜ × 12¼.
24345-1 Pa. $4.95

BEST SCIENCE FICTION STORIES OF H. G. WELLS, H. G. Wells. Full novel *The Invisible Man*, plus 17 short stories: "The Crystal Egg," "Aepyornis Island," "The Strange Orchid," etc. 303pp. 5⅜ × 8½. (Available in U.S. only)
21531-8 Pa. $6.95

AMERICAN SAILING SHIPS: Their Plans and History, Charles G. Davis. Photos, construction details of schooners, frigates, clippers, other sailcraft of 18th to early 20th centuries—plus entertaining discourse on design, rigging, nautical lore, much more. 137 black-and-white illustrations. 240pp. 6⅛ × 9¼.
24658-2 Pa. $6.95

ENTERTAINING MATHEMATICAL PUZZLES, Martin Gardner. Selection of author's favorite conundrums involving arithmetic, money, speed, etc., with lively commentary. Complete solutions. 112pp. 5⅜ × 8½.
25211-6 Pa. $2.95

THE WILL TO BELIEVE, HUMAN IMMORTALITY, William James. Two books bound together. Effect of irrational on logical, and arguments for human immortality. 402pp. 5⅜ × 8½.
20291-7 Pa. $7.95

THE HAUNTED MONASTERY and THE CHINESE MAZE MURDERS, Robert Van Gulik. 2 full novels by Van Gulik continue adventures of Judge Dee and his companions. An evil Taoist monastery, seemingly supernatural events; overgrown topiary maze that hides strange crimes. Set in 7th-century China. 27 illustrations. 328pp. 5⅜ × 8½.
23502-5 Pa. $6.95

CELEBRATED CASES OF JUDGE DEE (DEE GOONG AN), translated by Robert Van Gulik. Authentic 18th-century Chinese detective novel; Dee and associates solve three interlocked cases. Led to Van Gulik's own stories with same characters. Extensive introduction. 9 illustrations. 237pp. 5⅜ × 8½.
23337-5 Pa. $5.95

Prices subject to change without notice.

Available at your book dealer or write for free catalog to Dept. GI, Dover Publications, Inc., 31 East 2nd St., Mineola, N.Y. 11501. Dover publishes more than 175 books each year on science, elementary and advanced mathematics, biology, music, art, literary history, social sciences and other areas.